Combinatorial Algorithms

D0068679

T. C. Hu
University of California, San Diego

ADDISON-WESLEY PUBLISHING COMPANY
Reading, Massachusetts • Menlo Park, California
London • Amsterdam • Don Mills, Ontario • Sydney

Reproduced by Addison-Wesley from camera-ready copy supplied
by the author.

ISBN 0-201-03859-5
ABCDEFGHIJ-AL-8987654321

To my wife Jane Pu-chu,

the *Source* of 21% of my trouble

and *Root* of 62% of my happiness.

PREFACE

This book presents some combinatorial algorithms common in computer science and operations research. The presentation is to stress intuitive ideas in an algorithm and to illustrate it with a numerical example. The detailed implementation of the algorithms in PASCAL are in a separate manual. No background in linear programming and advanced data structure is needed. Most of the material can be taught to undergraduates while more difficult sections are only suitable to graduate students. Chapters can be read somewhat independently so that the instructor can select a subset of chapters for his course. This book should also be useful as a reference book since it contains much material not available in Journals or any other books.

Chapters One and Two can be used in a one quarter course in network theory or graph algorithms. Chapter One goes in-depth into several shortest-path problems and introduces a decomposition algorithm for large sparse networks. Chapter Two deals with network flows, and contains a large amount of new material, such as the algorithms of Dinic and Kazanov which have never appeared in English before, the optimum communication spanning tree and the description of PERT in terms of longest paths and cheapest cuts. Also in Chapter Two is a section on multi-terminal flows where a subset of nodes are terminal nodes.

Chapters Three and Four cover dynamic programming and backtrack (branch and bound) which are two general optimization techniques. Both topics are usually not covered in detail in computer science departments. Chapter Three introduces the concept of dynamic programming by using examples carefully selected to show the variety of problems solvable by dynamic programming. After the knapsack problem is solved, the periodic nature of the solutions is discussed. (The solution to the two-dimensional knapsack problem is based on the papers of Gilmore and Gomory.) This chapter ends with a brief discussion of the work of Dr. F.F. Yao. Chapter Four includes standard material on backtracking as well as a detailed description of $\alpha-\beta$ pruning in a game tree. It also gives an example of the Monte Carlo technique of estimating the size of the decision tree.

Chapters Five and Six contain a large amount of new material which should be of interest to computer scientists and operations researchers. Chapter Five introduces the Huffman algorithm, the Hu-Tucker algorithm, including a new reconstruction phase, and the generalization of both algorithms to regular cost functions. This generalization is based on the paper by Hu, Kleitman and Tamaki. Chapter Five also describes and illustrates the Garsia-Wachs construction. Chapter Six deals with heuristic algorithms. It contains the one-point theorem of Magazine, Nemhauser and Trotter and the new bin-packing algorithm of Yao. The treatment of job-scheduling for the tree-constraint is a revision of the author's paper published in 1961.

The subject of Chapter Seven is matrix multiplications. This chapter contains two combinatorial results, the Strassen's result on the multiplication of two large matrices and the results on the optimum order of multiplying a chain of matrices of different dimensions. Although the problem of optimum order can be solved by an $O(n^3)$ algorithm based on dynamic programming, the problem can now be solved by an $O(n\log n)$ algorithm based on combinatorial insights. Since the subject of finding the optimum order is a book by itself, we give the main theorems on the subject and a heuristic $O(n)$ algorithm which has a 15% error bound.

The final chapter, Chapter Eight, introduces the concepts of NP-complete problems. The purpose here is to give the reader some intuitive notions but not a complete treatment since a book has been published dealing with this subject in detail.

It is a pleasure to thank all persons who helped to make this book possible. To the National Science Foundation and Dr. J. Chandra and Dr. P. Boggs of the U. S. Army Research Office for their financial help. To Drs. F. Chin, S. Dreyfus,

F. Ruskey, W. Savitch, A. Tucker, M. Wachs, F. Yao for reading various parts of the drafts. To Professor L. E. Trotter, Jr. and Professor Andrew Yao for reading the next-to-final version of the whole book and made many valuable suggestions. To Mrs. Mary Deo for her effort in editing the earlier versions. To Mrs. Annetta Whiteman for her excellent technical typing of so many versions of the book. To Ms. Sue Sullivan, for skillfully converting the material into the book formats using the UNIX system. To Mr. Y.S. Kuo for preparing the index and writing parts of the manual. And last but most to Dr. Man-Tak Shing, for writing the manual and his technical and general assistance throughout the writing and production.

La Jolla, California

October 19, 1981

T. C. Hu

CONTENTS

Chapter 3. Dynamic Programming

Chapter 4. Backtracking

Chapter 5. Binary Tree

Chapter 6. Heuristic and Near Optimum

Chapter 7. Matrix Multiplication

Chapter 8. NP-complete

CHAPTER 1. SHORTEST PATHS

There is no shortest path to success.

§ 1.1 GRAPH TERMINOLOGY

When we try to solve a problem, we often draw a graph. A graph is often the simplest and easiest way to describe a system, a structure, or a situation. The Chinese proverb "A picture is worth one thousand words" is certainly true in mathematical modeling. This is why graph theory has a wide variety of applications in physical, biological, and social sciences. Due to the wide variety of applications, we also have diverse terminology. Papers on graph theory are full of definitions, and every author has his own definitions. Here, we introduce a minimum number of definitions which are intuitively obvious. The notation and terminology adopted here is similar to that of Knuth [18].

A graph consists of a finite set of vertices and a set of edges joining the vertices. We shall draw small circles to represent vertices and lines to represent edges. A system or a structure can often be represented by a graph where the lines indicate the relations among the vertices (the elements of the system). For example, we can use vertices to represent cities and edges to represent the highways connecting the cities. We can also use vertices to represent persons and draw an edge joining two vertices if the two persons know each other.

The reader should keep in mind that graph theory is a theory of relations, *not* a theory of definitions; however, a minimum number of definitions is needed here. Vertices are also called nodes, and edges are also called arcs, branches, or links. We usually assume that there are n vertices in the graph G and at most one edge joining any two vertices and there is no edge joining a node to itself. The vertices are denoted by V_i (i = 1,2,...,n) and the edge joining V_i and V_j is denoted by e_{ij}. Two vertices are *adjacent* if they are joined by an edge (the two vertices are also called *neighbors*); two edges are adjacent if they are both incident to the same vertex. A vertex is of *degree* k if there are k edges incident to it.

A sequence of vertices and edges

$$(V_1, e_{12}, V_2, e_{23}, V_3, ..., V_n)$$

is said to form a *path* from V_1 to V_n. We can represent a path by only its vertices as

$$(V_1, V_2, ..., V_n)$$

or by only the edges in the path as

$$(e_{12}, e_{23}, ..., e_{n-1,n}).$$

A graph is *connected* if there is a path between any two nodes of the graph. A path is of length k if there are k edges in the path. A path is a *simple path* if all the vertices V_1, V_2, ..., V_{n-1}, V_n are distinct. If $V_1 = V_n$, then it is called a cycle. In other words, a cycle is a path of length three or more from a vertex to itself. If all vertices in a cycle are distinct, then the cycle is a simple *cycle*. Unless otherwise stated, we shall use the word "path" to mean a simple path, "cycle" to mean a simple cycle, and "graph" to mean a connected graph.

If an edge has a direction (just like a street may be a one-way street), then it is called a *directed edge*. If a directed edge is from V_i to V_j, then we cannot follow this edge from V_j to V_i. Thus in the definition of a path, we want an edge to be undirected or to be a directed edge from V_i to V_{i+1}. In all other definitions, the directions of edges are ignored. A graph is called a *directed graph* if all edges are directed and a *mixed graph* if some edges are directed and some are not. A cycle formed by directed edges is called a *directed cycle* (or *circuit*). A directed graph is called *acyclic* if there are no directed cycles. The words "graph" and "edge" are used for an undirected graph and an undirected edge throughout this section.

A *tree* is a connected graph with no cycles. If a graph has n vertices, then any *two* of the following conditions characterize a tree and automatically imply the third condition.

1.   The graph G is connected.

2.   The graph has n-1 edges.

3.   The graph contains no cycles.

We shall denote a graph by $G = (V; E)$ where "V" is the set of nodes or vertices, and "E" is the set of edges in the graph. A graph $G' = (V'; E')$ is a *subgraph* of $G = (V; E)$ if $V' \subseteq V$ and $E' \subseteq E$.

A subgraph which is a tree and which contains all the vertices of a graph is called a *spanning tree* of the graph. We shall illustrate these intuitive definitions of graph theory in Figure 1.1.

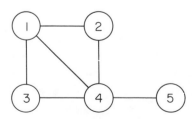

Figure 1.1

There are three paths between V_1 and V_5, namely (V_1, V_2, V_4, V_5), (V_1, V_4, V_5), (V_1, V_3, V_4, V_5). The edges e_{14}, e_{24}, e_{34}, and e_{45} form a spanning tree and so do the edges e_{12}, e_{24}, e_{34}, and e_{45}. Also, we may pick e_{12}, e_{13}, e_{34}, and e_{45} to be the spanning tree. Here the node V_1 is of degree 3 in the graph G but is of degree 2 in the last spanning tree. If the edge e_{45} was directed from V_4 to V_5, then there are still three paths from V_1 to V_5 but none from V_5 to V_1.

In most applications, we associate numbers with edges or vertices. Then the graph is called a *network*. All the definitions of graph theory apply to networks as well. In network theory, we usually use "nodes" and "arcs" instead of "vertices" and "edges".

§1.2 SHORTEST PATH

One of the fundamental problems in network theory is to find shortest paths in a network. Each arc of the network has a number which is the length of the arc.

In most cases, the arcs have positive lengths, but the arcs may have negative lengths in some applications. For example, the nodes may represent the various states of a physical system, where the length associated with the arc e_{ij} denotes the energy absorbed in transforming the state V_i to the state V_j. An arc with negative length then indicates that energy is released in transforming the state V_i into the state V_j. If the total length of a circuit or cycle is negative, we say that the network contains a negative circuit.

The length of a path is the sum of lengths of all the arcs in the path. There are usually many paths between a pair of nodes, say V_s and V_t, but a path with the minimum length is called a *shortest path* from V_s to V_t.

The problem of finding a shortest path is a fundamental problem and often occurs as a subproblem of other optimization problems. In some applications, the numbers associated with arcs may represent characteristics other than lengths and we may want optimum paths where optimum is defined by a different criterion. But the shortest path problem is the most common problem in the whole class of optimum path problems. The shortest path algorithm can usually be modified slightly to find other optimum paths. Thus we shall concentrate on the shortest paths.

If we denote a path from V_1 to V_k by $(V_1, V_2, ..., V_k)$, then $e_{i,i+1}$ must be either a directed arc from V_i to V_{i+1} or an undirected arc joining V_i and V_{i+1} $(i = 1,...,k-1)$. In most applications, we can think of an undirected arc between V_i and V_j as two directed arcs, one from V_i to V_j and the other from V_j to V_i. We usually are interested in three kinds of shortest-path problems:

(1)   The shortest path from one node to another.

(2)   The shortest paths from one node to all the other nodes.

(3)   The shortest paths between all pairs of nodes.

Since all algorithms solving Problem (1) and Problem (2) are essentially the same, we shall discuss the problem of finding shortest paths from one node to all other nodes in the network.

The problem of finding shortest paths is well-defined if the network does not contain a negative cycle (or a negative circuit). Note that a network can have some directed arcs with negative length and yet does not contain a negative cycle. We shall first study the case that all arcs have positive length.

Let us denote the length of the arc from V_i to V_j by d_{ij}, and assume that

$$d_{ij} > 0 \qquad \text{for all i,j} \qquad \text{condition 1}$$
$$d_{ij} \neq d_{ji} \qquad \text{for some i,j} \qquad \text{condition 2}$$
$$d_{ij} + d_{jk} \leqslant d_{ik} \qquad \text{for some i,j,k} \qquad \text{condition 3}$$

For convenience, we assume that $d_{ij} = \infty$ if there is no arc leading from V_i to V_j and $d_{ii} = 0$ for all i.

Condition 3 makes the shortest-path problem nontrivial. Otherwise, the shortest path from V_i to V_j consists of the single arc e_{ij}.

Assume that there are n nodes in the network and we want the shortest paths from V_0 to V_i (i = 1, 2, ..., n-1). If there are two or more shortest paths from V_0 to a node, then any one path is equally acceptable.

Usually, we would like to know the length of a shortest path as well as the intermediate nodes in the path.

Let us make some observations first. Let P_k be a path from V_0 to V_k, where V_i is an intermediate node on the path. Then the subpath from V_0 to V_i contains fewer arcs than the path P_k. Since all arcs have positive lengths, the subpath must be shorter than P_k. We state this as observation 1.

Observation 1. The length of a path is always longer than the length of any of its subpaths. (Note this is true only when all arcs are positive.)

Let V_i be an intermediate node on the path P_k (from V_0 to V_k). If the path P_k is a shortest path, then the subpath from V_0 to V_i must *itself* be a shortest path. Otherwise, a shorter path to V_i followed by the original route from V_i to V_k constitutes a path shorter than P_k. This would contradict that P_k is a shortest path. We state this as observation 2.

Observation 2. Any subpath (of a shortest path) must itself be a shortest path.

(Note that this does not depend on arcs having positive lengths.)

Observation 3. Any shortest path contains at most n-1 arcs. (This depends on arcs not forming negative cycles and that there are n nodes in the network.)

Based on these three observations, we can develop an algorithm to find the shortest paths from V_0 to all the other nodes in the network.

Imagine that all shortest paths from V_0 to all other nodes have been ordered according to their path lengths. *For convenience of discussion, we can rename the nodes such that the shortest path to V_1 is the shortest among all shortest paths.* We shall write

$$P_1 \leqslant P_2 \leqslant P_3 \leqslant ... \leqslant P_{n-1}$$

to denote that the lengths of these paths are monotonically increasing.

The algorithm will find P_1 first, P_2 second,..., until the longest of the shortest paths is found.

Let us motivate the ideas behind the algorithm. How many arcs are in the path P_1? If P_1 contains more than one arc, then it contains a subpath which is shorter than P_1 (observation 1). Thus P_1 must contain only one arc.

If P_k contains more than k arcs, then it contains at least k intermediate nodes on the path. Each of the subpaths to an intermediate node must be shorter than P_k, and we would have k paths shorter than P_k, a contradiction. Thus *the shortest path P_k contains at most k arcs.* We shall state this as observation 4.

Observation 4. The shortest path P_k contains at most k arcs.

To find P_1, we need only examine one-arc paths; the minimum among these must be P_1.

To find P_2, we need only one-arc or two-arc paths. The minimum among these must be P_2. If P_2 is a two-arc path where the last arc is e_{j2} ($j \neq 1$), then the single arc e_{0j} is a subpath of P_2 and hence shorter than P_2. Thus, the path P_2 must be either a one-arc path or a two-arc path where the arc e_{12} is the last arc on the path P_2.

In what follows, we shall write numbers on the nodes and call these numbers labels. There are two kinds of labels, temporary and permanent labels. The permanent label on a node is the true shortest distance from the origin V_0 to that node. A temporary label is the length of a path from the origin to that node. Since the path may or may not be a shortest path, a temporary label is an upper bound on the true shortest distance.

When we search for P_1, we write on every node V_i the length of the arc d_{0i}. These are called the temporary labels of V_i (since these labels may be changed later). Among all the temporary labels, we select the minimum and change the label to be permanent. Thus we have V_1 permanently labelled. (A node permanently labelled is called a permanent node.)

To find P_2, we do not have to find all two-arc paths; only those where the first arc is e_{01}. All the lengths of one-arc paths have already been written on the nodes as temporary labels. So we can compare d_{0i} (the length of one arc) with $d_{01} + d_{1i}$ (the length of the two-arc path), and the minimum of the two is written on V_i as the temporary label of V_i. Then among all temporary labels, the minimum is P_2.

The permanent label on a node V_i indicates the true shortest distance from V_0 to V_i. The temporary label on a node V_j indicates either the distance of the arc e_{0j} or the distance of a path from V_0 to a permanent node V_i followed by the arc e_{ij}.

Imagine that all arcs of the network were colored green. Whenever an arc is used in a shortest path, we recolor it brown. So we use one brown arc to reach V_1, one or two brown arcs to reach V_2, ..., at most k brown arcs to reach V_k. (The choice of color is such that the brown arcs form a tree, see EX. 2.) We see that the path P_{k+1} cannot contain nodes with temporary labels as intermediate nodes. Thus we can limit our search to those paths consisting of a sequence of brown arcs followed by one green arc reaching the node V_{k+1}. Two or more green arcs indicate a subpath of shorter distance than P_{k+1}.

To find the path P_{k+1} containing one green arc and possibly some brown arcs, we limit our search to the neighbors of V_0, V_1, ..., V_k. The search is made easy if we adopt the following rule:

Whenever a node V_i receives a permanent label, say l_i^* , we shall check all temporary labels of neighbors V_j of V_i to see if $l_i^* + d_{ij}$ is less than the current temporary label of V_j. If it is less, we shall replace the current temporary label by the smaller value. If not, we leave the temporary label unchanged.

To find P_{k+1}, we just find the minimum of temporary labels of all neighbors of V_0, V_1,...,V_k and change the minimum to a permanent label.

Now we can formalize the algorithm and use it in a numerical example. We will use l_i to denote the temporary shortest distances and l_i^* to denote the true shortest distances.

Dijkstra's Algorithm

Step 0.   All nodes V_i receive temporary labels l_i with value equal to d_{0i} ($i = 1,2,...,n-1$). For convenience, we can take $d_{0i} = \infty$ if there is no arc joining V_0 and V_i.

Set $l_i = d_{0i}$ (i = 1,...,n-1)

Step 1.   Among all temporary labels l_i

Pick $l_k = \min_i l_i$.

Change l_k to l_k^* .

Stop if there is no temporary label left.

Step 2.   Let V_k be the node that just received a permanent label in Step 1. Replace all temporary labels of the neighbors of V_k by the following rule:

$l_i \leftarrow \min[l_i, l_k^* + d_{ki}]$

Return to Step 1.

Consider the network shown in Figure 1.2 where the numbers are arc lengths.

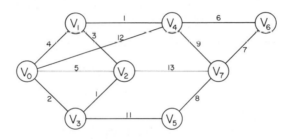

Figure 1.2

We shall put temporary labels inside each node and when the label becomes permanent, we shall add a star on the number. Whenever arcs are used in a shortest path, we shall use heavy lines to represent them.

Step 0.   All nodes receive temporary labels equal to d_{0i}, and the node V_0 gets permanent label 0. This is shown in Figure 1.3.

Step 1.   Among all temporary labels, V_3 has the minimum value 2, so V_3 receives a permanent label.

Step 2.   The node V_3 has neighbors V_2 and V_5

$l_2 \leftarrow \min[l_2, l_3^* + d_{32}] = \min[5, 2+1] = 3.$

$l_5 \leftarrow \min[l_5, l_3^* + d_{35}] = \min[\infty, 2+11] = 13.$

The result is shown in Figure 1.4.

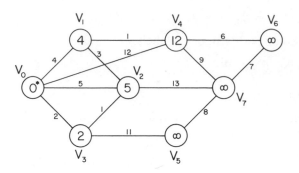

Figure 1.3

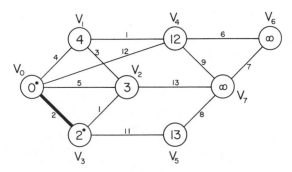

Figure 1.4

Step 1.   Among all temporary labels, the node V_2 has the minimum label 3. So V_2 receives a permanent label.

Step 2.   The neighbors of V_2 are V_1, V_7. (Note V_3 is also a neighbor, but since V_3 has become permanent it is excluded.)

$$l_1 \leftarrow \min[l_1, l_2^* + d_{21}] = \min[4, 3+3] = 4$$

$$l_7 \leftarrow \min[l_7, l_2^* + d_{27}] = \min[\infty, 3+13] = 16$$

Step 1.   The node V_1 receives the permanent label 4.

Step 2. $l_4 \leftarrow \min[l_4, l_1^* + d_{14}] = \min[12, 4+1] = 5.$

This is shown in Figure 1.5.

Step 1. V_4 gets a permanent label.

Step 2. $l_6 \leftarrow \min[l_6, l_4^* + d_{46}] = \min[\infty, 5+6] = 11$

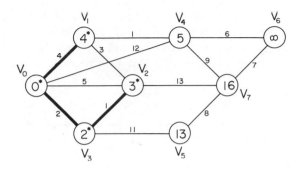

Figure 1.5

$$l_7 \leftarrow \min[l_7, l_4^* + d_{47}] = \min [16, 5+9] = 14$$

Step 1. V_6 gets a permanent label.

Step 2. $l_7 \leftarrow \min[l_7, l_6^* + d_{67}] = \min [14, 11+7] = 14$

Step 1. V_5 gets a permanent label.

Step 2. $l_7 \leftarrow \min[l_7, l_5^* + d_{57}] = \min[14, 13+8] = 14$

Step 1. V_7 gets a permanent label.

The final result is shown in Figure 1.6.

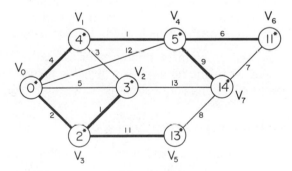

Figure 1.6

We have computed the shortest distances from V_0 to all other nodes in the network, but we have not given the shortest paths which achieve these shortest distances. This situation is like knowing that one can drive from New York to Los Angeles in 72 hours but not knowing which route one should use. One way to trace the intermediate nodes is as follows. If the permanent labels are written on the nodes, we can look for all neighbors of a node V_j to see which neighbor has a label that differs from V_j by exactly the length of the connecting arc. In this way, we can trace back from every node the shortest path from the origin to that node. In Figure 1.7, we have written two numbers on every node. The first number is the permanent label indicating the true shortest distance from the origin to that node; the second number indicates the last intermediate node on the shortest path.

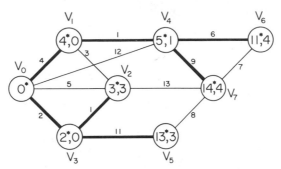

Figure 1.7

Since the algorithm consists of comparisons and additions, we shall count the number of comparisons and additions.

There are $n-2$ comparisons the first time and $n-3$ comparisons the second time, so that there are $(n-2)+(n-3)+...+1 = (n-1)(n-2)/2$ comparisons in Step 1. Similarly, there are $(n-1)(n-2)/2$ additions and the same number of comparisons in Step 2. Thus, the algorithm is $0(n^2)$. Since there are $0(n^2)$ arcs in a network of n nodes and every arc must be examined at least once, it is safe to say that there exists no algorithm which needs $0(n \log n)$ steps in general.

We shall discuss the problem of finding shortest paths from one origin to each of the other nodes when the network has negative arcs in section 1.6. Next, we turn to the problem of finding shortest paths between all pairs of nodes.

§1.3 MULTITERMINAL SHORTEST PATHS

In this section, we look for shortest paths between all pairs of nodes in a network. We allow the arcs to have negative length as long as there is no negative circuit. For computational purposes, we can regard an undirected arc as two directed arcs both with the same length. Thus, a negative undirected arc is equivalent to a negative cycle formed by two directed arcs. If there is only one directed arc with length d_{ij} leading from the node V_i to the node V_j, then we can imagine that there is another arc from V_j to V_i with $d_{ji} = \infty$.

As we have mentioned in section 1.2, any subpath of a shortest path must itself be the shortest. Let

$$e_{ij},\ e_{jk},\ e_{kl},\ ...,\ e_{pq}$$

be a shortest path from V_i to V_q. Then the shortest path from V_i to V_j must be the single arc e_{ij}, the shortest path from V_j to V_k must be the single arc e_{jk}, and so forth. We define an arc e_{ij} to be a *basic arc* if it is the shortest path from V_i to V_j. With this definition, we see that a shortest path must consist of basic arcs only. Also the brown arcs defined in section 1.2 are basic arcs but not all basic arcs are brown arcs.

We will present an algorithm which replaces all nonbasic arcs by basic arcs. In other words, we create an arc between each pair of nodes not connected by a basic arc. The length of the created arc is equal to the shortest distance between the two nodes. Let us consider a simple operation defined for a given node V_j:

$$d_{ik} \leftarrow \min(d_{ik}, d_{ij} + d_{jk}) \tag{1}$$

We perform this operation for a *fixed* j and all possible $i, k \neq j$. For three nodes V_i, V_j, and V_k and the three arcs with lengths d_{ik}, d_{ij}, and d_{jk}, the operation compares the length of an arc e_{ik} with the length of a path of two arcs with the intermediate node V_j. This situation is shown in Figure 1.8. The operation (1) is called a *triple operation*.

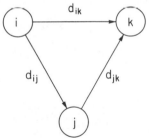

Figure 1.8

We try all possible pairs of nodes V_i and V_k which are neighbors of V_j.

If $d_{ik} \leqslant d_{ij} + d_{jk}$,

we do not change anything.

If $d_{ik} > d_{ij} + d_{jk}$,

we create a new arc from V_i to V_k with $d_{ik} = d_{ij} + d_{jk}$. We first fix $j=1$ and perform the triple operation (1) for all $i,k = 2,3,...,n$. Then we fix $j=2$ and perform the triple operation (1) for all $i,k = 1,3,...,n$. Note that when $j=2$, all the new arcs created when $j=1$ are used. We claim that once all triple operations are computed for $j=n$, the network consists of just basic arcs. That is to say, the number associated with every directed arc leading from V_p to V_q represents the shortest distance from V_p to V_q. Now we shall justify this assertion.

Take *any* shortest path from V_p to V_q in the original network. The shortest path must consist of basic arcs in the original network. If the triple operation would create an arc with its length equal to the sum of lengths of all basic arcs in the shortest path, then this would prove that the algorithm is correct.

Let us consider any shortest path such as the one shown in Figure 1.9.

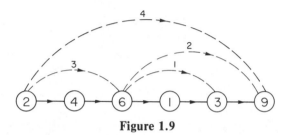

Figure 1.9

When j=1, the triple operation creates a new arc with $d_{63} = d_{61} + d_{13}$.

When j=2, the triple operation does not affect this particular shortest path.

When j=3, the arc with $d_{63} = d_{61} + d_{13}$ has already been created; thus, the triple operation will create an arc with $d_{69} = d_{63} + d_{39} = (d_{61} + d_{13}) + d_{39}$.

When j=4, an arc with $d_{26} = d_{24} + d_{46}$ is created.

When j=6, an arc with $d_{29} = d_{26} + d_{69}$

$$= (d_{24} + d_{46}) + (d_{63} + d_{39})$$
$$= d_{24} + d_{46} + d_{61} + d_{13} + d_{39}$$

is created. In Figure 1.9, we show these basic arcs created successively by dashed lines. The numbers beside these dashed lines indicate the order in which they are created. Thus, the basic arc e_{63} is created first, and the basic arc e_{69} is created second. Some basic arcs, such as e_{41}, will also be created by triple operations, but they are not shown in the figure since they are irrelevant to the shortest path that we are considering. Note that any of the arcs created by the triple operation cannot be replaced by another arc or a path of shorter distance. If so, it would contradict that the original path is a shortest path. If there are no negative cycles, then any shortest path must be a simple path and consist of at most n-1 arcs and at most n-2 distinct intermediate nodes. We have shown that the algorithm works for a particular shortest path, but we can easily generalize the idea to any arbitrary shortest path and supply a formal proof.

This algorithm is easy to program on a computer. The arc lengths of an n-node network are given by an n×n matrix. For example, a network is shown in Figure 1.10 and its distance matrix in Table 1.1.

When j=1, we compare every entry d_{ik} $(i{\neq}1, k{\neq}1)$ with $(d_{i1} + d_{1k})$. If the entry d_{ik} is greater than the sum of d_{i1} and d_{ik}, then the entry d_{ik} is replaced by the sum $(d_{i1} + d_{1k})$. Otherwise the entry remains the same. Likewise, when j=2, we compare every entry d_{ik} $(i \neq 2, k \neq 2)$ with $(d_{i2} + d_{2k})$. The minimum of d_{ik} and $(d_{i2} + d_{2k})$ becomes the new value of d_{ik}. Note that in the above computation for j=2, we have already used the results for j=1. For a fixed value of j, we have to check entries in a $(n{-}1){\times}(n{-}1)$ matrix (the diagonal entries are always zero). Each entry is compared with the sum of two other entries, one in the same row and one in the same column. The algorithm is completed when we finish the computation for j=n.

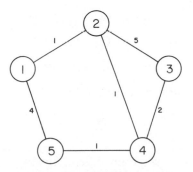

Figure 1.10

Table 1.1

	①	②	③	④	⑤
①	0	1	∞	∞	4
②	1	0	5	1	∞
③	∞	5	0	2	∞
④	∞	1	2	0	1
⑤	4	∞	∞	1	0

Let us do the triple operation for $j = 1, 2, 3, 4, 5$ and only record the computation where there is a change in the data. Note all the lengths of an undirected network are symmetric, so we shall only calculate one of the lengths.

For $j=1$,

$$d_{25} \leftarrow \min (d_{25}, d_{21} + d_{15}) = \min (\infty, 1+4) = 5.$$

For $j=2$,

$$d_{13} \leftarrow \min (d_{13}, d_{12} + d_{23}) = \min (\infty, 1+5) = 6,$$

$$d_{14} \leftarrow \min (d_{14}, d_{12} + d_{24}) = \min (\infty, 1+1) = 2,$$

$$d_{35} \leftarrow \min (d_{35}, d_{32} + d_{25}) = \min (\infty, 5+5) = 10.$$

For $j=3$,

Nothing is changed.

For $j=4$,

$$d_{13} \leftarrow \min (d_{13}, d_{14} + d_{43}) = \min (6, 2+2) = 4,$$

$$d_{15} \leftarrow \min (d_{15}, d_{14} + d_{45}) = \min (4, 2+1) = 3,$$

$$d_{23} \leftarrow \min (d_{23}, d_{24} + d_{43}) = \min (5, 1+2) = 3,$$

$$d_{25} \leftarrow \min (d_{25}, d_{24} + d_{45}) = \min (5, 1+1) = 2,$$

$$d_{35} \leftarrow \min (d_{35}, d_{34} + d_{45}) = \min (10, 2+1) = 3.$$

For $j=5$,

Nothing is changed.

Note that d_{25} was first ∞, then 5, and finally 2. But when $d_{25} = 5$, it is never used as an arc in any shortest path. Any arc with length equal to the sum of lengths of basic arcs in a shortest path cannot be replaced by another arc of shorter length. Otherwise, it will contradict the assumption that the path is shortest. The matrix of shortest distances between all pairs of nodes is shown in Table 1.2.

Having found the shortest distances between every pair of nodes, we still have to find the intermediate nodes in a shortest path. To keep track of the intermediate nodes, we use a matrix $[p_{ik}]$, where the entry in the ith row and kth column indicates the *first intermediate* node on the path from V_i to V_k. If $P_{ik} = j$, then the shortest path is $V_i, V_j, ..., V_k$. Then if $P_{jk} = s$, the shortest path is $V_i, V_j, V_s, ..., V_k$. Initially, we set $P_{ik} = k$ for all i,k. For example, corresponding to Table 1.1, we have Table 1.3.

This means each arc is assumed to be a basic arc (until proven otherwise), and in order to go from V_i to V_k the *first* intermediate node is V_k itself.

Table 1.2

	①	②	③	④	⑤
①	0	1	4	2	3
②	1	0	3	1	2
③	4	3	0	2	3
④	2	1	2	0	1
⑤	3	2	3	1	0

Table 1.3

	①	②	③	④	⑤
①	1	2	3	4	5
②	1	2	3	4	5
③	1	2	3	4	5
④	1	2	3	4	5
⑤	1	2	3	4	5

When we perform the triple operation on Table 1.1, we also update the information in Table 1.3. The entries in Table 1.3 are changed according to the following rule.

$$p_{ik} = \begin{cases} p_{ij} & \text{if } d_{ik} > d_{ij}+d_{jk} \\ \text{unchanged} & \text{if } d_{ik} \leqslant d_{ij}+d_{jk} \end{cases} \tag{2}$$

For example, when we set d_{25} to $d_{21} + d_{15} = 5$, we also set

$$p_{25} = p_{21} = 1.$$

When we set d_{14} to $d_{12} + d_{24} = 2$, we also set

$$p_{14} = p_{12} = 2.$$

When we set d_{15} to $d_{14} + d_{45}$, we also set

$$p_{15} = p_{14} = p_{12} = 2.$$

When we set d_{25} to $d_{24} + d_{45}$, we also set

$$p_{25} = p_{24} = 4.$$

So at the end of the computation, we have

$$p_{15} = 2, \ p_{25} = 4.$$

Since the arc e_{45} is a basic arc, $p_{45} = 5$ throughout the computation.

$p_{15} = 2$ means V_2 is the first intermediate node in going from V_1 to V_5,

$p_{25} = 4$ means V_4 is the first intermediate node in going from V_2 to V_5,

$p_{45} = 5$ means V_5 is the first intermediate node in going from V_4 to V_5.

Thus we can trace out all the intermediate nodes from V_1 to V_5 as V_1, V_2, V_4 and V_5.

In general, to find the shortest path from V_s to V_t, we look at the entry p_{st} and find the first intermediate node.

$$\text{If } p_{st} = a, \quad \text{we look for } p_{at} = \ ?$$
$$\text{If } p_{at} = b, \quad \text{we look for } p_{bt} = \ ?$$

This is continued until

$$p_{zt} = t.$$

Then we know $V_s, V_a, V_b, ..., V_z, V_t$ are the nodes on the shortest path.

The computation (2) is performed in Table 1.3 at the same time the computation (1) is performed in Table 1.1. When we have Table 1.2 of shortest distances at the end of computation (1), we also have Table 1.4 of intermediate nodes at the end of computation (2).

Table 1.4

	①	②	③	④	⑤
①	1	2	2	2	2
②	1	2	4	4	4
③	4	4	3	4	4
④	2	2	3	4	5
⑤	4	4	4	4	5

Note that although Table 1.2 is symmetric, Table 1.4 is not. In order to get the whole Table 1.4, we actually need to do all the calculations in Table 1.1, not just the half of the computations that we did in the example. (e.g., When we set

$d_{52} = d_{51} + d_{12} = 5,$

we also set $p_{52} = p_{51} = 1$.)

§1.4 DECOMPOSITION ALGORITHM

In most applications, a network is very sparse, and we need not do all the triple operations as discussed in the last section. We can regard a sparse network as several small networks overlapping each other, and do the triple operations on each small network. We can save a lot of computation by using the decomposition algorithm. For example, we can consider the network in Figure 1.11 as two small overlapping networks, one network consists of nodes labeled A or X and their connecting arcs, the other network consists of nodes labeled B or X and their connecting arcs.

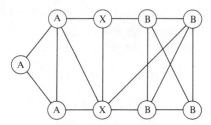

Figure 1.11

Take a subset of nodes in a network and denote it by A. Let X be another subset of nodes. We call the set X a *cut set* of A if it has the following property: If the set X together with its incident arcs are deleted from the network, then the network becomes two or more disconnected components, one component containing all the nodes of A and no other nodes. A cut set X of A is called a *minimal cut set* if no proper subset of X has this disconnecting property. Clearly, the set of all neighboring nodes of A constitutes a minimal cut set of A. First we shall consider the decomposition algorithm in its simplest form; i.e., how to decompose a network into two parts. Let us assume that the network N is partitioned into three sets of nodes such that $N = A \cup X \cup B$, where X is a minimal cut set of A. If the nodes in set A are assigned the indices $1,2,...,|A|$ (here $|A|$ denotes the cardinality of the set A) and the nodes in X are assigned the indices $|A|+1,|A|+2,...,|A|+|X|$, then the associated distance matrix is shown in Table 1.5, where $D_{AA} = [d_{ij}]$ with $V_i \in A$ and $V_j \in A$, $D_{AB} = [d_{ij}]$ with $V_i \in A$ and $V_j \in B$, etc. Initially, all entries in D_{AB} and D_{BA} are infinite. Sometimes it is convenient to use d_{AB} to represent one of the entries in D_{AB}.

Let us introduce a new term "*a conditional shortest* path". A conditional shortest path is a shortest path subject to the restriction that nodes in the path

Table 1.5

D_{AA}	D_{AX}	D_{AB}
D_{XA}	D_{XX}	D_{XB}
D_{BA}	D_{BX}	D_{BB}

We shall use d_{ij}^* to denote the true shortest distance (using any number of arcs) from V_i to V_j. Now we use $d_{ij}^*(Y)$ to denote the distance of the conditional shortest path from V_i to V_j, where Y is the subset of nodes in which the conditional shortest path must lie. The matrix of conditional shortest distances $[d_{ij}^*(Y)]$ with $V_i \in A$ and $V_j \in B$ is denoted by $D_{AB}^*(Y)$, and $d_{AB}^*(Y)$ represents one of its entries. If N is used to denote the whole network, then $d_{ij}^*(N) = d_{ij}^*$. If we know that the shortest paths lie in the set Y, then

$$d_{AB}^*(Y) = d_{AB}^*(N).$$

Let $\overline{A}$ denote $A \cup X$ and $\overline{B}$ denote $B \cup X$. We consider the original network as two networks overlapping each other. One network, called the $\overline{A}$-network, consists of nodes V_i $(V_i \in \overline{A})$ and arcs e_{ij} $(V_i, V_j \in \overline{A})$. The other network, called the $\overline{B}$-network, consists of nodes V_k $(V_k \in \overline{B})$ and arcs e_{kl} $(V_k, V_l \in \overline{B})$. First, we shall perform the triple operations in the $\overline{A}$-network. This will give the conditional shortest distances between any two nodes in $\overline{A}$. Then we shall do the triple operations on the $\overline{B}$-network, where the distances between nodes in X have been replaced by the conditional shortest distances calculated from the $\overline{A}$-network. After performing the triple operations in the $\overline{B}$-network, we shall do the triple operations in the $\overline{A}$-network again. The following two theorems give the foundations for the decomposition algorithm for two overlapping networks.

Theorem 1 Let $N = A \cup X \cup B$, where X is a cut set of A. Then the shortest distances between any two nodes in the $\overline{B}$-network can be obtained by considering only the $\overline{B}$-network, provided that the conditional shortest distances $D_{XX}^*(\overline{A})$ are known. (Note that $\overline{A} = N - B$.)

Proof. If the shortest path in N lies entirely in $\overline{B}$, then $d_{BB}^*(N) = d_{BB}^*(\overline{B})$, which means it is sufficient to do the triple operations on the $\overline{B}$-network. Assume that there are many subpaths of a shortest path which contain nodes in $\overline{A}$. This is shown symbolically in Figure 1.12a.

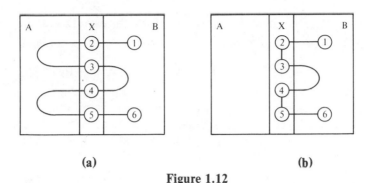

(a)   (b)

Figure 1.12

Consider a shortest path from V_1 to V_6. Since both the starting node and the terminal nodes are in $\overline{B}$, and X is a cut set of B, any subpath that contains nodes in A must begin and end in the set X. In Figure 1.12a the subpath from V_2 to V_3 and the subpath V_4 to V_5 are two such subpaths. If $d_{23}^*(\overline{A}) = d_{23}^*(N-B)$ and $d_{45}^*(\overline{A}) = d_{45}^*(N-B)$ are known, we have effectively in the $\overline{B}$-network, two arcs e_{23} with distance $d_{23}^*(N-B)$ and e_{45} with distance $d_{45}^*(N-B)$. In Figure 1.12b we have replaced the two subpaths by the arcs e_{23} and e_{45}.

The shortest path from V_1 to V_6 then consists of the subpath from V_1 to V_2, e_{23}, the subpath from V_3 to V_4, e_{45} and the subpath from V_5 to V_6, all of which contain only arcs in the $\overline{B}$-network. Thus, it is sufficient to consider only the $\overline{B}$-network. Note that the above reasoning is independent of the number of subpaths which contain nodes of $\overline{A}$.

Clearly, if we interchange A and B, and $\overline{A}$ and $\overline{B}$, then the theorem is also true. Since we first perform triple operations on $\overline{A}$, we only get the conditional shortest distance $D_{\overline{A}\,\overline{A}}^*(\overline{A})$. By the time $\overline{B}$ is finished, we have all $D_{\overline{B}\,\overline{B}}^*(N)$. Thus, we need to perform triple operations on $\overline{A}$ again to get $D_{\overline{A}\,\overline{A}}^*(N)$. Now, we turn to the problem of calculating the $D_{AB}^*(N)$ and $D_{BA}^*(N)$.

Theorem 2 Let $N = A \cup X \cup B$, where X is a cut set of A. Then

$$d_{AB}^*(N) = \min_X [d_{AX}^*(N)+d_{XB}^*(N)] , \tag{1}$$

$$d_{BA}^*(N) = \min_X [d_{BX}^*(N)+d_{XA}^*(N)] . \tag{2}$$

Proof. To get from any node V_i in A to any node V_k in B we must pass at least one node V_j in X. If the minimum is taken over all V_j in X, then it is certainly the minimum distance in N. ∎

Let the distance matrix $D^*_{AX}(N)$ be of dimension $r \times s$ and the distance matrix $D^*_{XB}(N)$ be $s \times t$. Then the operation as carried out for a given i and k is

$$d^*_{ik} = \min_j \ (d^*_{ij} + d^*_{jk}) \quad (V_j \in X, \ V_i \in A, \ V_k \in B). \tag{3}$$

The total number of additions is then $r \times s \times t$ with the same number of comparisons. The operation (3) is analogous to an ordinary matrix multiplication with $+$ replacing $\times$ and min replacing summation. We shall refer to (3) as a matrix minisummation.

Now we shall state the decomposition algorithm for the two overlapping networks.

Step 1.   Execute the triple operations for each of the entries of the matrix

$$\begin{vmatrix} D_{AA} & D_{AX} \\ D_{XA} & D_{XX} \end{vmatrix}$$

At the end of the step, we have $D^*_{AA}(\overline{A})$, $D^*_{AX}(\overline{A})$, $D^*_{XA}(\overline{A})$, and $D^*_{XX}(\overline{A})$.

Step 2.   Execute the triple operations on the matrix

$$\begin{vmatrix} D^*_{XX}(\overline{A}) & D_{XB} \\ D_{BX} & D_{BB} \end{vmatrix}$$

At the end of the step we have, from Theorem 1, $D^*_{XX}(N)$, $D^*_{XB}(N)$, $D^*_{BX}(N)$, and $D^*_{BB}(N)$.

Step 3.   Execute the triple operations on the matrix

$$\begin{vmatrix} D^*_{AA}(\overline{A}) & D^*_{AX}(\overline{A}) \\ D^*_{XA}(\overline{A}) & D^*_{XX}(N) \end{vmatrix}$$

At the end of this step we have, from Theorem 1, $D^*_{AA}(N)$, $D^*_{AX}(N)$, $D^*_{XA}(N)$, and $D^*_{XX}(N)$.

Step 4.   Use (3) to obtain $D^*_{AB}(N)$ and $D^*_{BA}(N)$.

For a matrix of dimension $n \times n$, we need approximately n^3 elementary operations to find the multiterminal shortest paths by the straightforward methods in section 1.3. Now, suppose we can decompose the original network into 3 subsets A, X, and B, where X is a cut set of A and where $|A| = n_1$, $|X| = n_2$, and $|B| = n_3$, we can use the decomposition algorithm to find the multiterminal shortest paths. We need

$$(n_1+n_2)^3 \qquad \text{operations in Step 1}$$
$$(n_2+n_3)^3 \qquad \text{operations in Step 2}$$
$$(n_1+n_2)^3 \qquad \text{operations in Step 3}$$
$$2(n_1 \cdot n_2 \cdot n_3) \qquad \text{operations in Step 4.}$$

If $n_1 = 4n/10$, $n_2 = n/10$ and $n_3 = 5n/10$, then the total number of operations is $(506/1000)n^3$ which is roughly half of the computation by treating the network as a whole.

When the network is extremely large and loosely connected, it is advantageous to decompose the network into four overlapping networks as shown in Table 1.6, where the white areas indicate entries that are originally infinite.

To construct such a distance matrix as in Table 1.6, we proceed as follows. Label any subset of nodes as A. Then its minimal cut set is X_A. Let B be a cut set of $A \cup X_A$, and X_B be the minimal cut set of $A \cup X_A \cup B$. (Note that the minimal cut set of B is $X_A \cup X_B$.) Let C be a cut set of $A \cup X_A \cup B \cup X_B$ and X_C be the minimal cut set of $A \cup X_A \cup B \cup X_B \cup C$. Continue until no further decomposition is desired. In Table 1.6, the original network is decomposed into four overlapping ones: $\overline{A}$−network $(\overline{A} = A \cup X_A)$, $\overline{B}$−network $(\overline{B} = X_A \cup B \cup X_B)$, $\overline{C}$−network $(\overline{C} = X_B \cup C \cup X_C)$, and $\overline{D}$−network $(\overline{D} = X_C \cup D)$.

We shall state the general decomposition algorithm for m overlapping networks: $\overline{A}$−network, $\overline{B}$−network, ..., $\overline{G}$−network, $\overline{H}$−network.

Step 1.   Do the triple operations on the m-1 networks $\overline{A}, \overline{B}, ..., \overline{G}$, successively, where conditional shortest distances obtained in one network will replace original distances in the succeeding network.   That is to say, $D^*_{X_A X_A}(\overline{A})$ will replace $D_{X_A X_A}$ before we perform the triple operations on $\overline{B} = X_A \cup B \cup X_B$.

To apply Theorem 1 to the case of several overlapping networks, we can first identify A, X_A, and $(B \cup X_B \cup ... \cup H)$ with A, X, and B of Theorem 1. Then we can identify

$$(A \cup X_A \cup B), \quad X_B, \quad (C \cup X_C \cup ... \cup H)$$

as   A ,   X ,   B   of Theorem 1.

It is easy to see that we get

$$D^*_{AA}(\overline{A}), D^*_{BB}(\overline{A} \cup \overline{B}), ..., D^*_{GG}(\overline{A} \cup \overline{B} \cup \cdots \cup \overline{G}).$$

Table 1.6

	A	X_A	B	X_B	C	X_C	D
A	D_{AA}	D_{AX_A}	D_{AB}	D_{AX_B}	D_{AC}	D_{AX_C}	D_{AD}
X_A	D_{X_AA}	$D_{X_AX_A}$	D_{X_AB}	$D_{X_AX_B}$	D_{X_AC}	$D_{X_AX_C}$	D_{X_AD}
B	D_{BA}	D_{BX_A}	D_{BB}	D_{BX_B}	D_{BC}	D_{BX_C}	D_{BD}
X_B	D_{X_BA}	$D_{X_BX_A}$	D_{X_BB}	$D_{X_BX_B}$	D_{X_BC}	$D_{X_BX_C}$	D_{X_BD}
C	D_{CA}	D_{CX_A}	D_{CB}	D_{CX_B}	D_{CC}	D_{CX_C}	D_{CD}
X_C	D_{X_CA}	$D_{X_CX_A}$	D_{X_CB}	$D_{X_CX_B}$	D_{X_CC}	$D_{X_CX_C}$	D_{X_CD}
D	D_{DA}	D_{DX_A}	D_{DB}	D_{DX_B}	D_{DC}	D_{DX_C}	D_{DD}

Step 2.   Perform the triple operation on the m networks, $\overline{H}, \overline{G}, ..., \overline{B}, \overline{A}$, successively, where the distances obtained in one network will replace the distances of the succeeding network, that is $D^*_{X_GX_G}(N)$ will replace $D^*_{X_GX_G}(N-H)$. From Theorem 1, we have

$$D^*_{\overline{H}\,\overline{H}}(N), D^*_{\overline{G}\,\overline{G}}(N), ..., D^*_{\overline{B}\,\overline{B}}(N), D^*_{\overline{A}\,\overline{A}}(N) \ .$$

Step 3.   Find the shortest distances between any two nodes which are not both in one of the sets $\overline{A}, \overline{B}, ..., \overline{H}$ by minisummation (3). We shall use the notation $A \oplus X_A \oplus B$ to denote the matrix minisummation with $V_i \in A$, $V_j \in X_A$, and $V_k \in B$. Though both $A \oplus X_A \oplus B$ and $B \oplus X_A \oplus A$ should be calculated, for simplicity we shall write only one of them. The order in which the matrix minisummations should be executed is as follows:

(A) $\oplus X_A \oplus$ (B $\cup$ X_B),

(A $\cup$ X_A $\cup$ B) $\oplus X_B \oplus$ (C $\cup$ X_C),

(A $\cup$ X_A $\cup$ B $\cup$ X_B $\cup$ C) $\oplus X_C \oplus$ (D $\cup$ X_D),

•

•

•

(A $\cup$ X_A $\cup$ ... $\cup$ F) $\oplus X_F \oplus$ (G $\cup$ X_G),

(A $\cup$ X_A $\cup$ ... $\cup$ G) $\oplus X_G \oplus$ (H).

In the above matrix minisummation, the $D^*_{AX_B}(N)$ obtained in the first min-isummation are used in the second minisummation.

The decomposition technique just mentioned can be classified as a linear decomposition, since the network is partitioned linearly into m overlapping networks as shown in Figure 1.13(a). If the m overlapping networks form a tree as shown in Figure 1.13(b), then there is a special order that we should perform on the triple operations on each of the small networks (see Blewett and Hu [2], Shier [25]).

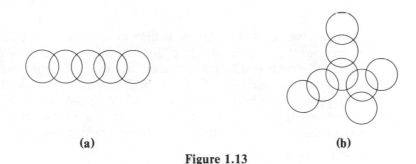

(a)   (b)

Figure 1.13

§1.5 ACYCLIC NETWORKS

In section 1.2, we gave an algorithm for finding shortest paths from the origin to each of the other nodes. In this section, we want the longest path from the origin to each of the other nodes. This problem of longest path with positive and negative arcs is well-defined only when the directed network is *acyclic.*

When the network is acyclic, the nodes are partially ordered and can be indexed such that all directed arcs are from V_i to V_j, where $i<j$. We shall assume that the nodes are already so numbered (see EX. 6). The origin is denoted by V_0 and we are seeking the longest paths from V_0 to V_i ($i = 1,2,...,n-1$).

Let us denote the longest distance from V_0 to V_i by l_i, then we have $l_0 = 0$, $l_1 = d_{01}$, and for l_k

$$l_k = \max_j (l_j+d_{jk}) \quad (j<k) \tag{1}$$

Thus

$$l_2 = \max [(l_0+d_{02}),\ (l_1+d_{12})]$$

$$l_3 = \max [(l_0+d_{03}),\ (l_1+d_{13}),\ (l_2+d_{23})]$$

$$\vdots$$

$$l_{n-1} = \max\ (l_j + d_{j,n-1}) \qquad (j = 0,1,...,n-2)$$

In equation (1), we define $d_{ij} = -\infty$ if there is no directed arc from V_i to V_j.

We can also use (1) to find the shortest paths from V_0 to V_i where there are negative arcs in the acyclic network simply be replacing max by min in (1) and letting l_i be the shortest distance. In the case of shortest paths in an acyclic network, we let $d_{ij} = \infty$ if there is no directed arc from V_i to V_j.

Note that there are two additions and one comparison in calculating l_2, three additions and two comparisons in calculating l_3. So the total number of additions is $(1 + 2 + ... + n-1) = n(n-1)/2$ and the total number of comparisons is $(n-1)(n-2)/2$. The bound of $0(n^2)$ is valid for both the longest path and for the shortest path with negative arcs. When the network is not acyclic, we have to use successive approximations to find shortest paths from the origin to each of the other nodes. Two successive approximation techniques are discussed in section 1.6.

§1.6 SHORTEST PATHS IN A GENERAL NETWORK

Consider a network with positive and negative arcs, and without negative cycles. We want to find the shortest paths from V_0 to each of the other nodes. (Recall that the Dijkstra algorithm requires positive arcs.) Since the network contains no negative cycles, a shortest path must be a simple path and hence contains at most n-1 arcs. We shall find all the shortest paths using successive approximations where the first order approximations give the shortest distances from V_0 to V_i using only one arc, and the kth order approximations give the shortest distances from V_0 to V_i (i = 1,2,...,n-1) using at most k arcs. The (n-1)st order approximations then give the true shortest distances.

The algorithm presented here is due to Ford[10] and Bellman[1]. We shall denote the shortest distance from V_0 to V_j using at most k arcs by $l_j^{(k)}$. Let $l_j^{(1)} = d_{0j}$ (j = 1,2,...,n-1). (We define $d_{ij} = \infty$ if there is no arc leading from V_i to V_j.)

It is easy to see that $l_j^{(1)} = $ (j = 1,2,...,n-1) are the shortest distances using one arc. When $l_j^{(k)}$ (j = 1,...,n-1) are all known, we can calculate $l_j^{(k+1)}$ recursively by the following equation.

$$l_j^{(k+1)} = \min\ \{(l_j^{(k)}, \underset{i}{\min}\,(l_i^{(k)} + d_{ij})\} \qquad (1)$$

To see (1), we reason as follows: the shortest path to V_j using at most $(k+1)$ arcs may actually consist of k arcs or less. If this is the case, then

$$l_j^{(k+1)} = l_j^{(k)} \; ,$$

which is the first term on the righthand side of (1).

On the other hand, if the shortest path to V_j consists of exactly $k+1$ arcs, then let the intermediate node adjacent to V_j be V_i. So the shortest path to V_j can be viewed as a shortest path of k arcs to V_i followed by an arc e_{ij}. Trying all possible i's, we have the second term on the righthand side of (1).

Actually, the computation of (1) can be reduced. We now describe an improved algorithm due to Yen[29].

Consider an arbitrary shortest path with the intermediate nodes, say

$$V_0, V_3, V_4, V_7, V_5, V_2, V_8$$

Note that the index of the nodes first increases from 0 to 7 then decreases to 2 and then increases to 8. We define an increasing sequence of indices or a decreasing sequence of indices as a *block*. Here the shortest path consists of three blocks. It is easy to see that a shortest path consists of at most (n-1) blocks.

Now we shall attach *new* meaning to $l_j^{(k)}$, and let $l_j^{(k)}$ be the shortest distance from V_0 to V_j of a path with at most k *blocks*.

Here $l_j^{(1)}$ may be the distance of a shortest path of n-1 arcs where the indices of the intermediate nodes increase from 0 to j; i.e., it contains only one block. We define

$$l_j^{(0)} = d_{0j} \qquad \qquad \text{for all j.}$$

$$l_j^{(1)} = \min\left[l_j^{(0)}, \min_{i<j} (l_i^{(1)}+d_{ij})\right] \qquad \text{(for } j = 1,2,...,\text{n-1)} \quad (2)$$

$$l_j^{(2)} = \min\left[l_j^{(1)}, \min_{i>j} (l_i^{(2)}+d_{ij})\right] \qquad \text{(for } j = \text{n-1},...,1) \quad (3)$$

In general

$$l_j^{(k)} = \min\left[l_j^{(k-1)}, \min_{i<j} (l_i^{(k)}+d_{ij})\right] \quad \text{(k odd)} \quad \text{(for } j = 1,2,...,\text{n-1)} \quad (4)$$

$$l_j^{(k)} = \min\left[l_j^{(k-1)}, \min_{i>j} (l_i^{(k)}+d_{ij})\right] \quad \text{(k even)} \quad \text{(for } j = \text{n-1},...,1) \quad (5)$$

Let us apply this algorithm to our example in Figure 1.14, assuming all other arcs not present have infinite length. In Figure 1.14, we show successively how the shortest path is obtained. The underlying concept is very much like that of triple operations except that all paths begin at V_0.

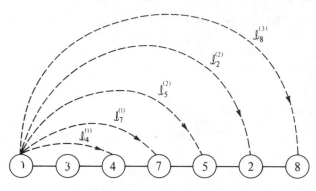

Figure 1.14

We shall only record the relevant information. (All other $l_i^{(k)}$ are infinite.)

$$l_3^{(0)} = d_{03}$$

$$l_3^{(1)} = \min \left[l_3^{(0)}, \min_i \left(l_i^{(1)} + d_{i3} \right) \right] \quad i = 1,2$$

$$= l_3^{(0)}$$

$$l_4^{(1)} = \min \left[l_4^{(0)}, \min_i \left(l_i^{(1)} + d_{i4} \right) \right] \quad i = 1,2,3$$

$$= l_3^{(1)} + d_{34}$$

$$= d_{03} + d_{34}$$

$$l_7^{(1)} = \min \left[l_7^{(0)}, \min_i \left(l_i^{(1)} + d_{i7} \right) \right] \quad i = 1,2,...,6$$

$$= l_4^{(1)} + d_{47}$$

$$= d_{03} + d_{34} + d_{47}$$

$$l_7^{(2)} = \min \left[l_7^{(1)}, \min_i \left(l_i^{(2)} + d_{i7} \right) \right] \quad i = 8$$

$$= l_7^{(1)}$$

$$l_5^{(2)} = \min \left[l_5^{(1)}, \min_i \ (l_i^{(2)} + d_{i5}) \right] \qquad i = 8,7,6$$

$$= l_7^{(2)} + d_{75}$$

$$l_2^{(2)} = \min \left[l_2^{(1)}, \min_i \ (l_i^{(2)} + d_{i2}) \right] \qquad i = 8,7,6,...,3$$

$$= l_5^{(2)} + d_{52}$$

$$l_2^{(3)} = l_2^{(2)}$$

$$l_8^{(3)} = \min \left[l_8^{(2)}, \min_i \ (l_i^{(3)} + d_{i8}) \right] \qquad i = 1,2,...,7$$

$$= l_2^{(3)} + d_{28}$$

$$= d_{03} + d_{34} + d_{47} + d_{75} + d_{52} + d_{28}$$

Note that in calculating $l_j^{(1)}$ we increase j from 1 to 8 and try all possible $i<j$; while in calculating $l_j^{(2)}$, we decrease j from 8 to 1 and try all possible $i>j$.

It is easy to see that the algorithm should terminate if $l_j^{(k+1)} = l_j^{(k)}$ for all j. If $l_j^{(k+1)} \neq l_j^{(k)}$ for some j when k=n-1, then a negative cycle exists.

For a fixed j, we either try those i which are less than j or try those i which are greater than j. Thus we do only half of the work of the algorithm of Ford [10] or Bellman [1]. Furthermore, the present algorithm can be terminated when $l_j^{(k+1)} = l_j^{(k)}$ for all j where k ⩽ n-1 in general. Note also that the storage requirement is reduced since $l_j^{(k)}$ can be erased as soon as $l_j^{(k+1)}$ is created.

§1.7 MINIMUM SPANNING TREE

Given an undirected network N, we can select a subset of arcs which form a tree T in which there is a path between every pair of nodes in the network. This kind of tree is called a *spanning tree* of the network. If there are costs d_{ij} associated with the arcs, the cost of a spanning tree is the sum of d_{ij} for arcs in the tree. A spanning tree with minimum cost among all spanning trees is called a *minimum spanning tree.* In section 1.2, we have a tree which consists of all arcs used in the shortest paths from the origin. In general, the minimum spanning tree is different from the tree of shortest paths.

The following two lemmas seem obvious but their proofs require careful study.

Lemma 1 Let e_{ax} be a shortest arc among all arcs adjacent to an arbitrary node V_a. Then there exists a minimum spanning tree T* which contains the arc e_{ax}. Proof. Let T be a minimum spanning tree, and A be the subset of arcs adjacent to V_a, say $A = \{e_{ab}, e_{ac}, e_{ad}, e_{ax}\}$. Assume the arc e_{ax} is a shortest arc adjacent to V_a but does not belong to T. Since T is a spanning tree, there must be a path in T from V_x to V_a which contains one of the arcs in A, say e_{ad}. We shall denote this path by (P_{xd}, e_{da}) where P_{xd} is the path from V_x to V_d. Replacing e_{ad} by e_{ax}, we have T*. If e_{ax} is shorter than e_{ad}, we claim that T* is a spanning tree of less cost. First, in the tree T*, V_a is connected to V_x by e_{ax} and to V_d by the path (e_{ax}, P_{xd}). The rest of the nodes V_b, V_c are still connected to V_a and hence to the rest of the network, so T* is a spanning tree. Second, the cost of T* is less than T since e_{ax} is shorter than e_{ad}. This contradicts the assumption that T is a minimum spanning tree. If e_{ad} is of the same length as e_{ax}, then we can still replace e_{ad} by e_{ax} and obtain a minimum spanning tree T* containing e_{ax}.

Lemma 2 If a subset of edges forming a subtree F is known to be part of a minimum spanning tree, then there exists a minimum spanning tree containing F and a minimum edge connecting F and N-F.
Proof. The proof is exactly like that of Lemma 1 except we replace V_a by F in the argument.

By Lemma 1, we can start from any vertex and select the minimum adjacent arc. Since we know the arc just selected is part of a minimum spanning tree, we can consider it to be F of Lemma 2 and select the minimum arc incident to F. We can keep selecting a minimum edge incident to the component we already have selected. This is essentially Prim's algorithm for a minimum spanning tree. Note the similarity of Prim's algorithm for minimum spanning tree and Dijkstra's algorithm for shortest paths.

Again, we label the nodes connected by arcs in the spanning tree with permanent labels and those nodes not yet connected with temporary labels.

Prim's Algorithm

Step 0.   Pick an arbitrary node, call it V_1, and label it permanent with value zero (i.e., $P_1 = 0$). Label all other nodes temporary with values T_j equal to d_{1j} for V_j.

Step 1.   Among all the temporary labels, pick the one (say, T_j) with minimum value and make it permanent. Include the arc with value $d_{ij} = T_j$ in the minimum spanning tree where V_i is a permanent node and $T_j = d_{ij}$.

Step 2.   Let V_j be the last node that just became permanent. For each temporary node V_k, let

$$T_k \leftarrow \min \{T_k, d_{jk}\} \ .$$

If there is no temporary label, stop. Otherwise go back to Step 1.

Analysis of Prim's Algorithm There are $(n-1) + (n-2) + \dots + 1 = 0(n^2)$ comparisons in Step 1. In Step 2, we have $(n-2) + \dots + 1 = 0(n^2)$ comparisons. So this algorithm is again an $0(n^2)$ algorithm.

There are other algorithms [5], [28], which need less computation asymptotically. See the suggested reading.

We have defined the cost of a spanning tree to be the sum of d_{ij} for arcs in the tree. The spanning tree of minimum cost is called a minimum spanning tree. In the same manner, we can define a maximum spanning tree. Then Prim's algorithm can be used for maximum spanning trees simply by replacing minimum by maximum (here $d_{ij} = -\infty$ if there is no arc). Now we illustrate Prim's algorithm for a network with the d_{ij} as shown in Table 1.7.

Table 1.7

	①	②	③	④	⑤	⑥
①	0	∞	1	∞	3	∞
②	∞	0	∞	6	∞	8
③	1	∞	0	4	2	∞
④	∞	6	4	0	6	7
⑤	3	∞	2	6	0	∞
⑥	∞	8	∞	7	∞	0

When the data of the network are in a matrix form, Prim's algorithm can be stated as follows:

Step 0.   Cross out all entries in the first column and make a mark on the first row.

Step 1.   Select the minimum entry among all entries in rows which have been marked, say the minimum entry is d_{ij} (crossed out entries cannot be selected). If all entries in checked rows have been crossed out, stop.

Step 2.   Cross out the jth column and make a mark on the jth row. Return to Step 1.

If we apply Prim's algorithm to Table 1.7, then the computation would look like Table 1.8 after two entries have been selected (selected entries are circled).

Table 1.8

	①	②	③	④	⑤	⑥	
①	0	∞	①	∞	3	∞	X
②	∞	0	∞	6	∞	8	
③	1	∞	0	4	②	∞	X
④	∞	6	4	0	6	7	
⑤	3	∞	2	6	0	∞	X
⑥	∞	8	∞	7	∞	0	

§1.8 BREADTH-FIRST-SEARCH AND DEPTH-FIRST-SEARCH

In many applications, we have to visit all the nodes of a graph in a certain order. The two common ways are called breadth-first-search (BFS) and depth-first-search (DFS). We shall use BFS in Chapter 2 and DFS in Chapter 4.

Breadth-First-Search We arbitrarily choose a node of the graph G, call the node V_0 and then visit all neighbors of V_0 in any order, say the nodes $V_1, V_2, ..., V_i$. When we have finished all the neighbors of V_0, we start again from V_1 (the first visited neighbor of V_0) and visit all the neighboring nodes of V_1, say, $V_{11}, V_{12}, ..., V_{1j}$, and then all the neighboring nodes of V_2, say $V_{21}, V_{22}, ..., V_{2k}$. Systematically, we have

Order of Visits	Neighboring Nodes
V_0	$V_1, V_2, ..., V_i$
V_1	$V_{11}, V_{12}, ..., V_{1j}$
V_2	$V_{21}, V_{22}, ..., V_{2k}$
•	
•	
•	
V_i	$V_{i1}, V_{i2}, ..., V_{ip}$
V_{11}	$V_{111}, V_{112}, ...$
V_{12}	$V_{121}, V_{122}, ...$

In Figure 1.15, we can pick V_a as V_0, then we can visit the nodes in the order

$$V_a, V_b, V_c, V_d, V_e, V_f$$
$$V_0, V_1, V_2, V_{11}, V_{21}, V_{111} \ .$$

If we pick V_b as V_0, then we can visit the nodes in the order

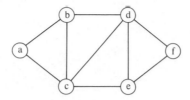

Figure 1.15

$$V_b, V_a, V_c, V_d, V_e, V_f$$
$$V_0, V_1, V_2, V_3, V_{21}, V_{31} .$$

Note that after visiting a new node, we can visit the neighbors of the new node in any order. Here we use the convention that we will visit the nodes in alphabetical order when a choice can be made.

If we label an arc connecting a visited node to a node being visited the first time, then all these labeled arcs form a spanning tree of the graph G; and if each arc has length 1, then the spanning tree is a shortest-path tree from V_0 to all the other nodes in G.

Depth-First-Search We arbitrarily choose a vertex V_0 and then follow an edge e_{01} to V_1, then follow an edge e_{12} to a neighbor V_2 of V_1. In general, when we visit a node V_i, we follow an edge e_{ij} to V_j if V_j has not been visited before. Then we apply the same process recursively to V_j and choose an edge e_{jk} to V_k. If the vertex V_j has been visited, we return to V_i and choose another edge. If all edges incident to V_i have been chosen and no new vertex can be found, we backtrack from V_i to its father which led to V_i and then examine edges incident to the father.

If we start with V_b in Figure 1.15, we might visit the nodes in the following order (the ordering is not unique):

$$V_b, V_c, V_a, V_d, V_e, V_f .$$

The arcs which lead to new vertices form a spanning tree. These arcs are

$$e_{bc}, e_{ca}, e_{cd}, e_{de}, e_{ef} ,$$

and they are shown in heavy lines in Figure 1.16.

The reader should compare the two ways of visiting nodes. In BFS, we would examine all edges incident to a node before moving to a new node. So the operation is "fanning-out" from nodes successively. In DFS, we would move to a new node as soon as a new node is found, and penetrate deeply into the graph. Only when all edges lead to old vertices do we back-up to a previous node and start DFS from there again.

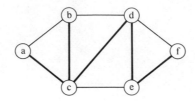

Figure 1.16

EXERCISES

1. Are the following statements right or wrong? For each statement, prove it if it is correct; construct a counterexample if it is wrong.

    (i)   In an undirected network with positive arc distances, the shortest arc in the network always belongs to the tree of shortest paths.

    (ii)   If all arcs in a network have different lengths, then the shortest path tree from V_0 to all the other nodes is unique.

    (iii)   In an acyclic network, to find the longest path, we use $d_{ij}' = k - d_{ij}$ where k is a large constant and find the shortest path. Would this transformation work? Why?

    (iv)   Partition a network into two parts and construct the minimum spanning tree for each part. Then connect the two parts by the shortest arc connecting the two parts. The resulting tree is the minimum spanning tree for the whole network.

    (v)   We get n shortest-path trees with every node as the origin. At least one of them would be a minimum spanning tree.

2. Prove that the brown arcs in the Dijkstra algorithm form a tree if the directions of arcs are ignored.

3. If every node as well as every arc has a length, can you find the shortest path between two nodes? (Hint: transform the network.)

4. The matrix shown in Table 1.7 is the adjacency matrix of a network. State Dijkstra's algorithm in terms of the matrix and then apply the algorithm to the matrix. (As we did for the Prim algorithm.)

	①	②	③	④	⑤	⑥	⑦
①	0	4	5	12	∞	∞	∞
②	4	0	3	∞	1	∞	∞
③	5	3	0	1	∞	∞	13
④	12	∞	1	0	∞	11	∞
⑤	∞	1	∞	∞	0	∞	9
⑥	∞	∞	∞	11	∞	0	8
⑦	∞	∞	13	∞	9	8	0

5.　If the shortest paths between all pairs of nodes are not unique, which path would be chosen by the triple operations? Can anything be done so that we always choose the path with the least number of arcs? (Assume that all data are integers.)

6.　How do you label the nodes of an acyclic directed network such that all directed arcs are from V_i to V_j where $i < j$.

7.　If we use the triple operations to find shortest paths between all pairs of nodes, what is the result after the computation $j=2$.

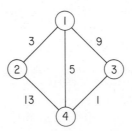

Figure 1.17

8.　Let us change the triple operations slightly as follows:

$$P_{ik} = \begin{cases} P_{ij} & \text{if } d_{ik} \geq d_{ij} + d_{jk} \\ \text{unchanged} & \text{if } d_{ik} < d_{ij} + d_{jk} \end{cases}$$

If the shortest paths between all pairs are not unique, which path would be chosen by the modified triple operations?

9.　In section 4, suppose that the shortest path between any two nodes in X consists of nodes entirely in X. Would this make the decomposition algorithm simpler? (suggested by Canuto and Villa)

10　If we perform triple operations for $j = 1,2,...,m$ $(m<n)$ and then stop, what do the d_{ik} represent?

CHAPTER 1

BIBLIOGRAPHIC NOTES AND SUGGESTED READING

For general information on the shortest path problem, see the books and survey articles by Dreyfus [8], Hu [14], Johnson [16], Murchland [23], and Yen [31].

For the Dijkstra algorithm, see Dijkstra [7]. For the triple operations, see Dantzig [6], Floyd [9], and Warshall [27].

The decomposition algorithms are discussed in Blewett and Hu [2], Hu [13,14], Hu and Torres [15], Land and Stairs [20], Shier [25], and Yen [30].

Section 1.6 is based on Bellman [1], Ford [10], and Yen [29].

For minimum spanning trees, see Cheriton and Tarjan [5], Kruskal [19], Prim [24], and Yao [28].

Sometimes, we are also interested in the second shortest path or the kth shortest path of a network. There are many papers on this subject: See [4], [12], [21], and [22].

To find shortest paths between all pairs of nodes we have the Floyd-Warshall algorithm which takes $0(n^3)$ operations. The average running time can be reduced, see the paper by Spira [26] and its correction by J. S. Carson and A. M. Law [3]. Another algorithm for finding shortest paths between all pairs of nodes is Dantzig's algorithm [6]. Dantzig's algorithm uses an inductive approach. The algorithm first finds conditional shortest paths between nodes 1,2,...,k where the conditional shortest paths must pass only nodes in the set {1,2,...,k}. Then all conditional shortest paths are updated when the node $k+1$ is added to the set. The algorithm terminates when the node n is added.

If we are only interested in the shortest distance between all pairs of nodes but not the paths themselves, we can get all the shortest distances in $0(n^{2+t})$, see the paper by M. Fredman [11].

1.   R. E. Bellman, "On a Routing Problem", Quart. Applied Math. 16 (1958), pp. 87-90.

2.   W. J. Blewett and T. C. Hu, "Tree Decomposition Algorithm for Large Networks", Networks 7 (4) (1977), pp. 289-296.

3.   J. S. Carson and A. M. Law, "A Note on Spira's Algorithm for All-pairs Shortest Paths problem", SIAM J. Computing 6 (4) (1977), pp. 696-699.

4.   S. Clarke, A. Krikorian, and J. Rausen, "Computing the Nth Best Loopless Path in a Network", SIAM J. Appl. Math. 11 (4) (1963), pp. 1096-1102.

5.   D. Cheriton and R. E. Tarjan, "Finding Minimum Spanning Trees", SIAM J. Computing 5 (4) (1976), pp. 724-742.

6.   G. B. Dantzig, "All Shortest Routes in a Graph", Operations Research Report, TR-66-3, Stanford University, Nov. 1966.

7.   E. W. Dijkstra, "A Note on Two Problems in Connection with Graphs", Numerische Mathematik 1 (1959), pp. 269-271.

8.   S. E. Dreyfus, "An Appraisal of Some Shortest-Path Algorithms", ORSA 17 (3) (1969), pp. 395-412.

9.   R. W. Floyd, "Algorithm 97, Shortest Path", Comm. ACM 5 (1962), pp. 345.

10.   L. R. Ford, Jr., "Network Flow Theory", The RAND Corp. (1956), p-923.

11.   M. L. Fredman, "New Bounds on the Complexity of the Shortest Path Problem", SIAM J. Computing 5 (1976), pp. 83-89.

12.   W. Hoffman and R. Pauley, "A Method for the Solution of the Nth Best Path Problem", J. ACM 6 (1959), pp. 508-514.

13.   T. C. Hu, "Decomposition Algorithm for Shortest Paths in a Network", J. ORSA 16 (1) (1968), pp. 91-102.

14.   T. C. Hu, "Integer Programming and Network Flows", Addison-Wesley, 1969.

15. T. C. Hu and W. T. Torres, "A Short Cut in Decomposition Algorithms", J. IBM Res. & Devel. 13 (4) (1969), pp. 387-390.

16. D. B. Johnson, "Algorithms for Shortest Paths", Ph.D. Thesis, Cornell University, 1973.

17. E. L. Johnson, "On Shortest Paths and Sorting", Proc. ACM 25th Annual Conference (1972), pp. 510-517.

18. D. E. Knuth, "Fundamental Algorithms", Addison-Wesley, 2nd edition, 1973.

19. J. B. Kruskal, Jr., "On the Shortest Spanning Tree of a Graph and the Traveling Salesman Problem", Proc. AMS 7 (1956), pp. 48-50.

20. A. H. Land and S. W. Stairs, "The Extension of the Cascade Algorithms to Large Graphs", Management Sci. 14 (1967), pp. 29-33.

21. E. L. Lawler, "Comment on Computing the k Shortest Paths in a Graph", Comm. of ACM 20 (8) (1977), pp. 603-604.

22. E. Minieka, "On Computing Sets of Shortest Paths in a Graph", Comm. of ACM 17 (1974), pp. 351-353.

23. J. D. Murchland, "Bibliography of the Shortest Route Problem", London School of Business Studies LBS-TNT-6.2 (1969).

24. R. C. Prim, "Shortest Connection Networks and Some Generalization", Bell System Technical J. 36 (1957), pp. 1389-1401.

25. D. R. Shier, "A Decomposition Algorithm for Optimality Problems in Tree-structured Networks", Discrete Math. 6 (1973), pp. 175-189.

26. P. M. Spira, "A New Algorithm for Finding all Shortest Paths in a Graph of Positive Arcs in Average Time $0(n^2 \log^2 n)$", SIAM J. Computing 2 (1) (1973), pp. 28-32.

27. S. Warshall, "A Theorem on Boolean Matrices", J. ACM 9 (1962), pp. 11-12.

28. A. C. Yao, "An $0(|E| \log\log |V|)$ Algorithm for Finding Minimum Spanning Trees", Information Processing Letters 4 (1975), pp. 21-23.

29.   J. Y. Yen, "An Algorithm for Finding Shortest Routes from All Source Nodes to a Given Destination in General Networks", Quart. Applied Math. 27 (1970), pp. 526-530.

30.   J. Y. Yen, "On Hu's Decomposition Algorithm for Shortest Paths in a Network", ORSA 19 (1971), pp. 983-985.

31.   J. Y. Yen, "Shortest Path Network Problems", Math. Systems in Economics 18, Verlag Anton Hain, 1975.

ANSWERS TO EXERCISES IN CHAPTER 1

1.

   (i)   Wrong.

   (ii)   Wrong.

   (iii) It cannot work because the number of arcs in the longest paths are not the same.

   (iv)   Wrong.

   (v)   A four-node counter example can be constructed.

3. If a node has length k, we can add k/2 to each arc which is adjacent to the node.

5. Let a shortest path have intermediate nodes $V_i, V_j, ..., V_p$ were the maximum index is given by

$$\max(i, j, ..., p) = q \ .$$

The shortest path with the minimum maximum index will be chosen.

    Assume that all arc lengths are integers, we can add a small decimal d nd < 1.

6. Label all nodes with inward degree zero with numbers 1,2,... . Erase all these nodes and their out-going arcs. Repeat.

8. The maximum index is maximum.

CHAPTER 2. MAXIMUM FLOW

There is a bottleneck in every system.

§2.1 MAXIMUM FLOWS

In this chapter, we shall study the so-called maximum flow problem of a network. Here, a number is associated with every arc of the network. This number is *not* the length of the arc, but more like the width of the arc. If we think of the network as a railroad network with the nodes representing railroad stations, then the number associated with the arc may represent the number of tracks between two stations. If we think of the network as a pipeline system and the nodes as the junctions, then the number represents the cross-sectional area of the pipeline between two junctions. We shall introduce a new concept of flows in a network, and use the number to indicate the maximum amount of liquid that can go through the arc. We call this number the *arc capacity*. The arc capacity of the arc e_{ij} is denoted by b_{ij}. In this section and the next, we shall not be concerned with the lengths of arcs, but with arc capacities only; we assume that $b_{ij} \geqslant 0$ for all i,j.

To specify a network, we shall specify the arc capacities of all the arcs. We also specify two special nodes, called the *source* and the *sink* of the network. The problem is to find the maximum amount of flow that can go through from the source to the sink. First, we have to define precisely what we mean by the flow in a network, since our flow does not behave exactly like water or any other liquid. The arc flow from V_i to V_j in the arc e_{ij} is denoted by x_{ij}. We have the constraint in the arc,

$$0 \leqslant x_{ij} \leqslant b_{ij} \tag{1}$$

Besides the constraint (1) we also want the inflow to any node to be equal to the outflow of any node; i.e., the flow is conserved at every node (except at the source and the sink). If we denote the source by V_s and the sink by V_t, then the constraint at every node V_j is

$$\sum_i x_{ij} = \sum_k x_{jk} \qquad \text{for all } j \neq s,t \tag{2}$$

Since the flow is conserved at every node, the input from the source must be equal to the output of the sink. Thus

$$\sum_i x_{si} = v = \sum_j x_{jt} \tag{3}$$

where v is called the *value* of the flow.

We can replace an undirected arc e_{ij} by two directed arcs, one from V_i to V_j and one from V_j to V_i, both with arc capacity equal to b_{ij}. The set of x_{ij} satisfying (1), (2), and (3) is called a flow in the network. A flow with maximum possible value is called *maximum flow*.

There are great differences between the flows in a network defined by (1), (2), (3) and the electric currents in an electrical network. The constraint (2) is just like the "node law" of the electrical current which says the amount of current entering a node is the same as the amount of current leaving the node, but there is no "loop law" governing our flows. Also the constraint (1) is not like Ohm's law of linear resistance. It is a very peculiar kind of arc that gives no resistance to flow until the flow reaches the upper limit b_{ij}. Then the resistance becomes ∞.

This new kind of flow is very useful in many applications. For example, what is the minimum number of arcs that has to be removed to disconnect two special nodes of a graph? This question is purely a problem of graph theory, but can be easily solved using the concept of flow. Other applications are discussed in § 2.5.

If the network consists of a path only, say $(V_s, V_1, V_2, ..., V_n, V_t)$, then the maximum amount of flow that can go from V_s to V_t satisfying (1), (2), and (3) is

$$\min (b_{s1}, b_{12}, b_{23}, \ldots, b_{nt}) \tag{4}$$

Here, the arc with the minimum arc capacity is the bottleneck of the network. Now, we shall define the notion of a bottleneck in a general network. A bottleneck of a general network is called a cut.

A *cut* is the collection of all arcs from a subset of nodes to its complement. It is denoted by $(X, \overline{X})$, where X is the subset of nodes and $\overline{X}$ its complement. Thus a cut $(X, \overline{X})$ is a set of all arcs e_{ij} with either $V_i \in X$ and $V_j \in \overline{X}$ or $V_j \in X$ and $V_i \in \overline{X}$. The removal of all the arcs in a cut will disconnect the network into two or more components. A cut separating V_s and V_t is a cut $(X, \overline{X})$ with $V_s \in X$ and $V_t \in \overline{X}$.

Symbolically, we show a network in Figure 2.1a where the real network might be like that in Figure 2.1b or Figure 2.3, for example.

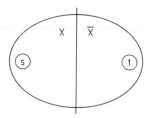

Figure 2.1a

The *capacity* or *value* of a cut $(X,\overline{X})$, $c(X,\overline{X})$, is $\sum_{i,j} b_{ij}$ with $V_i \in X$ and $V_j \in \overline{X}$. Note that in defining a cut, we count all the arcs that are between the set X and the set $\overline{X}$; but in calculating its capacity, we count the capacity only of arcs from X to $\overline{X}$, but not the directed arcs from $\overline{X}$ to X. Therefore, $c(X,\overline{X}) \neq c(\overline{X},X)$, in general.

Some authors define a cut $(X,\overline{X})$ as the set of arcs leading from X to $\overline{X}$ but do not include the set of arcs leading from $\overline{X}$ to X. In any case, $c(X,\overline{X}) \neq c(\overline{X},X)$ in general unless the network consists of undirected arcs only.

A cut $(X,\overline{X})$ separating V_s and V_t is then analogous to a bottleneck. Consider any cut $(X,\overline{X})$ which separates V_s from V_t, and assume that some arcs are directed from X to $\overline{X}$ and others from $\overline{X}$ to X. Since the flow is conserved, the amount of flow coming out of V_s must be equal to the amount going into V_t. Due to constraint (2), this amount is also equal to the net amount across any cut $(X,\overline{X})$ (i.e., the amount from X to $\overline{X}$, minus the amount from $\overline{X}$ to X). Due to constraint (1), the maximum flow value cannot exceed $c(X,\overline{X})$ for any cut $(X,\overline{X})$. What is surprising, perhaps, is that the maximum flow value is always equal to the minimum capacity of all cuts separating V_s and V_t. A cut separating V_s and V_t with minimum capacity is called a *minimum cut.* (For simplicity, we will sometimes omit the phrase "separating V_s and V_t" in describing a cut.) The fact that the maximum flow value is always equal to the capacity of a minimum cut was proved first by Ford and Fulkerson [6]. This is the central theorem in network flow theory.

We shall give a constructive proof of the theorem (see Ford and Fulkerson [7]), which constructs a maximum flow and locates a minimum cut. The proof shows that there always exists a flow with value equal to the capacity of a minimum cut. Since the maximum flow is always equal to or less than the capacity of any cut, in particular the minimum cut, this will prove the theorem.

Theorem 1 Max-Flow Min-Cut Theorem [6] [7]. For any network with integer arc capacities, the maximum flow value from the source to the sink is equal to the capacity of a minimum cut separating the source and the sink.

Proof. The constructive proof goes as follows:

If the current flow value equals the capacity of a cut, then the theorem is proved. If the flow value does not equal the capacity of a cut, we search for a path from V_s to V_t so that we can send additional flow along the path. This would increase the value of the flow. We keep doing this until no such path can be found. Then we prove that the flow value equals the capacity of a cut. Now we describe a systematic way of searching for such a path.

We start with any set of x_{ij} satisfying (1) and (2) (for example, $x_{ij} = 0$ for all i and j). Based on the current flow in the network we shall define a subset X of the nodes recursively by the following rules.

0. $V_s \in X$.

1.   If $V_i \in X$ and $x_{ij} < b_{ij}$, then $V_j \in X$.

2.   If $V_i \in X$ and $x_{ji} > 0$, then $V_j \in X$.

Any nodes not in X then belong to $\overline{X}$. Using these rules to define the set X, we have two possible outcomes.

Case 1 V_t is in $\overline{X}$. This implies that for all arcs from X to $\overline{X}$ we have $x_{ij} = b_{ij}$ (due to rule 1) and there is no arc flow x_{ji} from $\overline{X}$ to X (due to rule 2). Then

$$\sum_{\substack{i \in X \\ j \in \overline{X}}} x_{ij} = \sum_{\substack{i \in X \\ j \in \overline{X}}} b_{ij} \text{ and } \sum_{\substack{i \in X \\ j \in \overline{X}}} x_{ji} = 0.$$

Hence we have a flow with value equal to $c(X,\overline{X})$.

Case 2 V_t is in X. This implies that there is a path from V_s to V_t and the path is formed by arcs satisfying rule 1 or rule 2.

Let the path be

$$V_s,...,V_i,e_{ij},V_j,...,V_t.$$

Every arc in the path must satisfy either rule 1 or rule 2. If the arc satisfies rule 1, i.e.,

$$x_{ij} < b_{ij} ,$$

Then we can send additional flow from V_i to V_j. This would increase the amount of flow in the arc. This kind of arc is called a *forward arc*.

If the arc satisfies rule 2, i.e.,

$$x_{ji} > 0 ,$$

then we can send flow from V_i to V_j, effectively canceling the existing flow in the arc. The net effect is to reduce the amount of flow in the arc. This kind of arc is called a *backward arc*. This path is called a *flow-augmenting path* with respect to the current flow. For example, we have a network in Figure 2.3 (in section 2.2) where numbers indicate the arc capacities. If the arc flows are $x_{s1} = x_{12} = x_{2t} = 1$, and every other $x_{ij} = 0$, then $e_{s3}, e_{32}, e_{21}, e_{14}, e_{4t}$ would be a flow-augmenting path with e_{21} being a backward arc.

Assume all arc capacities are integers, and let $\epsilon_1 =$ minimum of all differences $b_{ij} - x_{ij}$ in the path, let $\epsilon_2 =$ minimum of x_{ji} in the path, and let $\epsilon = \min(\epsilon_1, \epsilon_2) =$ positive integer. Then we can increase the arc flows by ϵ on all forward arcs of the path and decrease the arc flows by ϵ on all backward arcs of the path. In this way the value of the flow is increased by ϵ and the new x_{ij} satisfies all the constraints (1) and (2). Now we can redefine the set X again based on the new flow. If V_t is still in X, we can again increase the flow value by some ϵ. Since the capacity of a minimum cut is a finite number and we increase the value of the flow by at least one unit, after a finite number of steps we always obtain the maximum flow.   **Q.E.D.**

We shall use F_{st} to denote the set of nonnegative integers x_{ij} satisfying (1), (2), and (3). Then we have the following corollary.

Corollary 1 A flow F_{st} is maximum if and only if there is no flow augmenting path with respect to F_{st}.

Several comments are in order. The value of a maximum flow is certainly unique in any network, but there may be many flows that give the same maximum flow value. Also there may be many minimum cuts in the network. For example, consider the network in Figure 2.1b.

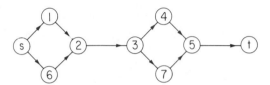

Figure 2.1b

Assume that every arc has a capacity of one unit. Then both the arc e_{23} and the arc e_{5t} are minimum cuts. The maximum flow value is certainly 1, but the maximum flow can be $x_{s1} = x_{12} = x_{23} = x_{34} = x_{45} = x_{5t} = 1$ or $x_{s6} = x_{62} = x_{23} = x_{37} = x_{75} = x_{5t} = 1$.

If the flow were water, then it would be impossible to have $x_{s1} = x_{12} = x_{23} = x_{34} = x_{45} = x_{5t} = 1$ and $x_{s6} = x_{62} = x_{37} = x_{75} = 0$ since this would mean some pipes were saturated and others completely dry. This is how our flow behaves differently from water.

Let $(X,\overline{X})$ and $(Y,\overline{Y})$ be two cuts. The two cuts are said to *cross* each other if and only if every one of the following four sets consists of at least one node

$$X \cap Y \quad , \quad X \cap \overline{Y}$$
$$\overline{X} \cap Y \quad , \quad \overline{X} \cap \overline{Y} \ .$$

Theorem 2 Let $(X,\overline{X})$ and $(Y,\overline{Y})$ be minimum cuts. The $(X \cup Y, \overline{X \cup Y})$ and $(X \cap Y, \overline{X \cap Y})$ are also minimum cuts.

Proof. If $X \subset Y$, then $X \cup Y = Y$ and $X \cap Y = X$, so

$$(X \cup Y, \overline{X \cup Y}) = (Y,\overline{Y}) \text{ and}$$
$$(X \cap Y, \overline{X \cap Y}) = (X,\overline{X}) \quad .$$

Now consider the case where $X \not\subset Y$ and $Y \not\subset X$, as shown in Figure 2.2. In other words, the two cuts cross each other. Define the four disjoint sets as follows:

$$Q = X \cap Y \ , \quad S = X \cap \overline{Y}$$
$$P = \overline{X} \cap Y \ , \quad R = \overline{X} \cap \overline{Y}$$

where $V_s \in Q$ and $V_t \in R$ by definition. Note that

$$X = Q \cup S \ , \quad \overline{X} = P \cup R$$
$$Y = P \cup Q \ , \quad \overline{Y} = R \cup S \ .$$

Let $c(P,Q) = \sum b_{ij}$ for all $i \in P, j \in Q$, and similarly for other notations.

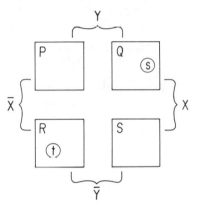

Figure 2.2

Since $(X,\overline{X})$ and $(Y,\overline{Y})$ are minimum cuts and $(P \cup Q \cup S, R)$ and $(Q, P \cup R \cup S)$ are cuts separating V_s and V_t, we must have

$$c(X,\overline{X}) + c(Y,\overline{Y}) \leqslant c(P \cup Q \cup S, R) + c(Q,P \cup R \cup S) \qquad (5)$$

or $\quad c(Q,P) + c(Q,R) + c(S,P) + c(S,R) + c(P,R) + c(P,S) + c(Q,R) + c(Q,S)$

$$\leqslant c(P,R) + c(Q,R) + c(S,R) + c(Q,P) + c(Q,R) + c(Q,S) \qquad (6)$$

or $\quad c(P,S) + c(S,P) \leqslant 0 \qquad (7)$

Since $c(P,S) + c(S,P)$ has to be nonnegative, we see that (5) must be an equality, i.e.

$$c(X,\overline{X}) + c(Y,\overline{Y}) = c(P \cup Q \cup S,R) + c(Q,P \cup R \cup S)$$

or $\quad c(X,\overline{X}) + c(Y,\overline{Y}) = c(X \cup Y, \overline{X \cup Y}) + c(X \cap Y, \overline{X \cap Y}) \qquad (8)$

Since neither term on the RHS of (8) can be strictly less than the capacity of a minimum cut, both must be equal to minimum cut capacity.

The reader should note that $c(P,S) \neq c(S,P)$ in general but both $c(P,S)$ and

$c(S,P)$ are nonnegative. Theorem 2 says that if there are two minimum cuts (separating V_s and V_t) which cross each other, then there are two other minimum cuts which do not cross each other.

§2.2 ALGORITHMS FOR MAXIMUM FLOW

We have seen in section 2.1 that a flow is a maximum flow if and only if there is no flow-augmenting path from V_s to V_t in the network. The constructive proof in the last section can also be implemented as an algorithm which systematically searches for flow-augmenting paths in the network. In fact, the first algorithm for finding maximum flow, due to Ford and Fulkerson, is based on their constructive proof [7].

To understand the algorithm, we first give a numerical example to illustrate some concepts.

Consider Figure 2.3, where numbers inside the square brackets are the arc capacities. We could send one unit of flow along the path (V_s,V_1,V_2,V_t) and another unit of flow along the path $(V_s,V_3,V_2,V_1,V_4,V_t)$. The superposition of the two flow-augmenting paths is equivalent to two flow-augmenting paths (V_s,V_3,V_2,V_t) and (V_s,V_1,V_4,V_t). Note that the arc e_{12} is first used to ship flow from V_1 to V_2 and then used to ship flow from V_2 to V_1. The net effect is that e_{12} is empty. Normally, the arc e_{12} is a directed arc and could only be used to ship flow from V_1 to V_2. But when $x_{12} > 0$, we have the option of shipping flow from V_2 to V_1 which amounts to canceling the existing arc flow.

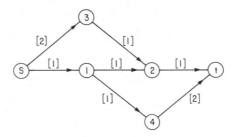

Figure 2.3

§2.2.1 FORD-FULKERSON ALGORITHM

The Ford-Fulkerson algorithm is a systematic way of searching for a flow-augmenting path. The algorithm is called a labeling method and can easily be implemented if the input data are given in adjacent-list form. (The reader unfamiliar with data structures can ignore comments about them in this book.)

The Ford-Fulkerson algorithm consists of two steps. Step 1 assigns labels to nodes to search for a flow-augmenting path. Step 2 increases the flow along the flow-augmenting path found in Step 1. We start with zero flow value (i.e., $x_{ij} \equiv 0$ for all i,j and then we repeat Step 1 and Step 2 until the flow is maximum.

Step 1. Labeling Process: Every node is always in one of three states:

    (i)   Unlabeled: if the node receives no label. In the beginning, every node is unlabeled.

    (ii)   Labeled and unscanned: if the node has a label and not all its neighbors have been labeled.

    (iii)   Labeled and scanned: if the node has a label and all its neighbors have also been labeled.

A node V_j gets a label consisting of two numbers (a,b). The first number a indicates the maximum additional amount of flow we can ship from V_s to V_j and the second number b indicates the last intermediate node on the flow-augmenting path from V_s to V_j. (Note the similarity between the label here and the label used in shortest path problems in section 1.2.)

To start the algorithm, we give V_s the label $[\infty, s]$ and all the neighbors V_i get $[b_{si}, s]$. Suppose a labeled node V_i has neighbor V_j which has not been labeled. Then V_j gets $[\epsilon(j), i]$ where

$$\epsilon(j) = \min[b_{si}, b_{ij}] .$$

In general, we can ship additional flow from V_i to V_j if

$$x_{ij} < b_{ij}$$

    or $$x_{ji} > 0 .$$

So let us assume V_i has a label $[\epsilon(i), r^+]$. Then V_j gets the label $[\epsilon(j), i^+]$ if

$$x_{ij} < b_{ij} \text{ where } \epsilon(j) = \min[\epsilon(i), b_{ij} - x_{ij}] > 0 .$$

The node V_j gets the label $[\epsilon(j), i^-]$ if

$$x_{ji} > 0 \text{ where } \epsilon(j) = \min[\epsilon(i), x_{ji}] > 0 .$$

The i^+ or i^- both indicate that V_i is the last intermediate node, but + indicates that the arc e_{ij} is a forward arc, and − indicates that the arc e_{ij} is a backward arc. Note that the node V_j gets labeled only if $\epsilon(j)$ is strictly positive.

At first, V_s is labeled and unscanned, then becomes labeled and scanned when all the neighbors of V_s are labeled. Then the neighbors of V_s also become labeled and scanned when all the neighbors of neighbors are labeled. The labeling process continues until either

    (i) V_t is labeled

or (ii)   No more labels can be assigned and V_t is unlabeled.

In case (ii), all the labeled nodes (scanned or unscanned) constitute the set X; while unlabeled nodes constitute the set $\overline{X}$. The cut $(X,\overline{X})$ is the minimum cut and the current flow is maximum. The algorithm terminates.

Step 2.   Flow Change: When V_t is labeled, we can trace back from V_t to V_s and change arc flows in the flow-augmenting path. Assume that V_t is labeled $[\epsilon(t), k^+]$, and V_k is labeled $[\epsilon(k), j^-]$, and V_j is labeled $[\epsilon(j), s^+]$. Then we add $\epsilon(t)$ to x_{kt} and x_{sj} and subtract $\epsilon(t)$ from x_{jk}; i.e., we add $\epsilon(t)$ to arc flows in forward arcs and decrease $\epsilon(t)$ from arc flows in backward arcs.

    Erase all labels and return to Step 1.

    The original Ford-Fulkerson algorithm does not specify the order that we give labels to nodes or inspect labeled and unscanned nodes. If we follow the rule of first-label-first-scan, then we are always using a shortest flow-augmenting path (shortest means the minimum number of arcs in the path). This modification is due to Edmonds and Karp [4]. In computer science, the rule of first-label-first-scan is more commonly known as breadth-first search (see § 1.8). If we use the breadth-first search for flow-augmenting paths and apply it to the network in Figure 2.3, we may get Figure 2.4 where the numbers beside the arcs are the current arc flows. (The numbers inside the square brackets are arc capacities.)

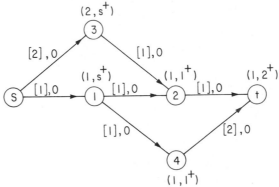

Figure 2.4

    After we add one unit of flow along the path (V_s, V_1, V_2, V_t) and execute the labeling process again, we have the following labels in Figure 2.5.

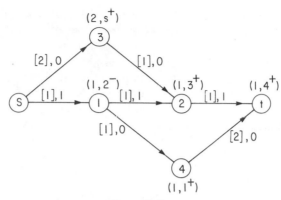

Figure 2.5

Based on the flow-augmenting path $(V_s,V_3,V_2,V_1,V_4,V_t)$ and the labels on these nodes, we add one unit of flow to $x_{s3},x_{32},x_{14},x_{4t}$ and subtract one unit from x_{12}. After this flow-change, we have

$$x_{s3} = x_{32} = x_{2t} = 1 \text{ and } x_{s1} = x_{14} = x_{4t} = 1.$$

If we do the labeling process again, then V_s and V_3 will be labeled and V_1, V_2, V_4, $\overline{V}_t$ will not be labeled; and the maximum flow is 2 while the minimum cut is $(X,\overline{X}) = (s,3 \mid 1,2,4,t)$.

Conceptually, an arc with capacity b_{ij} and arc flow x_{ij} is equivalent to an arc with capacity b'_{ij} where

$$b'_{ij} = b_{ij} - x_{ij} .$$

If the arc e_{ji} is a directed arc with arc flow $x_{ji} > 0$, then it is equivalent to an arc with capacity $b'_{ij} = b_{ij} + x_{ji}$.

Given any set of arc flows, the network constructed with b'_{ij} is called the *residue network* induced by the existing flow. As long as b'_{ij} is not zero, we say there is a *useful arc* from V_i to V_j.

Let us review briefly the Ford-Fulkerson algorithm.

1.   Based on the current flow, we construct the residue network with b'_{ij}.

2.   Systematically search for a flow-augmenting path in the residue network and increase the flow along the flow-augmenting path.

If all the arc capacities are integers, then each increment of flow is also an integer and the algorithm will terminate correctly. If arc capacities can be irrational, then it is possible to construct an example so that the algorithm will converge to the wrong limit and take an infinite number of steps (see [8]).

If we use the breadth-first search suggested by Edmonds and Karp, then we always increase the flow along the shortest flow-augmenting path. A flow-augmenting path is considered to be of length k if there are k arcs in the path. We first use a flow-augmenting path of length 1. When there are no flow-augmenting paths of length 1, we use a flow-augmenting path of length 2. This is repeated until the shortest flow—augmenting path is of length n-1. We divide the computation into n−1 phases. Each phase consists of increasing flows on aug-menting paths of a given length k (k = 1,2,...,n−1). (We will show that the shortest augmenting path increases in length from phase to phase.) At the end of each phase, we construct the residue network induced by the existing flow. In the beginning of each phase, we have a residue network with arc capacity b'_{ij}.

We divide all nodes of the network into different layers. By definition, the source V_s is at layer zero. We regard every arc to be of length 1. Then a node V_i is at layer k if the shortest distance from V_s to V_i is k. (In other words, the shortest path from V_s to V_i consists of k useful arcs.)

In Figure 2.6, we show a network partitioned into four layers.

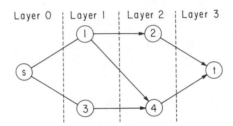

Figure 2.6

Note that V_t is at layer 3. Hence the shortest flow-augmenting path is of length 3. If we send flow in the network such that there is no flow-augmenting path of length 3, then the flow is called *maximal.* For example, in Figure 2.6, assuming all arcs have capacities 1, we can send one unit of flow along the path (e_{s1}, e_{14}, e_{4t}). Then there is no flow-augmenting path of length 3 and we declare the current flow (of one unit) to be *maximal,* although the *maximum* flow in this net-work is 2 units.

We call the part of the algorithm which

(i)   finds the residue network

(ii)   partitions the nodes into layers

(iii)   finds the *maximal* flow in the layered network

a *phase.* The algorithm consists of a sequence of these phases with increasing shortest flow-augmenting paths so that there are at most n−1 phases.

For a given network, assume that the shortest flow-augmenting path consists of k arcs. Let N(f) be the residue network induced by the flow f and let $\widetilde{N}(f)$ be the residue *subnetwork* consisting only of useful arcs connecting layer i to layer i+1 (i = 0,1,2,...,k−1). If the flow is increased as much as possible using augmenting paths of length k, then the new residue network and new residue subnetwork are denoted by $N(f_1)$ and $\widetilde{N}(f_1)$, respectively. We write

$$l(t) = k$$

to denote that V_t is at the layer k in $\widetilde{N}(f)$. We shall show that

$$l(t) > k \text{ in } \widetilde{N}(f_1).$$

When we partition nodes into layers in the residue network N(f), we can classify all useful arcs into five classes:

Class A: useful arcs leading from layer i to layer i+1

Class B: useful arcs leading from layer i to layer j where j > i+1.

Class C: useful arcs leading from layer i+1 to layer i

Class D: useful arcs leading from layer j to layer i where j > i+1

Class E: useful arcs leading from layer i to layer i.

Actually, the class B is empty, or it would contradict the definition of layers. On the other hand, the arcs in classes C, D, and E are in N(f) but not in $\widetilde{N}(f)$ so these arcs are not affected by the flow changes.

Now arcs in class A may be used in augmenting paths if i+1 ⩽ k and at least one arc in each augmenting path will become useless. Let $e_{i,i+1}$ be such an arc. Then $e_{i+1,i}$ becomes a useful arc in $N(f_1)$.

We claim that the shortest augmenting path in $\widetilde{N}(f_1)$ is at least of length k+1; i.e., $l(t) \geqslant k+1$ in $\widetilde{N}(f_1)$.

If the shortest augmenting path in $\widetilde{N}(f_1)$ does not use the arc $e_{i+1,i}$, then the path must use arcs only in classes A, C, D, and E in N(f). If the path uses only arcs in A and reaches t then it means the previous phase is not completed. If the path uses any one arc in C, D, or E then the path must be of length k+1 or more.

If the augmenting path in $\widetilde{N}(f_1)$ uses the arc $e_{i+1,i}$, then the subpath from V_s to V_{i+1} must be of length i+1, and the subpath from V_i to V_t must be of length at least k−i. So the total length is at least (i+1) + 1 + (k−i) = k+2.

If the length of the augmenting path increases from phase to phase, then there are at most n−1 such phases. Assume that there are m arcs. During a phase, there are at most m augmenting paths and each path needs at most 0(m) steps to search. So the total amount of work is $0(m^2)$ in a phase and $0(nm^2)$ for the algorithm of Edmonds and Karp.

The upper bound $0(nm^2)$ is obtained assuming that we search each augmenting path in $N(f)$ independently. We can improve the upper bound to $0(n^2m)$ if we coordinate the search for augmenting paths of a given length in a phase. This improved bound is due to Dinic [3].

Dinic Algorithm

We first construct $\widetilde{N}(f)$ using breadth-first-search. Once the network $\widetilde{N}(f)$ is constructed, we search for augmenting paths in $\widetilde{N}(f)$ using a depth-first-search to reach V_t. If we reach V_t, we increase flow along the path, update the capacities of arcs when we trace back the augmenting path, and delete arcs whose capacities become zero.

If we have to "back-up" from a node V_i during the depth-first-search for augmenting paths, then we cross out all the arcs adjacent to V_i in $\widetilde{N}(f)$. The depth-first-search for an augmenting path takes at most $0(n)$ time, and there are at most m augmenting paths in a phase, so the total amount of work is $0(nm)$ in a phase and $0(n^2m)$ for all the phases. (A detailed analysis of all flow algorithms is given in § 2.2.4.)

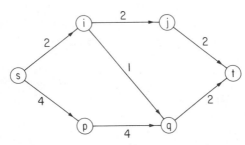

Figure 2.7

Consider the $\widetilde{N}(f)$ network in Figure 2.7 where the numbers beside the arcs are the capacities. If the depth-first-search gets the augmenting path

$$V_s \ [\infty, s^+], \ V_i \ [2, s^+], \ V_q \ [1, i^+], \ V_t \ [1, q^+],$$

then we assign the flow $x_{si} = x_{iq} = x_{qt} = 1$ and delete e_{iq} from the $\widetilde{N}(f)$ network.

If the next depth-first-search gets

$$V_s[\infty, s^+], \ V_p[4, s^+], \ V_q[4, p^+], \ V_t[1,q^+]$$

we assign $x_{sp} = x_{pq} = x_{qt} = 1$ and delete e_{qt} from the network.

If the next depth-first-search gets

$$V_s[\infty, s^+], \ V_p[3, s^+], \ V_q[3, p^+]$$

and we have to "back up" from V_q, to V_p (hence cross out e_{pq}) and back up from V_p to V_s (hence cross out e_{sp}), and then start a new depth-first-search

$$V_s[\infty, s^+], \ V_i[1, s^+], \ V_j[1, i^+], \ V_t[1, j^+] \ .$$

Note that the depth-first-search takes at most $0(n)$ time to get an augmenting path, and each search would delete at least one arc. The Dinic algorithm is to saturate one arc at a time in constructing *maximal* flow in a phase. Now we shall describe an algorithm due to Karzanov [21] which saturates at least one node at a time in constructing maximal flow in a phase and has a upper bound of $0(n^3)$.

§2.2.2 KARZANOV'S ALGORITHM

Before we can describe Karzanov's algorithm, we have to first describe the concept of *preflow* in a network. A set of x_{ij} is said to form a *preflow* in a network if

(i)   At every arc

$$x_{ij} \leqslant b_{ij} \tag{1}$$

(ii)   At every node V_j with incoming arcs e_{ij} and outgoing arcs e_{jk}, we have

$$\sum_{e_{ij} \in \alpha (V_j)} x_{ij} \geqslant \sum_{e_{jk} \in \beta (V_j)} x_{jk} \tag{2}$$

where $\alpha(V_j)$ denotes the set of arcs entering V_j

and $\beta(V_j)$ denotes the set of arcs leaving V_j.

A node with (2) satisfied as a strict inequality is called an *unbalanced* node.

If every node is balanced, then the preflow becomes a flow in a network.

The Karzanov algorithm consists of many phases where each phase is to find a *maximal* flow in a layered network. So the general setup is very much like Dinic's algorithm. But Karzanov's way of finding a maximal flow in a layered network is quite different.

Remember that in the Dinic algorithm, we find maximal flow in a residue subnetwork $\bar{N}(f)$ by saturating *one arc* at a time. Now, in the Karzanov algorithm, we find maximal flow in $\bar{N}(f)$ by saturating *one node* at a time. We start a phase by pushing the preflows from V_s and then from layer to layer until V_t is reached. Then we balance the preflow at every node until every node is balanced. Thus in a phase, we have two steps. Step 1 is called the advance of preflow and Step 2 is called the balance of preflow. The steps are iterated so that the flow becomes maximal in the residue subnetwork $\widetilde{N}(f)$.

Karzanov's Algorithm For Maximal Flow In A Layered Network

Step 0.   Based on the current flow in the network, construct the $\widetilde{N}(f)$ network.

Step 1.   Advance of the preflow in $\widetilde{N}(f)$.

Step 2.   Balance of the preflow in $\widetilde{N}(f)$.

Steps 1 and 2 are iterated until every node is balanced except V_s and V_t.

In finding a maximal flow in $\widetilde{N}(f)$ in a given phase we call an arc e_{ij} *closed* if we do not allow the current x_{ij} to be changed. An arc is called *open* if its arc flow can be changed. Initially, all arcs in the layered network are open. During Step 2, some arcs may be declared closed and the arc flows in these arcs then remain the same for the rest of the phase.

For a given node V_j all the arcs e_{jk} are ordered in a certain order; say, in the increasing order of the index k. When we try to advance flow from V_j to the next layer, we always try to put as much flow as possible in the first open arc which is not saturated; and then as much as possible in the second open arc, etc. So the arcs in $\beta(V_j)$ are like a *queue*.

This ordering of arcs is fixed during the phase. Thus, typically, among all open arcs in $\beta(V_j)$ we may have several arcs saturated to their capacities, and one arc with $x_{jk} < b_{jk}$, and several other arcs with zero flow.

The arcs in $\alpha(V_j)$ are not ordered at first, rather, we keep track of the order in which x_{ij} are added to the node V_j. If during the phase we want to reduce the incoming flow to V_j, we will reduce the latest addition first; in other words, we reduce the x_{ij} in the last-in-first-out fashion, so it is like a *stack*. Now we can describe the details of the algorithm.

Step 1 Advance of Preflow

The purpose of this subroutine is to push forward as much preflow as possible from the source to the sink.

We start at the source V_s (at the layer 0) and we push as much preflow as possible into nodes at the layer 1 by setting $x_{sj} = b_{sj}$ to all nodes V_j at the layer 1. And we consider that we have moved the preflow from the layer 0 to the layer 1.

In general, we consider the unbalanced nodes at the lowest layer and try to push preflow into the next layer and successively to V_t. The advance subroutine stops when it is impossible to push any preflow forward from any node V_j. This happens if arcs in $\beta(V_j)$ are either closed or are saturated to their capacities.

Step 2 Balance of Preflow

The purpose of this subroutine is to make unbalanced nodes balanced, and effectively to reduce preflows to regular flows.

We start with the highest layer which contains unbalanced nodes V_j. For every such node V_j, we reduce the incoming flows to the node in the last-in-first-out fashion, until the node is balanced. All the arcs in $\alpha(V_j)$ to the newly balanced node are marked closed. If all the unbalanced nodes are balanced in this layer we return to Step 1 (even if there may be unbalanced nodes in lower layers).

Note that the first time we use Step 1, we push preflow from the layer 0 to layer 1, layer 1 to layer 2, ..., until V_t is reached; and then go to Step 2. However, in the balance subroutine, we concentrate only on one layer, the highest layer j containing unbalanced nodes. The effect of balancing nodes in the layer j will create unbalanced nodes in layer $j-1$. Since all nodes in layer $j-2,...,0$ have been processed already, we can start Step 1 from layer $j-1$ and push as much preflow as possible to the sink t.

Now we shall give a numerical example which is constructed to show all the possibilities, and hence is very unfavorable to the Karzanov algorithm.

Consider the $\widetilde{N}(f)$ network in Figure 2.8 where all arcs are directed from left to right and the numbers beside the arcs are capacities (within a layer, we shall process the smallest index node first). We assume that the queue for the outgoing arcs at every node is to try the lower index arc first, thus e_{12} before e_{13}, and at the node V_3, e_{34} is before e_{35}.

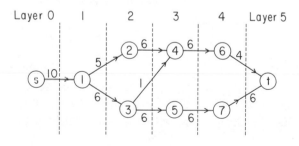

Figure 2.8

Step 1.   If we advance preflow from V_s to V_t, we have the preflow as shown in Figure 2.9. (The first number in square brackets is the arc capacity and the second number is the arc flow.)

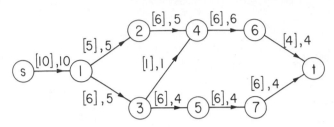

Figure 2.9

Step 2.   Now V_6 is the unbalanced node at the highest layer and we change x_{46} from 6 to 4 and mark e_{46} closed. All nodes at layer 4 are balanced so we go to Step 1.

Step 1.   We advance the preflow from layer 3 where V_4 is the only node which has excess flow. Since the only outgoing arc e_{46} is closed, the advance from V_4 ends, and we return to Step 2.

Step 2.   Now V_4 is the unbalanced node at the highest layer 3. We reduce x_{34} to zero, since it is the last addition to V_4 and reduce x_{24} to 4 and mark e_{34} and e_{24} closed.

Step 1.   The excess flow at V_2 cannot be advanced and the excess flow at V_3 can be advanced to V_5, to V_7, and then to V_t. The result is shown in Figure 2.10. (All closed arcs are marked ⇸.)

Step 2.   We reduce x_{12} to 4 and mark e_{12} closed, and return to Step 1.

Step 1.   The excess flow at V_1 is advanced through V_3, V_5, V_7 and to V_t. The result is shown in Figure 2.11.

(Note that we do not advance flow to e_{34} as the arc is closed.)

The flow in Figure 2.11 is maximum.

§2.2.3 MPM ALGORITHM

A very clever modification of Karzanov's algorithm is given by Malhotra, Pramodh Kamar and Maheshwari [24] for finding maximal flows in a layered network. For each node in the layered network, we define the flow potential of the node V_j by

$$\min\left(\sum_i b'_{ij}, \sum_k b'_{jk}\right)$$

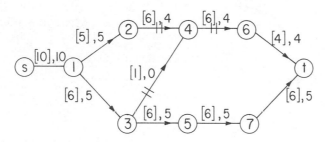

Figure 2.10

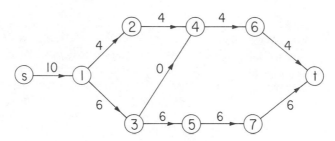

Figure 2.11

i.e., the minimum of the total incoming arc capacities or the total outgoing arc capacities at the node. Intuitively, the flow potential is the maximum amount of flow that can be forced through the node. Among all the nodes with non-zero flow potential in the layered network, the node with minimum flow-potential is called the reference node V_r. If the reference node has flow potential v, then it is possible to send v units of flow from V_s to V_t so that the flow potential of the reference node becomes zero.

It is easy to see that we can send v units of flow from the reference node V_r to V_t layer by layer since all the nodes have greater flow potential than V_r. (By a symmetry argument, we can also send v units of flow from V_s to V_r.) In sending flow through a node, we should leave at most one out-going arc partially saturated. We can delete all saturated arcs from the layered network. In particular, we can delete the reference node from the network since either all incoming arcs or all outgoing arcs are saturated in such an implementation.

To find the reference node, we need n−1 comparisons. Since the reference node is deleted each time, we need at most $O(n^2)$ time per phase. To update the capacity of arcs, we keep all outgoing arcs of every node in a circular list. There is at most one partial saturated arc per node. So the amount of updating arc capacity is again bounded by $O(n^2)$ per phase. There are at most m arcs in the layered network and an arc becomes saturated only once. So the total amount of work in deleting the arcs is $O(m)$. And the total work per phase is $O(n^2) + O(m) = O(n^2)$. (We could do the same procedure in sending v units of flow from V_s to V_r.)

If we implement the maximal flow algorithm per phase, and there are at most $n-1$ phases, we have $O(n^3)$ maximum flow algorithm.

§2.2.4 ANALYSIS OF ALGORITHMS

In this section we shall analyze the different algorithms for maximum flows discussed in the last section.

Ford and Fulkerson

If all the arc capacities are integers, then the labeling method will locate a flow-augmenting path with integer capacity; and the maximum flow value will also be increased by the same amount. The maximum flow value v is equal to the minimum cut capacity which is an integer. This algorithm needs at most v flow-augmenting paths where each flow-augmenting path needs at most $O(n^2)$ steps. Since v is unknown in the beginning, we do not have a bound in terms of m and n.

Edmonds and Karp

Edmonds and Karp suggested that the labeling method of Ford and Fulkerson should be implemented using the first-label-first-scan rule. This will give an $O(nm^2)$ upper bound.

To see this, we divide the computation into phases where each phase consists of finding all flow-augmenting paths of a given length. (Here the length of a path means the number of arcs in the path.)

In each phase, we first construct the residue network with the residue arc capacity b'_{ij} defined by

$$b'_{ij} = b_{ij} - x_{ij}$$

or $$b'_{ij} = |b_{ij}| + x_{ji} \quad \text{if } x_{ji} > 0.$$

This means that we look at an arc at most twice, once from each direction, so the total amount of work is $O(m)$.

The search for flow-augmenting paths by BFS takes at most $O(m)$ steps and there are at most m flow-augmenting paths in each phase. So the work in each phase is bounded by $O(m^2)$. Since the length of augmenting paths is strictly increasing from phase to phase, and there are at most $n-1$ phases, the total work is bounded by $O(nm^2)$. For a general network, $O(nm^2) = O(n^5)$.

Note that we find a maximal flow in each phase, and we find the maximum flow in the final phase.

Dinic's Algorithm

This algorithm has an upper bound of $O(n^2m)$ and the improvement is due to the way we search for flow-augmenting paths in a phase. After we find the residue network in each phase, which takes $O(m)$ steps, we can find a flow-augmenting path in $O(n)$ time.

Basically, we use DFS to find a flow-augmenting path. When we reach V_t, we increase the flow along the path and delete the arc whose residue capacity is zero. When we have to back up from a given node V_i, we delete all the incoming and outgoing arcs of V_i. In this way, we look at a node at most once in finding a flow-augmenting path, so the amount of work is $O(n)$ in one path, $O(nm)$ in all flow-augmenting paths in a phase, and $O(n^2m)$ total.

Karzanov's Algorithm

We shall show that Karzanov's algorithm for maximal flow in a layered network takes $O(n^2)$ units of time. Since there are at most n-1 phases, the total time is $O(n^3)$.

First, we define a vertex to be blocked if every path from that vertex to the sink V_t contains at least one saturated arc. Once a vertex is blocked, we cannot send more flow through the vertex.

Lemma 1 An unbalanced vertex becomes blocked after being processed during the advance of preflow. A blocked vertex remains blocked during the whole phase.

Proof. During the first advance of preflow, V_s becomes blocked since every outgoing arc from V_s is saturated. Also, every unbalanced vertex is blocked by the same reasoning. We shall prove this lemma by induction on the number of applications of the balance step. We shall prove that blocked vertex before a balance step remains a blocked vertex after the balance step.

A blocked vertex V_j at the highest layer cannot become unblocked since no arc flow x_{jk} can be decreased, and every path from V_j to V_t contains a saturated arc by definition.

Let the incoming flow of V_j be reduced during the "balance" step, and this reduction in turn reduces the outgoing arc flow of a blocked vertex V_i at the lower layer.

Since every path from V_i to V_t must go through a blocked vertex V_j, the vertex V_i remains blocked after the balance step.

Let V_i in a lower layer become unbalanced due to the reduction of outgoing flow. Then if V_i is processed in the next balance step, the vertex V_i will become balanced. Each outgoing arc of V_i is either saturated or is a closed arc. Every path from V_i containing a closed arc must go through a blocked vertex V_j. Thus V_i is blocked.

Lemma 2 Every vertex is being balanced at most once.

Proof. Assume that a vertex V_i is being balanced, we claim that from that time on all arc flows in layers higher than V_i cannot decrease in value. If this is not true, let b_{jk} be the arc which has x_{jk} reduced the first time. Since the vertex V_k is balanced at the time V_i is being balanced the only way V_k will be processed for balancing is when the total outflow from V_k reduces below the previous value. But this is impossible since we assume that b_{jk} is the first arc with its arc flow reduced. (Note that the incoming flows at a node are on a stack.)

Lemma 3 The flow achieved during a phase is a maximal flow.

Proof. The source V_s becomes blocked the first time, since every unbalanced vertex can be processed at most once and will remain blocked after processing. So after a while, all vertices become both balanced and blocked; and V_s remains blocked which shows that the flow is maximal.

Lemma 4 The maximal flow algorithm of Karzanov in a layered network is bounded by $O(n^2)$.

Proof. In the algorithm, there are balance steps and advance steps. In the balanced step, if an arc flow is reduced then that arc becomes closed, so the total number of flow reduction is bounded by the number of arcs $O(m)$. When the arc flow is increased, it is either saturated or unsaturated. But saturation can occur at most once for any arc, since any decrease in flow will close that arc. So the number of saturations is also bounded by $O(m)$. If an arc flow is increased but not to its limit, this can happen at most $n-1$ times in the initial preflow advancement, and of most $n-2$ times in the next preflow advancement, since some node has been balanced in the initial preflow advancement and hence is inaccessible. Continuing, we see that the number of steps increasing the flow but not to its limit is $(n-1) + (n-2) ... + 1 = O(n^2)$. So the algorithm is bounded by $O(m) + O(n^2) = O(n^2)$. Since there are n phases, the total time for Karzanov's algorithm is $O(n^3)$.

§2.3 MULTITERMINAL MAXIMAL FLOWS

If we consider the network as a communication network with the nodes as cities and arc capacities as communication channel capacities, then we may regard the maximum flow from V_s to V_t as the maximum rate of message flow from city V_s to city V_t. We assume that cities (other than V_s and V_t) serve as relay stations and do not communicate with each other. In reality, all the cities are communicating simultaneously. In this section, we shall study the maximum flows between all pairs of nodes in a network. To simplify the study of the mathematical structure of a network, we shall concentrate on *one pair of nodes at a time. At a given time* only one pair of nodes serves as the source and the sink while all other nodes serve as relay stations (or intermediate nodes). Thus, given an n-node network, we can pick $n(n-1)$ pairs as the source and the sink and find the maximum flow for each pair. *In this section,* we shall consider only undirected networks, i.e. $b_{ij} = b_{ji}$ for all i,j. Thus, we have the maximum flow values $f_{ij} = f_{ji}$ and we need to know $\binom{n}{2}$ maximum flows. (The reader should distinguish this problem from the problem of simultaneous maximum flows which will be discussed in section 2.3.4.)

There are three questions that we shall ask:

1. Realization condition. When the arc capacities of a network are given, we can find the maximum flows for each of the $\binom{n}{2}$ pairs of nodes. We shall denote the maximum flow value between V_i and V_j by f_{ij}. Since $b_{ij} = b_{ji}$, we have $f_{ij} = f_{ji}$ for all i,j. And we shall define $f_{ii} = \infty$ for all i. The maximum flow values can be displayed as an n×n matrix with the f_{ij} occupying the ith row and the jth column. This matrix is symmetric and has all diagonal elements equal to ∞. Is there any relation between the elements of the matrix besides $f_{ij} = f_{ji}$? Once the b_{ij} of a network are given, we can fill in the $[f_{ij}]$ matrix by computing maximum flows, but if we are given an arbitrary symmetric matrix $[f_{ij}]$, will there exist an n-node network whose f_{ij} are those numbers? The condition on the numbers $[f_{ij}]$ which assure the existence of a network is called the realization condition. What are the necessary and sufficient conditions for a set of $n(n-1)/2$ numbers to represent maximum flow values between pairs of nodes in some network?

2. Analysis. What are the maximum flow values between all pairs of nodes in a network? This question can certainly be solved by doing a maximum flow algorithm for each pair of nodes, but something better can be done.

3. Synthesis. If we set a lower bound on the maximum flow value between each pair of nodes, we can certainly build a network which has maximum flow values greater than the lower bounds. This can be done by assigning arbitrarily large arc capacities between all pairs of nodes. The problem of synthesis is to construct a network with maximum flows greater than all the lower bounds and with its total arc capacity minimum.

The reader should be reminded that in all three problems the maximum flow is between one pair of nodes at a given time. After a maximum flow is found, we pick another pair of nodes and find the maximum flow while all other nodes serve as intermediate nodes. All the arcs are now available for the new pair of source and sink. This is done for all the $\binom{n}{2}$ pairs on the same network.

This model of network flows is called the multi-terminal network flow model.

§2.3.1 REALIZABILITY (Gomory and Hu [12])

Realization condition For a given undirected network with arc capacities $b_{ij} = b_{ji}$, the maximal flow values f_{ij} are certainly symmetric, i.e., $f_{ij} = f_{ji}$. (For convenience, we shall let $f_{ii} = \infty$ for all i.) We now have the following theorem.

Theorem 3 Realizability. A necessary and sufficient condition for a set of non-negative numbers $f_{ij} = f_{ji}$ (i, j = 1,...,n) to be the maximum flow values of a network is

$$f_{ik} \geqslant \min (f_{ij}, f_{jk}) \quad \text{(for all i,j,k).} \tag{1}$$

Proof. **Necessity.** Considering V_i and V_k as the source and the sink, and using the max-flow min-cut theorem, we have for a cut $(X, \overline{X})$,

$$f_{ik} = c(X, \overline{X}), \tag{2}$$

where $V_i \in X$ and $V_k \in \overline{X}$. Now V_j either belongs to X or to $\overline{X}$. If $V_j \in X$, then $(X, \overline{X})$ is a cut separating V_j and V_k; hence

$$f_{jk} \leqslant c(X, \overline{X}) = f_{ik}. \tag{3}$$

If V_j belongs to $\overline{X}$, then $(X, \overline{X})$ is a cut separating V_i from V_j; hence

$$f_{ij} \leqslant c(X, \overline{X}) = f_{ik} . \tag{4}$$

Since at least one of the two conditions (3) and (4) must hold, we have

$$f_{ik} \geqslant \min (f_{ij}, f_{jk}). \tag{Q.E.D.}$$

It follows from (1) by induction that

$$f_{1,n} \geqslant \min (f_{12}, f_{23},...,f_{n-1,n}), \tag{5}$$

where $V_1, V_2,...,V_n$ is any sequence of nodes of the network.

Several comments are now in order. Take any three nodes of the network and consider the maximum flow values f_{ij}, f_{jk}, and f_{ik} between them. (Recall that $f_{ij} = f_{ji}$.) We claim that at least two of the flow values must be equal. For if these three values are distinct, putting the smallest value on the left-hand side of (1) will contradict (1). Furthermore, the flow value which is not equal to the other two flow values must be the largest; otherwise, (1) will again be contradicted. If we were to draw n(n-1)/2 links between nodes of the network with lengths of the links equal to the maximum flow values then each triangle would have two equal sides with the other side longer or the same length. Therefore (1) is like a "triangular inequality" which limits severely the values that can be maximum flow values of a network.

It follows from (5) that among the $n(n-1)/2$ flow values $f_{ij} = f_{ji}$, *there exist at most* $n-1$ *distinct flow values*. This can be seen as follows. Consider the complete graph with $n(n-1)/2$ links with lengths equal to their maximum flow values and select those links which will form a maximum spanning tree. We claim that each of the $n(n-1)/2$ flow values must be equal to one of the $(n-1)$ values associated with the spanning tree. Let f_{1n} be one of the $n(n-1)/2$ flow values not associated with the maximum spanning tree. There is a unique path from V_1 to V_n consisting of links of the maximum spanning tree. From (5), f_{1n} must be greater than or equal to the minimum value in this unique path. If it is greater, we can replace the minimum link in the path by f_{1n} and get another spanning tree with total value greater than the original maximum spanning tree, which is a contradiction.

Sufficiency This is proved by constructing a network which has the numbers n_{ij} satisfying (1) as its maximum flow values. To do this, consider the numbers n_{ij} satisfying (1) as lengths of links of a complete graph and select among the links a maximum spanning tree. Now consider a network which is of the same structure as the maximum spanning tree and with arc capacities $b_{ij} = n_{ij}$, where n_{ij} are given numbers which are to be realized as the flow values of some network. We claim that this tree network has $f_{ij} = n_{ij}$. For any pair of nodes of the network, we have

$$f_{ij} = \min \ (b_{i1}, b_{12}, ..., b_{qj})$$

$$= \min \ (n_{i1}, n_{12}, ..., n_{qj})$$

$$= n_{ij} \ (\text{since } n_{ij} \text{ does not belong the maximum spanning tree})$$

where $b_{i1}, b_{12}, ..., b_{qj}$ are the capacities of arcs which form the unique path from V_i to V_j. Note that in proving the sufficiency of (1), we have shown that there is always a tree network that will do the job.

Q.E.D.

§2.3.2 ANALYSIS (Gomory and Hu [12])

Given a network like the one shown in Figure 2.21, we can find the maximum flow values between all pairs of nodes by doing $\binom{6}{2}$ computations. There is another six-node network shown in Figure 2.29 which is of tree-shape. To find the maximum flow value between any two nodes in a tree-network is to pick the minimum arc capacity in the unique path connecting the two nodes. It turns out that the maximum flow values in the two networks are exactly the same for all corresponding pairs! We shall call two networks *flow-equivalent* if the maximum flow values between all pairs of nodes are the same. *We shall prove that any arbitrary undirected network is always flow-equivalent to a tree network.*

Furthermore, the tree-network can be obtained by doing only n−1 maximum flow problems. Consider a 1000-node network, the $1000(1000-1)/2 = 499500$ flow values can be obtained by doing 999 maximum flow problems. The aim of this section is to introduce an algorithm which will get the tree network flow-equivalent to the network of concern.

Assume that America has 1000 cities and we are interested in the maximum flow values between the capitals of the fifty states. Do we have to do 999 flow problems in order to get $50(50-1)/2 = 1225$ maximum flow values? It turns out that we can get the 1225 maximum flow values by doing $50-1 = 49$ maximum flow problems.

The problem here is: if we want maximum flow values between several nodes instead of between every pair, can we somehow reduce the amount of computation? Assume that we are interested in finding maximum flow values between p nodes where $2 \leqslant p \leqslant n$. Then instead of doing $p(p-1)/2$ maximum flow computations, *we need to do only* p − 1 *maximum flow computations*. Furthermore, each of the flow computations is done on a simplified network.

First we shall describe a process called "condensing a subset of nodes into a single node". The process regards a subset of nodes of the network as a single node; i.e., between every pair of nodes in the subset an arc of infinite capacity is added. (Consider the network shown in Figure 2.12.) The arcs directly connecting a node V_i, not in the subset, to any nodes in the subset are replaced by a single arc having a capacity equal to the sum of the capacities of the connecting arcs.

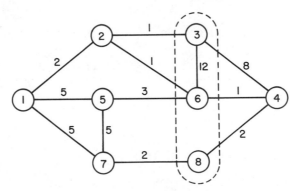

Figure 2.12

If we condense the nodes V_3, V_6, and V_8 into a single node, then the resulting network is as shown in Figure 2.13.

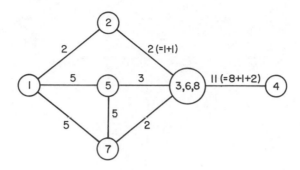

Figure 2.13

In the network of Figure 2.12, the maximum flow $f_{27} = c(Y,\overline{Y}) = 4$ and the minimum cut $(Y,\overline{Y}) = (2\,|\,1,3,4,5,6,7,8)$ consists of the arcs b_{21}, b_{23}, and b_{26}. *Increasing* arc capacities of arcs *not* in the minimum cut $(Y,\overline{Y})$ will not affect the value of $c(Y,\overline{Y})$ and, furthermore, may only *increase* the capacity of other cuts separating V_2 and V_7. Thus $(Y,\overline{Y})$ will remain as the minimum cut separating V_2 and V_7. Therefore, so far as calculating the maximum flow value f_{27} is concerned, we may, for example, condense $\{V_3, V_6, V_8\}$ into a single node and do the calculation in the network of Figure 2.13.

When we condense a subset of nodes, we have essentially a simplified network. This saves a lot of computation. We shall prove Lemma 5 which gives all the allowable conditions for condensing nodes. Lemma 5 is the key to the rest of the analysis.

As an illustration, assume that we find the minimum cut separating $V_i \in X$ and $V_j \in \overline{X}$. The network is symbolically represented as a circular disk and the cut $(X,\overline{X})$ as the solid line in Figure 2.14. If we then try to find the minimum cut separating V_e and V_k, the minimum cut may be like $(Y,\overline{Y})$ which is shown as the dotted line which crosses the solid line representing the $(X,\overline{X})$ cut.

Recall that two cuts $(X,\overline{X})$ and $(Y,\overline{Y})$ are said to cross each other if and only if each of the four sets $X \cap Y$, $X \cap \overline{Y}$, $\overline{X} \cap Y$, and $\overline{X} \cap \overline{Y}$ contains at least one node.

For example, in the network shown in Figure 2.15(a) a minimum cut separating V_i and V_j is $(X,\overline{X}) = (i,a\,|\,e,k,j)$ and a minimum cut separating V_e and V_k is $(Y,\overline{Y}) = (e,i\,|\,j,k,a)$ and the two minimum cuts cross each other.

If we condense the set X into a single node in Figure 2.15(a), we effectively increase the arc capacity b_{ia} to infinity. This would change the cut capacity $(Y,\overline{Y})$ which is the sum of $b_{ek} + b_{ia}$. So if $(Y,\overline{Y})$ *is the only* minimum cut separating V_e and V_k, we cannot condense X into a single node.

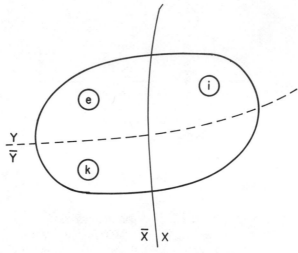

Figure 2.14

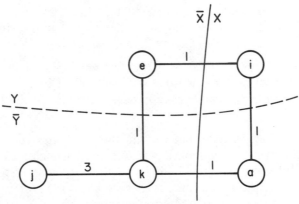

Figure 2.15 (a)

On the other hand, there is another minimum cut $\left[(Z,\bar{Z}) = (e\,|\,i,a,j,k)\right]$ separating V_e and V_k and this minimum cut does not cross $(X,\bar{X})$. Now, condensing X into a single node does not change the capacity of $(Z,\bar{Z})$ and will only increase the capacity of other cuts. Thus, $(Z,\bar{Z})$ will remain as a minimum cut separating V_e and V_k, and we can calculate the maximum flow f_{ek} in the network shown in Figure 2.15(b) where X is condensed.

To formalize the idea of condensing nodes, we now introduce Lemma 5 and consider an arbitrary network as shown in Figure 2.16.

Lemma 5 (non-crossing min cuts) Let $(X,\bar{X})$ be a minimum cut separating $V_i \in X$ and some other node, and let V_e and V_k be any two nodes contained in $\bar{X}$.

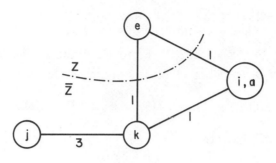

Figure 2.15(b)

Then there exists a minimum cut $(Z,\overline{Z})$ separating V_e and V_k such that $(Z,\overline{Z})$ and $(X,\overline{X})$ do not cross each other.

Proof. Assume that there is a minimum cut $(Y,\overline{Y})$ separating V_e and V_k which does cross $(X,\overline{X})$. Let

$$X \cap Y = Q \quad , \quad X \cap \overline{Y} = S,$$
$$\overline{X} \cap Y = P \quad , \quad \overline{X} \cap \overline{Y} = R,$$

as shown in Figure 2.16.

Note that $V_e \in P$ and $V_k \in R$.

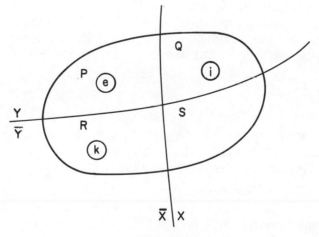

Figure 2.16

The network is now partitioned into four components and we shall prove that either $(P, Q \cup R \cup S)$ or $(P \cup Q \cup S, R)$ is the minimum cut $(Z,\overline{Z})$ which does not cross $(X,\overline{X})$.

We shall use the notation $c(Q,P)$ to denote the sum of capacities of all arcs connecting the components Q and P. In this notation

$$c(X,\overline{X}) = c(Q,P) + c(Q,R) + c(S,P) + c(S,R).$$

Case 1 Let $V_i \in Q$. Since $(X,\overline{X})$ is a minimum cut, we have

$$c(Q,P) + c(Q,R) + c(S,P) + c(S,R) \leqslant c(Q,P) + c(Q,R) + c(Q,S) . \tag{1}$$

Since $c(S,P) \geqslant 0$, we have from (1),

$$c(S,R) \leqslant c(Q,S). \tag{2}$$

$$c(P,R) + c(Q,R) = c(P,R) + c(Q,R), \tag{3}$$

and
$$0 \leqslant c(P,S). \tag{4}$$

Adding both sides of (2), (3), and (4) we have

$$c(P,R) + c(Q,R) + c(S,R)$$
$$\leqslant c(P,R) + c(Q,R) + c(Q,S) + c(P,S) . \tag{5}$$

But the left-hand side of (5) is the value of the cut $(P \cup Q \cup S,R)$ which is a cut separating V_e and V_k that does not cross $(X,\overline{X})$, and the right-hand side of (5) is the capacity of the minimum cut $(Y,\overline{Y})$. Thus $(P \cup Q \cup S,R)$ is the required $(Z,\overline{Z})$.

Case 2 $V_i \in S$. Similarly we can show that $(P,Q \cup R \cup S)$ is a cut separating V_e and V_k with a value not greater than that of $(Y,\overline{Y})$. Thus either $(P \cup Q \cup S,R)$ or $(P,Q \cup R \cup S)$ is the required minimum cut $(Z,\overline{Z})$ that does not cross $(X,\overline{X})$.

Q.E.D.

This means that if $(X,\overline{X})$ is a minimum cut, we can condense X into a single node in calculating the maximum flow values between two nodes in $\overline{X}$. (By symmetry, we can do the same thing for the maximum flow between two nodes in X.)

We shall need Lemma 5 in an algorithm which computes the maximum flow values between all pairs of nodes in a network. There are other conditions that allow us to condense nodes. One condition is Lemma 6.

Lemma 6 Let $(X,\overline{X})$ be a minimum cut separating V_i and some other node, and let V_k be any node that belongs to $\overline{X}$. Then there exists a minimum cut $(Z,\overline{Z})$ separating V_i and V_k such that $(X,\overline{X})$ and $(Z,\overline{Z})$ do not cross each other.

Proof. Assume that there is a minimum cut $(Y,\overline{Y})$ separating V_i and V_k which does cross $(X,\overline{X})$ and let (as before)

$$X \cap Y = Q \ , \quad X \cap \overline{Y} = S,$$
$$\overline{X} \cap Y = P \ , \quad \overline{X} \cap \overline{Y} = R,$$

where $V_k \in R$ and $V_i \in Q$ (see Figure 2.16).

Since $(X,\overline{X})$ is a minimum cut, by exactly the same argument, we have (5). But then the left-hand side of (5) is the value of a cut $(P \cup Q \cup S,R)$ which separates V_i and V_k and has a value not greater than that of $(Y,\overline{Y})$ whose capacity is the right-hand side of (5). Thus, $(P \cup Q \cup S,R)$ is the required $(Z,\overline{Z})$.

Q.E.D.

This means that if $(X,\overline{X})$ *is a minimum cut separating* V_i *and some other node and we want to find* f_{ik}, *where* V_k *is any node in* $\overline{X}$, *we can condense* X *into a single node.*

Remember that the aim of the section is to compute the maximum flows between all pairs of nodes in a network N, or the maximum flows between a subset of p nodes in the network N. It is convenient to think of the n nodes as cities in the U.S.A. and the subset of p nodes as capitals in the fifty states.

Let us call those p nodes *terminal nodes* and the other n - p nodes ordinary or intermediate nodes. Suppose there is another network N′ which consist of p nodes, and the maximum flow values between the p terminal nodes of N are the same as the maximum flow values of the network N′. (Two networks with the same maximum flow values between a set of nodes are said to be flow equivalent to each other with respect to that set of nodes.) Then we can get all the maximum flow values of the p nodes from the network N′. It turns out that there always exists an N′ which is a tree. The algorithm described below constructs from a network N the tree N′ which has the same maximum flow values. The algorithm for finding maximum flow values between p terminal nodes in an n-node network consists of two steps which are iterated until the tree network N′ (which is flow equivalent to the original network N with respect to the p nodes) is constructed. The network N′ can be obtained by doing p−1 maximum flow problems while the straightforward approach on the network N would need $\binom{p}{2}$ maximum flow problems. Note that the algorithm works for all values of p, $2 \leqslant p \leqslant n$. Let us first outline the algorithm before giving the detailed description. (The reader may skip the detailed description and the proof and study the numerical example shown in Figure 2.21 first.)

Outline: Pick two terminal nodes V_i and V_j in N and do a maximum flow computation and obtain the minimum cut $(X,\overline{X})$ with $V_i \in X$ and $V_j \in \overline{X}$, say. We then draw a diagram of two circles connected by a link of value v, where v is the maximum flow value just obtained. In one circle we list all the nodes in X and in the other circle all the nodes in $\overline{X}$. This is the first step in constructing the network N′. When we have created p circles after doing p−1 maximum flow problems, then the diagram of p circles is the flow-equivalent network N′.

In a general step, we shall compute a maximum flow in the network N where subsets of nodes are condensed into single nodes. The computed maximum flow is between two nodes in one circle, and the result will split the circle into two circles with a connecting link having the value of the maximum flow. So the computation is always done on the network N or its simplified form and we keep track of the results obtained so far in a diagram which looks like a tree. From the diagram, we decide which pair of nodes should be chosen as the next source and sink, and also what subsets of nodes can be condensed.

Now, we give the detailed description. First, select two terminal nodes arbitrarily and do a maximum flow computation on the original network. This gives a minimum cut $(X,\overline{X})$, which is represented symbolically by two circles connected by a link as in Figure 2.17. This is the first link of the tree network N'. The value v_1 written beside the link is the value of the minimum cut $(X,\overline{X})$. In one circle all the nodes of X are listed; in the other all nodes of X.

Second, from the tree diagram obtained so far, select any circle which contains two or more terminal nodes and do a maximum flow computation between the two terminal nodes on a network derived from the original network in which X or $\overline{X}$ is condensed. Let us say the two terminal nodes selected are in X. Then $\overline{X}$ is condensed into a single node. This will give another minimum cut. This is represented symbolically as in Figure 2.18, where v_2 is the value of the minimum cut just obtained, and $Y_1 \cup Y_2$ is the original set X.

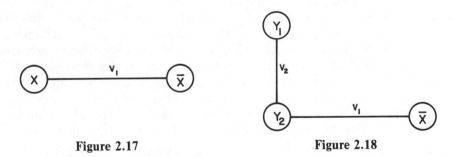

Figure 2.17   Figure 2.18

Note that $\overline{x}$ is attached to Y_2 if $\overline{X}$ and Y_2 are on the same side of the minimum cut with value v_2; $\overline{x}$ is attached to Y_1 if $\overline{X}$ and Y_1 are on the same side of the minimum cut with value v_2. The process of dividing a circle is continued. At any stage of the construction, we choose a circle Y which contains two or more terminal nodes as shown in Figure 2.19. If Y is removed from the tree diagram, the tree becomes several disconnected components. In doing a maximum flow for two terminal nodes in Y , all the nodes located in one of these components of the diagram are *condensed* into a single node. After p-1 maximal flow computations, a tree diagram is obtained in which each circle contains exactly one terminal node and possibly several other intermediate nodes. (Note that in doing the maximum flow computation, we are doing it on a network usually simpler than the original network due to condensation of nodes.)

We assert that if we consider the tree diagram as a network with arc capacities equal to the value associated with the links in the diagram, then the tree network will have the same maximum flow values as the original network.

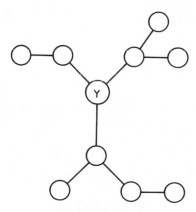

Figure 2.19

Theorem 4 The maximum flow value between any two terminal nodes V_i and V_j of the original network is equal to

$$f_{ij} = \min \ (v_{ia}, v_{ab}, ..., v_{dj}),\qquad(6)$$

where $v_{ia}, v_{ab}, ..., v_{dj}$ are values associated with links of the tree which form a unique path from V_i to V_j.

Proof. We shall first prove that

$$f_{ij} \leq \min \ (v_{ia}, v_{ab}, ..., v_{dj})\qquad(7)$$

and then

$$f_{ij} \geq \min \ (v_{ia}, v_{ab}, ..., v_{dj})\qquad(8)$$

Note that every link in the tree diagram represents a cut which separates V_i and V_j. Thus, the maximum flow value f_{ij} must be less than or equal to any of the values associated with the links, so we have the inequality (7).

Consider any stage of construction of the tree diagram, where a link with value v connects two circles X and Y, say. We shall prove that there is a terminal node V_i in X and a terminal node V_j in Y such that $f_{ij} = v$.

This assertion is certainly true when we construct the tree diagram of two circles, say X and $\overline{X}$. Since this tree diagram is created by computing the maximum flow between V_i and V_j, there is a node $V_i \in X$ and a node $V_j \in \overline{X}$ such that $f_{ij} = v$. We want to prove that this holds true when the tree diagram is further divided. Let us assume that we pick V_a and V_b in X and do another maximum flow problem which partitions X into Y_1 and Y_2 where $V_a \in Y_1$ and $V_b \in Y_2$. This is shown in Figure 2.20.

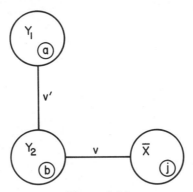

Figure 2.20

Naturally $f_{ab} = v'$ where $V_a \in Y_1$ and $V_b \in Y_2$. If $V_i \in Y_2$, we still have two nodes V_i and V_j in the two circles Y_2 and $\overline{X}$ with $f_{ij} = v$.

The difficulty is that V_i may be in Y_1. In this case, we shall show that $f_{bj} = v$.

In the original network we know

$$f_{ab} = v' \quad \text{and} \quad f_{ij} = v.$$

If the subset of nodes Y_1 is condensed into a single node and V_i is in Y_1, then in the condensed network, the maximum flow values between V_a and V_b and between V_i and V_j are not affected (Lemma 6). In the condensed network, we let all maximum flow values be represented by primes. Thus

$$f'_{ij} = f_{ij} = v$$
$$f'_{ab} = f_{ab} = v'$$

Note that $v' \geq v$ because $(Y_1, Y_2 \cup \overline{X})$ is a cut separating V_i and V_j.

It follows from (5) of § 2.3.1 that in the condensed network

$$f'_{jb} \geq \min \, [f'_{ji}, f'_{ia}, f'_{ab}]$$
$$= \min \, [v, \infty, v']$$

$$= v \qquad \text{(since } v' \geqslant v)$$

But $f_{jb} = f'_{jb}$ due to Lemma 5, so V_b and V_j are the two required nodes with maximum flow value equal to the value of the link connecting two circles.

Having established that the neighboring terminal nodes have a maximum flow value equal to the value of the connecting link, we have, from (5) of § 2.3.1, for any two terminal nodes connected by a series of links in the tree

$$f_{ij} \geqslant \min (f_{ia}, f_{ab}, \ldots, f_{dj})$$

$$= \min (v_{ia}, v_{ab}, \ldots, v_{dj}), \qquad (9)$$

where V_i and V_j are not neighboring terminal nodes in the tree. Equations (7) and (9) establish the desired result of the theorem. Q.E.D.

Let us do a numerical example illustrating the analysis technique. Consider the network in Figure 2.21, where the numbers beside the arcs denote arc capacities. Assume that we are interested in maximum flows between V_1, V_3, V_4, and V_5. First let us arbitrarily select V_1 and V_3 and do a maximum flow computation. We get a minimum cut $(V_1, V_2, V_6 \mid V_3, V_4, V_5)$ with value 13. This is indicated symbolically in Figure 2.22.

Now, we do a maximum flow computation between V_3 and V_4 in the network shown in Figure 2.23. We get the network in Figure 2.23 by condensing V_1, V_2, and V_6 in Figure 2.21 into a single node. The result of this computation is a minimum cut $(V_1, V_2, V_6, V_3, V_5 \mid V_4)$ with value 14 which is shown in Figure 2.24. Note that ③,⑤ is attached to ①,②,⑥ because they are on one side of the minimum cut separating V_3 and V_4. Now, we do a maximum flow computation between V_3 and V_5, which again should be done on the network shown in Figure 2.23. As a result of this, we have a minimum cut $(V_1, V_2, V_6, V_5, V_4 \mid V_3)$ with value 15. This is shown symbolically in Figure 2.25.

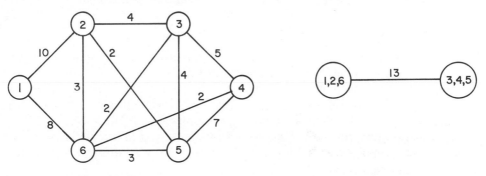

Figure 2.21   Figure 2.22

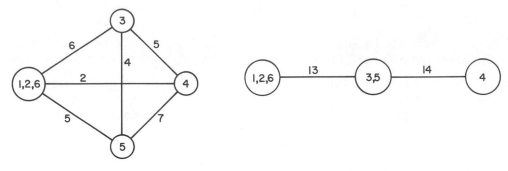

Figure 2.23   Figure 2.24

Now since each circle is the diagram contains only one terminal node, we can stop. The flow values are $f_{13} = f_{14} = f_{15} = 13$, $f_{34} = f_{45} = 14$, and $f_{35} = 15$. This network then has the same maximum flow values f_{13}, f_{14}, f_{15}, f_{34}, f_{35}, and f_{45} as the original network in Figure 2.21.

If we are interested in maximum flow values between all pairs of nodes, we simply continue the process and choose V_1 and V_6, say, and do the maximum flow computation on the network in Figure 2.26. The result is a minimum cut $(V_1, V_2 \mid V_6, V_3, V_4, V_5)$ with value 17, which is shown in Figure 2.27.

Now we choose V_1 and V_2 and do a maximum flow computation on the network in Figure 2.28. The result is a minimum cut $(V_1 \mid V_2, V_6, V_3, V_4, V_5)$ with value 18. This is shown in Figure 2.29. From Figure 2.29 we can easily reach the maximum flow values between all pairs of nodes, and they are listed in Table 2.1.

The reader should check that the networks in Figures 2.21 and 2.29 have the same maximum flow values for all pairs of nodes. Recall that two networks with the same f_{ij} are *flow equivalent* to each other. If the maximum flow values are same for pairs in a subset of nodes, then they are flow equivalent with respect to the set of nodes. Thus the network in Figure 2.21 and the network in Figure 2.25 are flow equivalent with respect to V_1, V_3, V_4, and V_5.

The method of analysis described above constructs a flow equivalent network which is a tree. Note that there are many trees that are flow equivalent to a given network. But the flow equivalent tree constructed above has another property; namely, each link of the tree represents a minimum cut of the original network. Therefore, it is called a *cut tree* by Gomory and Hu (also called the Gomory-Hu tree). A cut tree of n-nodes shows the n−1 minimum cuts of the original network which do not cross each other. The n-1 cuts are shown in dotted lines in Figure 2.30.

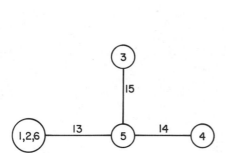

Figure 2.25

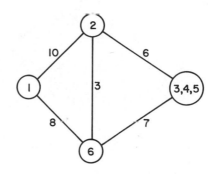

Figure 2.26

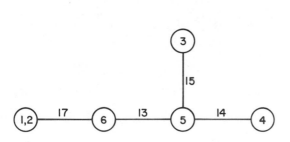

Figure 2.27

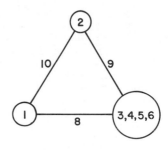

Figure 2.28

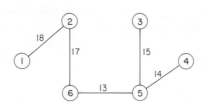

Figure 2.29

The cut tree shows precisely the n-1 minimum cuts which determine the maximum flows between all pairs of nodes, and is useful in section 2.5.3. We state this result as a theorem.

Theorem 5 (Gomory and Hu) Any network is flow-equivalent to a cut tree.

Table 2.1

	①	②	③	④	⑤	⑥
①	∞	18	13	13	13	17
②	18	∞	13	13	13	17
③	13	13	∞	14	15	13
④	13	13	14	∞	14	13
⑤	13	13	15	14	∞	13
⑥	17	17	13	13	13	∞

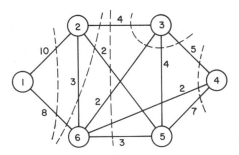

Figure 2.30

§2.3.3 SYNTHESIS (Gomory and Hu [12])

In the previous section we have shown how to find maximum flow values of a given network. Now we shall study the inverse problem; i.e., given $n(n-1)/2$ numbers r_{ij} which represent the lower bounds of maximum flow between V_i and V_j, what is the undirected network that will have $f_{ij} \geqslant r_{ij}$ and a minimum total arc capacity?

Let the $n(n-1)/2$ numbers r_{ij} be given. They may be drawn as a complete graph with n nodes. If we consider the r_{ij} as lengths of the links of the graph, we can form a maximum spanning tree of the graph. The requirements r_{ij} associated with the maximum spanning tree are called the dominant requirements. The maximum spanning tree is called the *dominant requirement tree*. If Figure 2.31(a) represents the required flow values in the network, then its dominant requirement tree is shown in Figure 2.31(b).

For any network to have $f_{ij} \geqslant r_{ij}$ for all i,j, it is necessary and sufficient to have $f_{ij} \geqslant r_{ij}$ for $r_{ij} \in T$, the dominant requirement tree. It is clearly necessary to have $f_{ij} \geqslant r_{ij}$ for $r_{ij} \in T$, since these are a subset of the original requirements. It is also sufficient since the missing r_{ip} satisfy the following relation, because T is a maximum spanning tree:

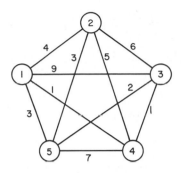

Figure 2.31 (a)

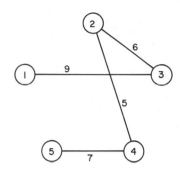

Figure 2.31 (b)

$$r_{ip} \leqslant \min \ (r_{ij}, r_{jk}, ..., r_{op}),$$ (1)

where r_{ij}, r_{jk}, etc., on the right-hand side of (1) are associated with the links forming the unique path in T from V_i to V_p. In any network satisfying the dominant requirements, any flow f_{ip} must automatically satisfy

$$f_{ip} \geqslant \min \ (f_{ij}, f_{jk}, ..., f_{op})$$
$$\geqslant \min \ (r_{ij}, r_{jk}, ..., r_{op})$$ (2)
$$\geqslant r_{ip} \ ,$$

and so all requirements are satisfied. Therefore, for the sake of convenience we shall consider only the dominant requirements.

The total arc capacity for any undirected network is $\frac{1}{2}\sum_{i \neq j} b_{ij}$. We now introduce a lower bound C_L for this quantity. Consider any node V_i of a network satisfying dominant requirements. Let $u_i = \max_j r_{ij}$ i.e., u_i is the largest flow requirement among those involving V_i. Any satisfactory network must have at least that much b_{ij} to allow the flow out of V_i, i.e., $\sum_j b_{ij} \geqslant u_i$. Since an arc is counted once in each of its two end nodes, a lower bound to the total arc capacity is then

$$C_L = \frac{1}{2} \sum_i u_i \leqslant \frac{1}{2} \sum_i \left(\sum_j b_{ij} \right) (i \neq j)$$

We shall now describe the synthesis procedure (Gomory and Hu [12]) for getting a satisfactory network at this lower bound. Note first that these u_i can be obtained by considering only the dominant requirements; i.e., selecting max r_{ij} for $r_{ij} \in T$ and adjacent to V_i. Now consider a fixed tree T with attached requirements r_{ij} and resulting lower bound C_L. If the r_{ij} are replaced by a new set of r'_{ij}, we get a new bound C'_L. Let us now use $r''_{ij} = r_{ij} + r'_{ij}$ as the requirements associated with the same tree and get a lower bound C''_L. Then, in general, we have

$$C''_L \leqslant C_L + C'_L,$$

since the $\max_j r_{ij}$ and $\max_j r'_{ij}$ may not coincide on every node V_i. But if r_{ij} (or r'_{ij}) are *uniform requirements*, i.e., $r_{ij} = r$ for all r_{ij} in T, then

$$C''_L = C_L + C'_L. \tag{3}$$

Now consider two networks, one with arc capacities b_{ij} and maximum flows f_{ij}, the other with b'_{ij} and f'_{ij}. If we form a third network having arc capacities $b''_{ij} = b_{ij} + b'_{ij}$, then the maximum flows f''_{ij} of the third network will certainly satisfy

$$f''_{ij} \geqslant f_{ij} + f'_{ij}. \tag{4}$$

Now let T be the dominant requirement tree which we want to satisfy. Let r_{min} be the smallest requirement in the tree and write any r_{ij} as $r_{min} + (r_{ij} - r_{min})$. We can then consider the original tree as the superposition of two trees, one with uniform requirements r_{min}, and one with $r_{ij} - r_{min}$. (The tree with $r_{ij} - r_{min}$ may consist of two or more components since $r_{ij} - r_{min} = 0$ for some i,j, or we can still consider it as one tree with some requirements zero.) For example, the tree T in Figure 2.31(b) can be considered as the superposition of the trees in Figure 2.32. For any part without uniform requirements, the decomposition procedure can be continued until each part has uniform requirements. For example, Figure 2.32 can be further decomposed into Figure 2.33.

Let us use the phrase "synthesizing a tree" to mean "constructing a network with maximum flows greater than or equal to the requirements in the tree." After a tree is decomposed into a sum of uniform trees, we can synthesize each uniform tree individually. If each uniform tree can be synthesized at its lower bound C_L, then the superposition of each satisfactory network will give a network capable of satisfying the original requirements, due to (4), and which is of minimum total arc capacity, due to (3).

Therefore, the problem is reduced to synthesizing a uniform tree with requirements all equal to r. This can be done by drawing any cycle through the nodes and then assigning r/2 to each of the arcs of the cycle. (When there are only two nodes, a single arc of capacity r is used.) Clearly such a network will meet the flow requirements and, furthermore, is of the minimal total capacity. (The total capacity is nr/2 for a network of n nodes, and the lower bound C_L for synthesizing a uniform tree is $\frac{1}{2}\sum_i u_i = \frac{1}{2}nr$.)

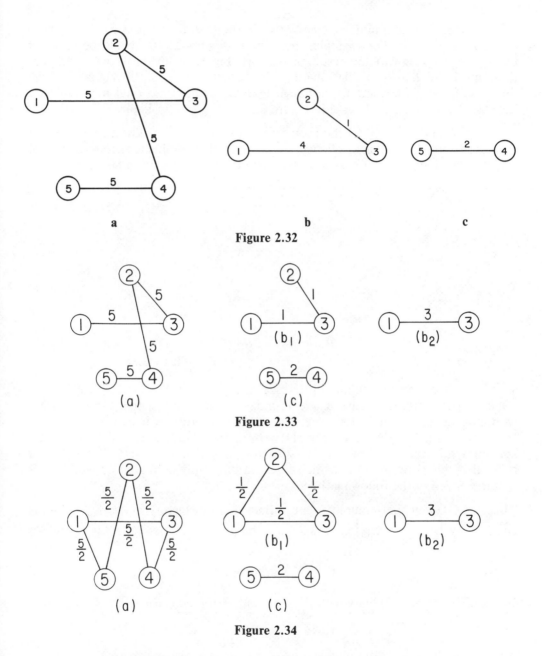

a   **b**   **c**

Figure 2.32

Figure 2.33

Figure 2.34

Take Figure 2.33 for example. Each of the uniform trees can be synthesized as shown in Figure 2.34. Upon superimposing the networks in Figure
2.34, we obtain Figure 2.35, which is a network satisfying all requirements of Figure 2.31(a) and is of minimum total arc capacity.

In synthesizing a uniform tree, we have the freedom of passing through the nodes in any order. For example, the cycle in Figure 2.34(a) could be replaced by Figure 2.36(a) with the resulting network Figure 2.36(b). If we check the flows in Figure 2.36(b) we find that $f_{ij} = r_{ij}$ for all i,j $\in$ T, but in Figure 2.35 we find that $f_{ij} > r_{ij}$ for some i,j, although both have the same total minimum arc capacity. (For example, $f_{24} = 6$ in Figure 2.35 but $f_{24} = 5$ in Figure 2.36(b)).

We shall first study (i) the problem of getting as much flow as possible and then study the (ii) problem of meeting all r_{ij} in the dominant requirement tree exactly. Of course, in both cases we want the total arc capacity to be minimum.

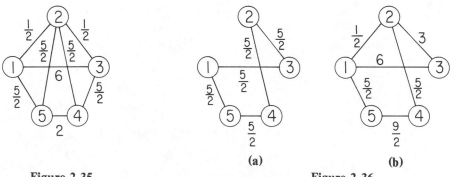

Figure 2.35   Figure 2.36

     (a)   (b)

(i) First, the total minimum arc capacity C_L is determined by the u_i, not the r_{ij}. Therefore, after the u_i are found, we can raise r_{ij} to $r_{ij}^* = \min(u_i, u_j)$ without changing the u_i or the lower bound C_L. Any further increase of r_{ij}^* would certainly change the lower bound. Now by a procedure described later we are able to synthesize the new tree T^* with resulting maximal flows $f_{ij}^* = r_{ij}^*$. We claim that this network N^* in some sense is a uniformly dominant network. This is summarized in the following theorem.

Theorem 6 Given the requirements r_{ij}, there is a satisfactory network N^* having capacity C_L^* $\left[C_L^* = \dfrac{1}{2}\sum_i u_i\right]$ with maximum flows

$$f_{ij}^* = r_{ij}^* = \min(u_i, u_j). \tag{5}$$

Let N' be any other network with $f_{ij}' \geq r_{ij}$, and with total capacity C'. Then either

$$C' > C_L^* \tag{6}$$

or $\qquad\qquad f_{ij}' \leq f_{ij}^* \quad \text{for all i,j} . \tag{7}$$

Proof. Assume that (6) does not hold, so that we have $f_{ij}' \geq r_{ij}$ and $C' \leq C_L^*$. We must show that $f_{ij}' \leq f_{ij}^*$. If $f_{ij}' \geq r_{ij}$, then

$$\sum_j b_{ij}' \geq u_i = \max_j r_{ij}$$

for each i. Since

$$\frac{1}{2} \sum_{i \neq j} b'_{ij} = C' \leqslant C_L^* = \frac{1}{2} \sum_i u_i,$$

we actually have $\sum_j b'_{ij} = u_i$. This implies that

$$f'_{ij} \leqslant \min\left(\sum_k b'_{ik} , \sum_s b'_{sj} \right) = \min(u_i, u_j) = f_{ij}^*. \qquad\qquad \text{Q.E.D.}$$

Now we attack problem (ii), synthesizing the flow requirements in the tree *exactly*, at minimal total capacity. The reason for getting excess flows is due to the superposition of networks which may not have the same partition of nodes as their minimum cuts. Therefore, in synthesizing a uniform tree, we want the cycle network to have the same capacities of cuts as those represented by the links of the uniform tree. For example, in the cycle network of Figure 2.34(a) the cut separating V_2 and V_4 $(V_1, V_2, V_3 \mid V_4, V_5)$ is of capacity 10, while the link between V_2 and V_4 in Figure 2.32(a) represents a cut of capacity 5. But in the cycle network of Figure 2.36(a) the cut $(V_1, V_2, V_3 \mid V_4, V_5)$ is also of capacity 5. If we synthesize trees so that the tree becomes a cut tree of the constructed cycle network, then in superimposing the cycle networks, minimum cuts are also superimposed to form minimum cuts and the original dominant flow f_{ip} of two nodes V_i and V_p satisfies

$$f_{ip} \leqslant \min(r_{ij}, r_{jk}, ..., r_{op}). \qquad\qquad (8)$$

Inequalities (2) and (8) imply

$$f_{ip} = \min(r_{ij}, r_{jk}, ..., r_{op}), \qquad\qquad (9)$$

so that all dominant requirements are met exactly.

To synthesize a cycle network with the uniform tree as its cut tree, we have to have two arcs of capacities $r/2$ corresponding to each link of the tree. The following DFS (see § 1.8 for DFS) labeling procedure will construct such a cycle network from a given tree T:

Step 1.   Label any node of T with the number 1.

Step 2.   Check if there is any unlabeled node adjacent to the current largest labeled node, which is node k. If yes, label it k+1. If there is more than one unlabeled node adjacent to the node k, then any of the nodes can be labeled k+1. If there is no unlabeled node adjacent to node k, check if there is any unlabeled node adjacent to node k-1. If yes, label it k+1: if not check any unlabeled node adjacent to k-2, etc.

Step 3.   When the nodes of T are all labeled, construct a cycle from node 1 to node 2, ... to node n and then back to node 1. This is the cycle network desired.

In Figure 2.37 we give two possible labelings of an n-node tree by the procedure just mentioned. To prove that this procedure gives a cycle network with T as its cut tree, we consider any link l_{ij} of the tree such as the link between V_1 and V_4 in Figure 2.37(a) or the link between V_2 and V_3 in Figure 2.37(b). Let the two nodes adjacent to the link be labeled i and j with i<j. If the link l_{ij} is removed, then the tree is disconnected into two components; one component contains V_i and one component contains V_j. Let k be the largest label which occurs in the component which contains j. Then the node with label k+1 must be in the component which contains i. (If k=n, then k+1 means 1.) Since i<j, the node with the label j−1 must also be in the component which contains i. Then the two arcs of the cycle network from j−1 to j and from k to k+1 correspond to l_{ij}. So the cycle network will have two arcs, each of capacity $\frac{r}{2}$, corresponding to the link of the cut tree.

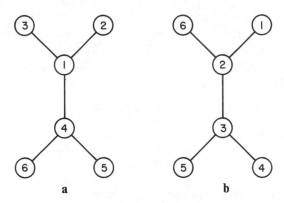

a   b

Figure 2.37

§2.3.4   MULTI-COMMODITY FLOWS

Let S_1 and S_2 be two centers of production and T_1 and T_2 be two centers of consumption. These centers are connected through other transhipment centers by arcs of various capacities. Essentially, we have a network with two sources and two sinks. Assume that the supplies at S_1 and S_2 are s_1 and s_2 and the demands at T_1 and T_2 are t_1 and t_2. The question is whether supply and demand can be met without violating the arc-capacity constraints. Obviously $s_1 + s_2 = t_1 + t_2$ is a necessary condition. Actually, this question can be converted to maximum flow problem. We can create a supersource S^* which has two arcs leading from S^* to S_1 and S_2, with the arc capacities s_1 and s_2. We also create a supersink T^* which has two arcs leading from T_1 and T_2 to T^*, with arc capacities t_1 and t_2. Then we can find the maximum flow from S* to T* in the new network. If the maximum flow is equal to $(s_1 + s_2)$ or $(t_1 + t_2)$, then the supply-and-demand can be met. If the maximum flow is less than $(s_1 + s_2)$, then there is a minimum cut of capacity less than $s_1 + s_2$ separating S_1 and S_2 from T_1 and T_2, which means that supply-and-demand cannot be met.

Similarly, any multiple-source and multiple-sink problem can be converted into a single-source and single-sink problem without much difficulty. The underlying assumption is that all sources give the same kind of supply, or there is only one kind of commodity flowing in the network. If the supply of S_1 is different than that of S_2, and the supply of S_1 must be shipped to T_1 and the supply of S_2 must be shipped to T_2, then the question of feasibility is much harder. Basically, when there are many commodity flows in the network all sharing the same arc capacities, the problem of feasibility has to be solved by linear programming techniques. The only exception is the problem of two-commodity flows in an undirected network. For the two-commodity flow problem and the multi-commodity flow problem, the reader is referred to Fulkerson [9], and Hu [16] [17].

§2.4 MINIMUM COST FLOWS

In this chapter, we have introduced the concept of arc capacity which indicates the maximum amount of flow that can go through an arc. Now we also assign a unit shipping cost of flow through every arc. We ask the following two questions:

1.   If a given amount of flow is to be shipped from V_s to V_t, what is the minimum cost?

2.   If a fixed budget is given, what is the maximum amount of flow that can be shipped from V_s to V_t?

If we denote the unit shipping cost along the arc e_{ij} by c_{ij}, then problem 1 can be stated formally as

$$\min \ z = \Sigma c_{ij} x_{ij}$$

$$\text{subject to} \ \sum_i x_{ij} - \sum_k x_{jk} = \begin{cases} -v & j = s \\ 0 & j \neq s,t \\ v & j = t \end{cases}$$

$$0 \leqslant x_{ij} \leqslant b_{ij}$$

where v is the required amount of flow.

Problem 2 can be stated as

$$\max \ v$$

$$\text{subject to } \sum c_{ij} x_{ij} \leqslant c \quad \text{(c is a given constant)}$$

$$\sum_i x_{ij} - \sum_k x_{jk} = \begin{cases} -v & j = s \\ 0 & j \neq s,t \\ v & j = t \end{cases}$$

$$0 \leqslant x_{ij} \leqslant b_{ij}.$$

If there are no capacity restrictions on the arcs, then we can regard the c_{ij} as the lengths of the arcs and find the cheapest path (the shortest path) from V_s to V_t and then ship the required amount of flow along the path. Even if arc capacity restrictions are imposed, the approach of shipping along the cheapest path still works if the minimum arc capacity on the path is greater than v. On the other hand, if the minimum arc capacity $b_{ij} < v$, then the arc will be saturated and further shipping along the path becomes impossible. Effectively, this is equivalent to having infinite cost on the arc. This motivates the idea of "modified cost" where the cost depends on the current flow in the arc.

We can now outline an algorithm for problem 1.

Step 0.   Start with all arc flows equal to zero and hence the flow value equal to zero.

Step 1.   Define the modified costs c_{ij}^* induced by the existing flows in the network as follows:

$$c_{ij}^* = c_{ij} \quad \text{if } 0 < x_{ij} < b_{ij}$$

$$c_{ij}^* = \infty \quad \text{if } x_{ij} = b_{ij}$$

$$c_{ij}^* = -c_{ji} \quad \text{if } x_{ji} > 0.$$

Step 2.   Find the cheapest path in terms of the modified costs c_{ij}^* obtained in Step 1, and ship ϵ units of flow along the path where

$$\epsilon \ = \ \min \ (\epsilon_1 , \ \epsilon_2)$$

$$\epsilon_1 = \text{min of } (b_{ij} - x_{ij}) \text{ of all forward arcs}$$

$$\epsilon_2 = \text{min of } (x_{ji}) \text{ of all backward arcs.}$$

Update the current flow value by ϵ units and return to Step 1. (Stop if the current flow is v.)

This algorithm actually gives minimum-cost flow of p units for $p = 1,2,...,v$. In finding the cheapest path in Step 1, we could use the shortest path algorithm of section 1.6 where negative length is allowed.

Let us use the algorithm to ship 4 units of flow at minimum cost in the network shown in Figure 2.38.

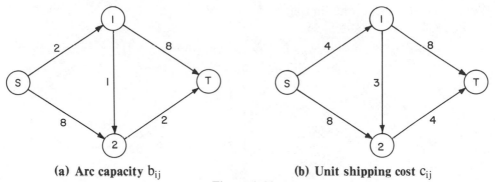

(a) Arc capacity b_{ij} (b) Unit shipping cost c_{ij}

Figure 2.38

We first would send one unit of flow along the path V_s, V_1, V_2, V_t and the arc e_{12} would be saturated. Then the residual capacity $b_{12} = 0$ and $b_{21} = 1$ and the modified costs $c_{12}^* = \infty$ and $c_{21}^* = -3$. We show the residual arc capacities and the modified costs in parentheses in Figure 2.39.

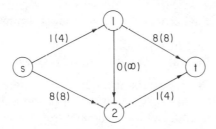

Figure 2.39

After two more units of flow have been shipped, we have Figure 2.40.

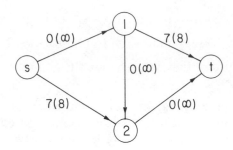

Figure 2.40

We are forced to ship one unit along V_s, V_2, V_1, V_t, and then the modified costs will be as shown in Figure 2.41.

The final residual arc capacities are shown in Figure 2.41.

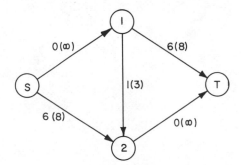

Figure 2.41

Note that the cheapest path is not used in the final flow.

For problem 2, the same algorithm can be used except that we stop the algorithm whenever the total cost reaches the budget limitation.

It is easy to prove that this modified cost algorithm gives the minimum-cost flow of v units or gives the maximum amount of flow with a given budget.

If a flow pattern in a network is optimum, then there is no cycle with negative cost in the network. On the other hand, the non-existence of such a cycle implies the current flow is optimum. For details, see [2] [17] [20].

§2.5 APPLICATIONS

In this section, we shall discuss some applications of network flow theory. More applications can be found in Ford and Fulkerson [8], Hu [17], and other books on mathematical programming. Intuitively speaking, we may think of the maximum flow value from V_s to V_t as a measure of the degree of connectedness. We may think of the capacity of the minimum cut as a measure of the amount of effort required to separate the source and the sink. Another way of expressing the **MAX-FLOW MIN-CUT** theorem is to say the *degree of connectedness is equal to the degree of separation.*

§2.5.1 SETS OF DISTINCT REPRESENTATIVES

A University has many professors who like to form committees. After the professors form many committees among themselves, they decide to have a committee on committees. The committee on committees consists of representatives who are the chairmen of the committees. The rule is that:

(i)   every committee has exactly one representative in the committee on committees,

(ii)   no one in the committee on committees shall be a representative for more than one committee.

Can this be done? In other words, can every committee have a chairman with no professor serving as the chairman of more than one committee?

To put this question into set terminology, let

$$V = \{V_1, V_2, ..., V_m\} \quad \text{be a set of members}$$

$$S = \{S_1, S_2, ..., S_n\} \quad \text{be a set of subsets of V}$$

where S_j consists of members from V.

Can we select distinct V_j ($j = i_1, ..., i_n$) such that there is one-to-one correspondence between S_j and V_j? Here the V_i ($i = 1, ..., m$) are the professors, V_j ($j = i_1, ..., i_n$) are the committee chairmen and S_j ($j = 1, ..., n$) are the committees.

For example, if

$$S_1 = \{2,4,5\},\ S_2 = \{1,5\},\ S_3 = \{3,4\},\ S_4 = \{1,4\},$$

we could let

$$2 \ \text{represent}\ S_1$$

$$1 \ \text{represent}\ S_2$$

$$3 \ \text{represent}\ S_3$$

$$4 \ \text{represent}\ S_4$$

If $S_1 = \{1,3,4\}$, $S_2 = \{1,3\}$, $S_3 = \{3,4\}$, $S_4 = \{1,4\}$, then it is impossible to select a set of distinct representatives for each committee, because there are only three professors 1,3,4, and four committees.

The theorem which settles the existence question is called the theorem on the system of distinct representatives and is due to Hall [8]. It is a fundamental theorem in combinatorics.

Theorem 7 System of Distinct Representatives (S.D.R.)

An SDR exists for S $= \{S_1,...,S_n\}$ *if and only if every collection of* k *sets of* S *contain at least* k *distinct members for* k $= 1,...,n$.

The necessary part of the theorem is obvious. The sufficiency is not so easy to prove. Furthermore, to check every union of k sets of S (for k $= 1,...,n$), we need to find 2^n unions. Even if both necessary and sufficient conditions are met, the theorem or its proof gives no procedure for obtaining the SDR.

If we convert this problem into a network flow problem, then we can give a constructive procedure which takes $O(n^3)$ steps. Actually, for this particular problem, we can solve it in $O(n^{2.5})$ steps. (See Hopcroft and Karp [14].)

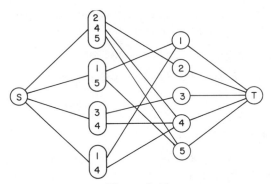

Figure 2.42

In Figure 2.42, we let each committee be a node and the four committees become four nodes in the left column. Each member also becomes a node and the five nodes on the right represent the five members. Connect S_j to V_i if S_j includes V_i as one of its members. Thus, we connect $S_1 = \{2,4,5\}$ to V_2, V_4, and V_5. Each of these lines is an arc of capacity one. To the left of S_j, we create a source node S which has arcs of capacity one to each S_j. To the right of the V_i, we create a sink T which is connected to every node V_i by an arc of capacity one. If the maximum flow from S to T is equal to the number of committees, then the SDR exists and the flow-path automatically picks out the representative. For example, the flow-path $S - S_2 - V_1 - T$ means that V_1 is the representative of S_2.

§2.5.2 PERT

One of the most celebrated applications of network flow theory is called P.E.R.T. (Program Evaluation and Review Technique). This technique is used to distribute money optimally among jobs of a project such that the project may be completed at the earliest time. Consider a large project consisting of many jobs. The jobs are partially ordered due to technical restrictions; for example, the job of washing has to be done before drying. We shall represent jobs by directed arcs. Thus in Figure 2.43, we have five jobs where the job e_{12} must precede the jobs e_{23} and e_{24}; likewise, the jobs e_{13} and e_{23} must both be finished before the job e_{34} can be started.

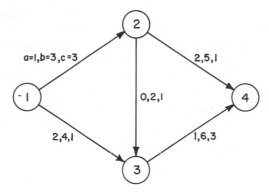

Figure 2.43

For each individual job, there is a normal completion time and an absolute minimum completion time. The more money spent on a job, the quicker the job will be completed. The problem is to finish the whole project as early as possible with a fixed budget. Another version of the same problem is to finish the whole project before a certain deadline with minimum amount of money. We assume that we are given enough money to finish all jobs at their normal completion time. Any additional money should be allocated among the jobs optimally so that the whole project is finished at the earliest time.

In Figure 2.43, we associate three numbers (a_{ij}, b_{ij}, c_{ij}) with each arc (job). The number a_{ij} denotes the minimum time, b_{ij} the normal completion time, and c_{ij} is the amount we have to spend on the job to decrease the normal completion time by one unit. Thus the job e_{12} normally takes three days but can be finished in 2 days if 3 dollars are spent, and in 1 day if 6 dollars are spent. (Since the job e_{12} has a minimum time $a_{12} = 1$, the job takes at least one day.)

Note that the arcs form an acyclic network and the longest path (in terms of b_{ij}) from V_1 to V_4 is

$$e_{12}, \ e_{23}, \ e_{34}$$

which takes $(b_{12} + b_{23} + b_{34}) = (3 + 2 + 6) = 11$ days. Obviously, any additional money should be spent on these jobs to decrease the completion time of the whole project, since this path is the most critical path. This is called critical path scheduling in the literature. Two fundamental papers on the subjects are due to Fulkerson [10] and Kelley [22] and both involve the concepts of mathematical programming. Another paper by Prager [24] explains the algorithm in terms of a mechanical analogue. Here we explain in terms of longest path.

Let us first explain the algorithm intuitively and then apply it to the network in Figure 2.43. For the network in Figure 2.43, V_1 is the starting node where all jobs start and V_4 is the terminating node where all jobs are finished. If a network has several starting nodes, we can create a new starting node V_s with arcs of zero length to all these starting nodes. Conceptually, we can consider that there is only one starting node V_s and one terminating node V_t. To shorten the completion time of the project, we have to shorten the longest path from V_s to V_t. Since there are many arcs in the longest path, we spend money on the arc (job) with the smallest c_{ij}. This would decrease the length of the longest path most efficiently. We continue to shorten the arc until either (i) or (ii) becomes true.

(i)   The arc is shortened to the minimum time a_{ij}.

(ii) The path is no longer the longest path.

When (i) occurs, we pick another arc in the path with the second smallest c_{ij} When (ii) occurs, we then have several paths, all of the longest length. To shorten these paths simultaneously, we have to shorten arcs which would disconnect these paths. We shall pick a set of such arcs with the total sum of c_{ij} a minimum.

This essentially covers the main idea of our algorithm. Sometimes, an arc e_{ij} of a path P_1 is first shortened to its minimum time at an earlier stage. At a later time, other arcs of P_1 are also shortened and consequently P_1 is not a longest path even if the arc e_{ij} is lengthened to its original length. (Note that lengthening an arc means that we can save money.)

To apply the algorithm to the network in Figure 2.43, we first redraw the network in Figure 2.44.

Arcs in solid lines are those in a longest path and arcs in dashed lines are not in any longest path. We shall call arcs in solid lines, *active arcs*, and those in dashed lines, *slack arcs*.

There are three active arcs forming the longest path from V_1 to V_4 and since e_{23} has the smallest cost c_{23}, we shall decrease its length until its length is 1. At that time, e_{13} becomes active, and we have two longest paths, namely:

$$e_{12}, \ e_{23}, \ e_{34}$$

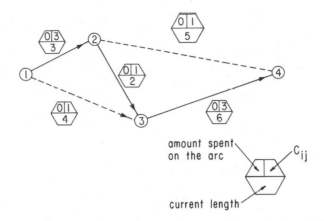

Figure 2.44

or $\qquad$ e_{13}, e_{34}

This is shown in Figure 2.45.

To shorten the two longest paths, we have three choices:

(a) decrease the lengths of e_{12} and e_{13} with $c_{12} + c_{13} = 4$

(b) decrease the lengths of e_{23} and e_{13} with $c_{23} + c_{13} = 2$

(c) decrease the length of e_{34} with $c_{34} = 3$.

Note that the cut $(V_1,V_2 \,|\, V_3,V_4)$ consists of three arcs but e_{24} is not active. Since the cut consisting of e_{23} and e_{13} is the cheapest, we shorten both of these arcs.

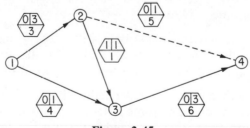

Figure 2.45

The result is shown in Figure 2.46. Then we have two cuts

(a) e_{12} and e_{13} with $c_{12} + c_{13} = 4$

(b) e_{34} with $c_{34} = 3$.

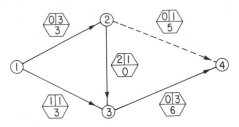

Figure 2.46

When we decrease the length of e_{34} to 5, then e_{24} becomes active and the situation is shown in Figure 2.47.

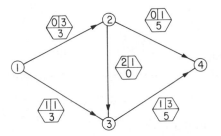

Figure 2.47

An arc, such as e_{23}, is called a *rigid arc* if its length has been reduced to its minimum completion time.

In Figure 2.47, we have two cuts both with costs 4, namely $(c_{12} + c_{13})$ or $(c_{24} + c_{34})$, we could decrease the arcs e_{12} and e_{13} to the length 2, and the arcs e_{24} and e_{34} to length 2, and the result is shown in Figure 2.48.

At this stage, both e_{13} and e_{24} have reduced to their minimum times and cannot be reduced any more. The same is true for e_{23}. If we reduce e_{12} and e_{34} also to their minimum time, then we could increase the length of e_{23} without affecting the length of the longest path. This situation is shown in Figure 2.49.

In Figure 2.49, we have a longest path (e_{12}, e_{24}) in which all arcs are rigid arcs. So the duration of the whole project cannot be reduced any more. The cost $(6 + 3 + 1 + 2 + 15)$ is the minimum cost to reduce the project to 3 days. In general, a configuration is of minimum cost when a longest path is formed by active arcs. Thus Figures 2.44, 2.45, 2.46, 2.47, 2.48, and 2.49 are of minimum

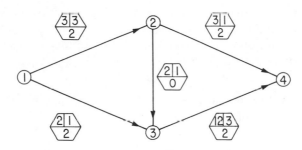

Figure 2.48

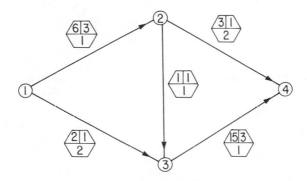

Figure 2.49

cost for their project times: $0 for 11 days, $1 for 10 days, $3 for 9 days, $6 for 8 days, $22 for 4 days, and $27 for 3 days.

We can outline an algorithm for PERT as follows

1. Based on the current lengths of arcs, find all longest paths from V_s to V_t. All arcs on longest paths are active arcs.

2. Consider C_{ij} of active arcs as the arc capacities of active arcs, find the maximum flow from V_s to V_t. (In finding the maximum flow, we locate the minimum cut which represents the cheapest way to reduce the duration of the whole project.)

3. If an arc becomes rigid, consider its arc capacity as infinity.

4. If the maximum flow becomes infinity in step 2, it means that the duration of the project cannot be decreased further.

5.   Find the distance from V_s to every node using only rigid arcs. The distance to a node V_i represents the shortest time that event (the node) can occur. If an active arc has length shorter than the difference of distances of its two nodes, then increase the length of the arc. (This is equivalent to a reduction in cost.)

Since this algorithm is equivalent to those algorithms in [11] [22] [24], we do not present a proof here.

§2.5.3 OPTIMUM COMMUNICATION SPANNING TREE

In section 1.7, we introduced the concept of a minimum spanning tree. A typical application of a minimum spanning tree might be to connect n cities with telephone lines and the objective is to have the minimum construction costs, where d_{ij} indicates the construction cost of connecting city i and city j. Since we want to connect all the cities, we need at least n−1 links, and since we want to minimize the construction cost, we want a minimum spanning tree.

Now, assume that we know the number of telephone calls r_{ij} between each pair of cities before the network is built and we would like to minimize the communication cost after the telephone network is built. Let the communication cost of placing a call between city i and city j be equal to the length of the telephone line connecting city i and city j. If there are r_{ij} calls, the cost would be multiplied by r_{ij}. Summing over all the pairs of cities, we have the total communication cost. Obviously, using this criterion of communication cost, we would build a telephone line along the shortest path between any two cities and then superpose all the shortest paths to get the best network.

In general, the best network would not be a spanning tree and would have more than (n−1) links, and hence have a large construction cost. To balance the construction cost and the communication cost, we want to pick, among all spanning trees, the one with minimum communication cost. We shall call this spanning tree, the *Optimum Communication Spanning Tree.*

To formalize the idea of optimum communication spanning trees, we consider six cities and their distances as shown in Figure 2.50.

Assume also the requirements between these cities are as shown in Figure 2.51.

If we construct a spanning tree as shown in Figure 2.52, then the communication cost would be

$$r_{12}(2+2) + r_{13}(2+3) + r_{14}(2+4+3) + \cdots + r_{46}(3+4) + r_{56}(4)$$
$$= 10(2+2) + 0(2+3) + 0(2+4+3) + \cdots + 2(3+4) + 3(4)$$
$$= 225$$

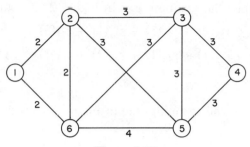

Figure 2.50

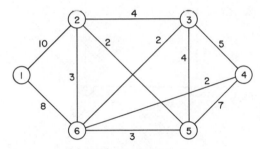

Figure 2.51

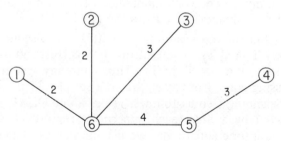

Figure 2.52

The problem of finding the optimum communication spanning tree turns out to be very difficult and the assumption that the cost of a call is equal to the length of the telephone line is rather unrealistic. So we shall deal with a special case with all $d_{ij} \equiv 1$. In other words, the cost of a call is equal to the number of arcs in the path connecting the two cities. Even for this special case (of $d_{ij} \equiv 1$ and r_{ij} arbitrary), the problem of the optimum communication spanning tree is still more difficult than the minimum spanning tree problem in section 1.7.

If all $d_{ij} \equiv 1$,   then the spanning tree in Figure 2.52 would cost

$$r_{12}(2) + r_{16}(1) + r_{23}(2) + r_{25}(2) + r_{26}(1) + r_{34}(3)$$
$$+ r_{35}(2) + r_{36}(1) + r_{45}(1) + r_{46}(2) + r_{56}(1)$$
$$= 82$$

On the other hand, the spanning tree in Figure 2.53 with the same r_{ij} would cost only 77.

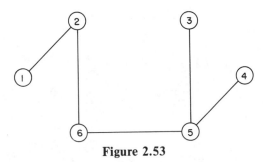

Figure 2.53

We shall introduce several lemmas which will be relevant to the problem we are discussing now.

Lemma 7 There is a one-to-one correspondence between $n-1$ links of a spanning tree of a graph and $n-1$ noncrossing cuts in the graph.

Proof. Remove any link of the spanning tree; this will disconnect the tree into two components, say T_1 and T_2. Then let this link correspond to the cut (T_1, T_2). Do the same process to the tree T_1 or T_2. Thus from any spanning tree, we get a set of $n-1$ noncrossing cuts. Conversely, from a set of $n-1$ noncrossing cuts, we can construct the spanning tree as follows. Take a cut $(X, \overline{X})$; we can draw two supernodes connected by a link (each supernode represents a set of ordinary nodes symbolically); in one supernode, we list the names of nodes in X, and in the other supernode, we list the names of nodes of $\overline{X}$. This creates one link of the spanning tree. Now consider another cut $(Y, \overline{Y})$. Since $(Y, \overline{Y})$ does not cross $(X, \overline{X})$, we have $Y \subset X$ and $\overline{Y} \supset \overline{X}$ (or $Y \supset X$ and $\overline{Y} \subset \overline{X}$); then we can create a tree with three supernodes Y, $(X-Y)$ and $\overline{X}$ as shown in Figure 2.54. After $n-1$ steps, we create a spanning tree of $n-1$ links.

Lemma 8 Given two spanning trees of a graph G, we shall refer to one as the "red" spanning tree and the other as the "blue" spanning tree. For any blue link B_{ij}, there exists a red link B_{pq} such that B_{pq} is one of the red links which forms the unique path from V_i to V_j in the red spanning tree. Furthermore, a one-to-one mapping between the blue links and red links can be established which satisfies the above condition.

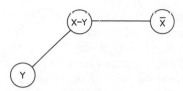

Figure 2.54

Before we give a proof of Lemma 8, let us illustrate it by an example.

We shall list the red links which form the unique path connecting V_i and V_j as a subset opposite the blue link B_{ij}. The underlined red link corresponds to the blue link B_{ij}. (See Figure 2.55.)

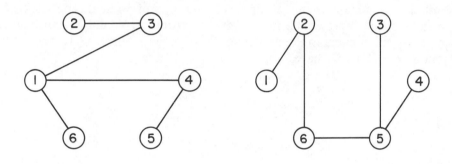

Red Spanning Tree   **Blue Spanning Tree**

Figure 2.55

Red Links		Blue Links
$B_{\underline{13}}$	B_{32}	B_{12}
$B_{\underline{23}}$ B_{31}	B_{16}	B_{26}
$B_{\underline{61}}$ B_{14}	B_{45}	B_{65}
B_{31} $B_{\underline{14}}$	B_{45}	B_{35}
	$B_{\underline{45}}$	B_{45}

Proof. For any blue link B_{ij}, if there exists a red link B_{ij} in the red spanning tree, let the red link B_{ij} be the unique image of the blue link B_{ij}. If there is no direct link connecting V_i and V_j in the red spanning tree, then there exists a path $B_{ip},...,$ B_{qj} which contains two or more links in the red tree. This set of red links forms the image of the corresponding blue link B_{ij}.

Take any subset of blue links which form p components. Let the number of nodes in the ith component be n_i and

$$\sum_{i=1}^{p} n_i = k.$$

This subset of nodes contains k−p blue links. The image of each component must be connected and incident to all the nodes in the component. Now consider the set of red links which is the union of the images of the p components. This set of red links must form p' ($\leqslant$p) components and be incident to all the k nodes. Thus the set contains at least $k-p'$ red links. From Theorem 7, sets of distinct representatives 2.5.1 (Hall's Theorem in [8]), we can select n−1 distinct red links to the image of the n−1 blue links in the spanning tree.

Lemma 9 The sum of the n−1 cut capacities of the n−1 noncrossing cuts represented by the cut tree (Gomory-Hu tree) is less than the sum of the cut capacities of any n−1 noncrossing cuts.

Proof. Any set of n−1 noncrossing cuts can be represented as a spanning tree (Lemma 7). Let this spanning tree be the red spanning tree and Gomory-Hu tree be the blue spanning tree in Lemma 8. For any blue link B_{ij}, there is a unique red link B_{pq} which represents a cut separating V_i and V_j in the network. Note that the blue link represents a minimum cut separating V_i and V_j and hence the value of the cut is equal to the maximum flow value f_{ij}. Since B_{pq} represents a cut separating V_i and V_j, we have

$$c(p,q) \geqslant f_{ij} = c(i,j) .$$

$$\text{red} \qquad\qquad \text{blue}$$

Thus,

$$\sum_{p,q} c(p,q) \geqslant \sum_{i,j} c(i,j)$$

$$\text{red} \qquad\qquad \text{blue}$$

Theorem 8 Given a set of $n(n-1)/2$ requirements r_{ij} between a set of n nodes, and a spanning tree T connecting the set of n nodes. The communication cost of the tree T for the set of r_{ij} can be calculated as follows:

(i)   Construct a network N with $b_{kl} \equiv r_{kl}$.

(ii)   In the network N, find the n−1 noncrossing cuts represented by T.

(iii)   The sum of cut capacities of the n−1 cuts in (ii) is the communication cost of the tree T for the set of r_{ij}.

Proof. Since $d_{ij} \equiv 1$, the communication cost for a pair of nodes V_p and V_q in a tree T is equal to r_{pq} multiplied by the number of links in the unique path in the tree T. Summing over $\binom{n}{2}$ pairs of nodes, we have the communication cost of the tree T. Alternatively, we could fix our attention on a link B_{ij} of T, and add all the r_{pq}'s which use the link B_{ij}, and let the sum be credited to the link B_{ij}; summing over the n−1 links of T, we also have the communication cost of T.

If we construct a network N with $b_{kl} \equiv r_{kl}$, then the capacity of a cut $(X, \overline{X})$ represented by a link b_{ij} of T is equal to

$$\sum b_{pq} \quad \text{with} \quad V_p \in X \quad \text{and} \quad V_q \in \overline{X}.$$

This is the same as the number of r_{pq}'s using the link B_{ij}.

Summing over the $n-1$ links, we have the theorem.

Theorem 9 For $d_{ij} \equiv 1$, $r_{ij} \geqslant 0$, the optimum communication spanning tree T for the set of r_{ij} can be obtained as follows

(i)   Construct a network N with $b_{kl} \equiv r_{kl}$.

(ii)   Construct the Gomory-Hu tree for the network N.

(iii)   The Gomory-Hu tree constructed in (ii) is the optimum communication tree T.

Proof. From Theorem 8, the communication cost of any spanning tree T is the sum of $n-1$ noncrossing cuts of a network N constructed with $b_{kl} = r_{kl}$.

From Lemma 9, the sum of $n-1$ noncrossing cut capacities is greater than the sum of cut capacities of the $n-1$ cuts represented by Gomory-Hu cut tree T^*.

Hence T^* is the optimum communication spanning tree.

For example, if a network of six nodes has requirements as shown in Figure 2.51, then according to Theorems 8 and 9, we regard these r_{ij} as arc capacities of a network. Then we can construct the Gomory-Hu cut tree as discussed in 2.3.2. (In Figure 2.21, we have exactly the same network as in Figure 2.51.) Hence we get the Gomory-Hu tree as shown in Figure 2.53 which is the same as Figure 2.29. Note the communication cost of the tree in Figure 2.53 can be obtained by summing over all the link values in Figure 2.29.

$$18 + 17 + 13 + 14 + 15 = 77$$

which was obtained by a direct calculation.

EXERCISES

1. Are the following statements correct? Explain.

    (i)   If all arcs in a network have different capacities, then there exists a unique minimum cut separating the source and the sink.

    (ii)   If all arcs in a network have different capacities, then there exists a unique set of arc flows that gives the maximum flow value.

2. Prove that any network is flow-equivalent to a tree which has only two nodes of degree one (i.e., the tree is of the shape of a path).

3. Prove that any four node network shown below is flow-equivalent to the three node network with respect to V_A, V_B, and V_C.

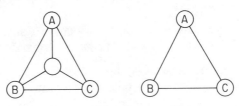

Figure 2.56

4. Assume that we represent jobs by nodes in the **PERT** network. Can we transform the nodes into arcs such that (i) the partial ordering relationship is maintained and (ii) there is a one-to-one corresponding between nodes and arcs?

5. A path from V_s to V_t with arc capacity

    $$(b_{s1}, b_{12}, ..., b_{ij}, ..., b_{kt})$$

    is called a maximum capacity route if

    $$\min(b_{s1}, b_{12}, ..., b_{ij}, ..., b_{kt})$$

    is maximum among all routes from V_s to V_t. Design an algorithm to find the maximum capacity routes between all pairs of nodes in a network.

6. Construct a four-node network such that the Ford-Fulkerson algorithm needs v iterations where v is the maximum flow value of the network.

7. Is it possible to have $x_{ij} > 0$ and $x_{ji} > 0$ at the same time? Modify the labeling method such that the above situation will be avoided.

8.   Use the modified version of labeling method. The node v_j gets the label $[\epsilon(j), i^-]$ if $x_{ji} > 0$ where $\epsilon(j) = \min[\epsilon(i), x_{ji} + b_{ij}]$. Then at least one arc will be saturated after a flow-change.

9.   Construct a network such that the maximal flow is one unit where the maximum flow is k units.

10.   If every arc has capacity zero or one, then the triangular inequality in § 2.3 is still necessary but no longer sufficient. What is the sufficient condition? (Open question)

CHAPTER 2

BIBLIOGRAPHIC NOTES AND SUGGESTED READING

The MAX-FLOW MIN-CUT theorem was discovered by Ford and Fulkerson [6], [7], [8]. The BSF search for flow-augmenting paths was discovered by Edmonds and Karp [4], and the successive improved new algorithms are by Dinic [3] and Karzanov [21]. Since both Dinic and Karzanov's papers are in Russian, two English exposition papers by Even [8] and Tarjan [28] are highly recommended.

The whole Section 2.3 Multi-terminal Flows is based on the paper by Gomory and Hu [12], although the exposition here is slightly different. Lemmas 5 and 6 should be read carefully. In fact, the cut $(X,\overline{X})$ in the lemmas does not have to be a minimum cut. Lemmas 5 and 6 are still true as long as there exist *no* other cut $(X',\overline{X}')$ such that

$$X' \subset X \quad \text{and}$$
$$c(X',\overline{X}') \leqslant c(X,\overline{X}).$$

A cut $(X,\overline{X})$ satisfying the above property is called a local minimum cut, and is used in Hu and Ruskey [19]. Lemmas 5 and 6 (commonly referred to as non-crossing cut lemmas) and the process of condensing nodes should have wide application in the graph and network theory. See also the interesting application of Network Flow Theory in [26] [27].

The multi-commodity flow problem in general is NP-complete (see Chapter 8) although a linear programming approach with column-generating techniques proves to be very efficient, see Fulkerson [9], Gomory and Hu [13], and Hu [17]. The special case of two commodity flows can still be handled by a labeling method, see Hu [16].

The minimum cost flow algorithms are based on the papers by Busacker and Gwen [2], Fulkerson [10], Hu [15], Iri [20], and Klein [23].

The proofs that PERT works can be found in Fulkerson [11], Kelley [22], and Prager [24]. Since the reader may not have mathematical programming background, we use the intuitive concepts of longest path and cheapest cut.

The optimum communication spanning tree in Section 2.5.3 is based on Hu [18].

1. A. E. Baratz, "Construction and Analysis of Network Flow Problem which forces Karzanov's Algorithm to $O(N^3)$ Running Time", M.I.T./LCS/TM-83, April 1977.

2. R. G. Busacker and P. J. Gowen, "A Procedure for Determining a Family of Minimal-Cost Network Flow Patterns", ORO Tech. Report 15, John Hopkins Univ., 1961.

3. E. A. Dinic, "Algorithm for Solution of a Problem of Maximum Flow in a Network with Power Estimation", Soviet Math. Dokl. 11 (1970), pp. 1277-1280.

4. J. Edmonds and R. M. Karp, "Theoretical Improvements in Algorithmic Efficiency for Network Flow Problems", J. ACM 19(2) (1972), pp. 248-264.

5. S. Even, "The Max Flow Algorithm of Dinic and Karzanov: An Exposition", M.I.T./LCS/TM-80, Dec. 1976.

6. L. R. Ford and D. R. Fulkerson, "Maximal Flow Through a Network", Canadian J. Math. 8(3) (1956), pp. 399-404.

7. L. R. Ford and D. R. Fulkerson, "A Simple Algorithm for Finding Maximal Network Flows and an Application to the Hitchcock Problem", Canadian J. Math. 9(2) (1957), pp. 210-218.

8. L. R. Ford and D. R. Fulkerson, "Flows in Networks", Princeton Unviersity Press, 1962.

9. D. R. Fulkerson, "Suggested Computation for Maximal Multi-commodity Network Flows", Man. Sci. 5(1) (1958), pp. 97-101.

10. D. R. Fulkerson, "Increasing the Capacity of a Network, the Parametric Budget Problem", Man. Sci. 5(4) (1959), pp. 472-483.

11. D. R. Fulkerson, "A Network Flow Computation for Project Cost Curves", Man. Sci. 7 (1961), pp. 167-178.

12. R. E. Gomory and T. C. Hu, "Multi-terminal Network Flows", J. SIAM 9(4) (1961), pp. 551-570.

13. R. E. Gomory and T. C. Hu, "Synthesis of a Communication Network", J. SIAM 12(2) (1964), pp. 348-369.

14.   J. E. Hopcroft and R. M. Karp, "An $n^{2.5}$ Algorithm for Maximum Matching in Bipartite Graphs", SIAM J. Computing 2 (1973), pp. 225-231.

15.   T. C. Hu, "Minimum Convex Cost Flows", Navy Res. Log. Quart. 13(1) (1966), pp. 1-9.

16.   T. C. Hu "Multi-commodity Network Flows", J. ORSA 11(3) (1963), pp. 344-360.

17.   T. C. HU, "Integer Programming and Network Flows", Addison-Wesley, 1969.

18.   T. C. Hu, "Optimum Communication Spanning Tree", SIAM J. Computing 3(3) (1974), pp. 188-195.

19.   T. C. Hu and F. Ruskey, "Circular Cut in a Network", to appear in Mathematics of Operations Research, Vol. 5, No. 3, August 1980, pp. 422-434.

20.   M. Iri, "A New Method of Solving Transportation Network Problems", J. O. R. Japan 3(no. 1 & 2) (1960), pp. 27-87.

21.   A. V. Karzanov, "Determining the Max Flow in a Network by the Method of Preflows", Soviet Math. Dokl. 15 (1974), pp. 434-437.

22.   J. E. Kelley, Jr., "Critical Path Planning and Scheduling Mathematical Basis", J. ORSA 9(2) (1961), pp. 296-320.

23.   M. Klein, "A Primal Method for Minimal Cost Flows", Man. Sci. 14(3) (1967), pp. 205-220.

24.   V. M. Malhotra, M. Pramodh Kumar and S. N. Maheshwari, "An $O(v^3)$ Algorithm for Finding Maximum Flows in Networks". Information Processing Letters, Vol. 7., No. 6 (1978), pp. 277-278.

25.   W. Prager, "A Structural Method for Computing Project Cost Polygons", Man. Sci. 9(3) (1963), pp. 394-404.

26.   G. S. Rao, H. S. Stone, and T. C. Hu, "Assignment of Tasks in a Distributed Processor System with Limited Memory", IEEE Transaction on Computers, Vol. C-28(4) (1979), pp. 291-299.

27.   C. P. Schnorr, "Bottlenecks and Edge Connectivity in Unsymmetrical Networks", SIAM J. Computing 8(2) (1979), pp. 265-274.

28.   R. Tarjan, "Lecture Notes on Flow Theory", Stanford University, 1976.

ANSWERS TO EXERCISES IN CHAPTER 2

1.   (i)   Wrong.

      (ii) Wrong.

2.   First construct the Gomory-Hu cut tree. Then convert the cut tree to a path as follows: Let V_1, V_2, V_3 be nodes of degree one and that they are adjacent to a node V_i. If the capacities of the links in the cut tree are b_{i1}, b_{i2}, b_{i3} where $b_{i1} < b_{i2} < b_{i3}$, We make a path from V_1, V_2, V_3, V_i and then connect to the rest of the cut tree.

4.   Sometimes we have to add dummy arcs to preserve the partial ordering relationship.

5.   We can have a modified triple operation as follows:

$$b_{ik} \leftarrow \min (b_{ik}, b_{ij} + b_{jk})$$

for $j = 1,2,...,n$ and all i,k not equal to j. (Compare the triple operation in Chapter 1.)

CHAPTER 3. DYNAMIC PROGRAMMING

Live optimally today, for today is the first day of the rest of your life.

§3.1 INTRODUCTION

Dynamic programming is an approach to optimization just as mathematical induction is an approach to proving theorems. Dynamic programming is a very useful approach to many optimization problems. It is one of the few *general* techniques for solving optimization problems and can be easily adapted to stochastic situations. Since the technique is so general, it may not use all the structure of a particular problem. Usually, we can find a tailor-made algorithm which is more efficient than the straight-forward algorithm based on dynamic programming.

In this chapter, we shall give several examples to show how the idea of dynamic programming is used. For some problems, a special algorithm could be used which is more efficient than the algorithm based on dynamic programming.

Example 1

Shortest Path

A road map is shown in Figure 3.1, where all the streets are one-way streets (from left to right). The numbers on the arcs are the lengths of these streets. The problem is to find a shortest path from any node S_i ($i = 1,...,5$) to any node T_j ($j = 1,2,...,5$). This is a special shortest-path problem to illustrate the idea of dynamic programming. The brute force approach is to consider all possible paths from S_i to T_j and compare their lengths and pick the shortest. Let us make three observations.

1) Assume that a path (S_2,A_1,B_2,C_2,T_3) is the shortest path. There are many subpaths such as (S_2,A_1,B_2), (A_1,B_2,C_2,T_3), (A_1,B_2,C_2) contained in the given shortest path. Each of the subpaths must be a shortest path itself; i.e., (S_2,A_1,B_2) is a shortest path from S_2 to B_2, the path (A_1,B_2,C_2,T_3) is a shortest path from A_1 to T_3. If the subpath (S_2,A_1,B_2) were not the shortest, then we could replace it by a shorter path (S_2,A_2,B_2) and form the path (S_2,A_2,B_2,C_2,T_3) which would be shorter than (S_2,A_1,B_2,C_2,T_3). This is a contradiction. This observation can be summarized in one sentence. *Any subpath of an optimum path must be optimum itself.*

2) If we really want to travel from S_i to T_j along the shortest path, we have to pick the correct S_i to start; but we do not need to know the entire path when we are at S_i. All we have to know is whether to go up or down at a given node. If there were signs at all intermediate nodes telling us where to

107

go, then we could trace out the optimum path step by step. The philosophy here is not to describe a curve as a whole but to prescribe the tangent at every point as we go along. In dynamic programming, we use the tangent approach.

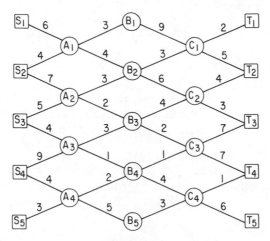

Figure 3.1

3)   Instead of starting from S_i, we could start from nodes C_i and think backward. If we are at a node C_i, should we go up or down? Since there are two choices at each node C_i, we can write u (for up) and d (for down) at every C_i, and the mileage from C_i to a terminal node T_j. (Note that no matter how we arrived at a node C_i, we must proceed optimally from that time on). Going back to nodes B_i, we again ask the up-or-down question. At a node B_3, we pick $\min(4+3, 2+7) = 7$ (see Figure 3.2), so we should go up. When all comparisons are made for the B_i, we have u or d written in every node B_i as well as the shortest distance from the node B_i to its nearest T_j. This is shown in Figure 3.2.

In making the decision at nodes A_i, we do *not* need the part of the network to the right of B_j. This is how we reduce the amount of computation. Going back to S_i, we can use the same approach. The only data that affect the decisions at S_i are the lengths of arcs from S_i and the numbers written on the A_j.

From Figure 3.2, we see that two shortest paths are possible; one from S_3 and one from S_5. A path can be traced out easily from either S_3 or S_5. From S_3, we go down to A_3, down to B_4, down to C_4, and up to T_4. From S_5, we go up to A_4, up to B_4, down to C_4, and up to T_4.

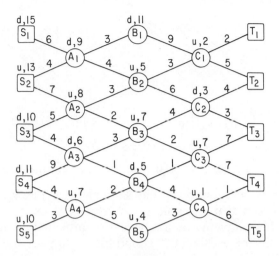

Figure 3.2

Note that in this problem, we define an optimum path as the path of shortest length. If we had defined an optimum path as the path of longest length, we could still use the same technique to find the optimum path. The key feature here is that *any subpath of an optimum path must be optimum itself.* This seemingly obvious statement can be generalized to many other problems, such as multistage decision problems, allocation processes, and so forth. Instead of using the word *path*, we use the word *policy* which is more suitable to decision problems. This idea has been called the "*principle of optimality*" by people using dynamic programming.

The principle of optimality. Any subpolicy of an optimum policy must itself be an optimum policy with regard to the initial and terminal states of the subpolicy.

The argument is very simple. If the subpolicy is not optimum, we can replace it with a better subpolicy with the same initial and terminal states. Then the total policy could be better, contradicting the assumption that the original policy is optimum.

The implicit assumption here is that a policy can be broken into many subpolicies, where the optimality of the policy implies that every subpolicy is optimum. Let us define an optimum path as one where the sum of all arc lengths (mod 10) is minimum, and consider the network in Figure 3.3.

There are two arcs between two successive nodes. The upper arc has length 1 while the lower arc has length 9. Since 1 (mod 10) is less than 9 (mod 10), we should use the upper arc in going from V_s to V_1, V_1 to V_2, etc. Then the value of the path using all upper arcs is

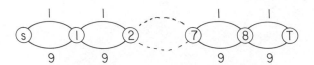

Figure 3.3

$$1 + 1 + 1 + \ldots + 1 \pmod{10} = 9$$

while the value of the path using all lower arcs is

$$9 + 9 + 9 + \ldots + 9 \pmod{10} = 81 \pmod{10} = 1 .$$

Note that the path is optimum but it has a subpath such as V_s to V_2 which is not optimum. The reason that dynamic programming does not work well in this problem is that this problem cannot be easily broken into many subproblems where the optimality of each of the subproblems implies the optimality of the whole problem. (See Exercise 9.)

For an optimization problem, we usually try to maximize or minimize a function subject to certain constraints. The dynamic programming approach is:

1)   Consider the problem as many subproblems. If the problem is to make many decisions simultaneously, the approach is to formulate the problem as a sequential decision process where some of the decisions have already been made, and then decide what should be the best decision under those conditions.

2)   When all the subproblems are solved, or when all partial optimum decisions are known, we can combine these partial solutions to get the optimal solution of the whole problem. The relationship of the subproblem to the whole problem can usually be defined recursively by a functional equation.

Books [1], [2], [4], [14], [15] have been written to show how the idea of dynamic programming can be used in various problems. Let us now consider another example.

Example 2

Allocation of money among enterprises

Given 1000 dollars to invest in 10 possible enterprises, how should we allocate the money?

Let x_i = the amount of money invested in the ith enterprise, $f_i(x_i)$ = the amount of return from the ith enterprise when x_i dollars are invested.

So the problem is to find

$$\max \; [f_1(x_1) + f_2(x_2) + \cdots + f_{10}(x_{10})]$$
$$\text{subject to} \;\; x_1 + x_2 + \cdots + x_{10} = 1000$$
$$x_i \geqslant 0, \text{integers} \; (i = 1, ..., 10).$$

We assume that $f_i(0) = 0$ and all functions are monotonically increasing.

An optimum policy here is to determine the exact amount of x_i in each of the ten enterprises. Instead of deciding how much we should invest in each of the enterprises, we ask the following type of questions:

If 450 dollars have already been spent on the first four enterprises, how should we spend the rest of the money among the six remaining enterprises?

Here the subpolicy is to spend $550 among six enterprises. If we do not use the $550 optimally, then the total policy is certainly *not* optimum. Note that we do not know whether we should spend $450 among the first four enterprises or not. If we know all the solutions to such subproblems, we can piece the subsolutions together to get the overall solution.

Let us try these ideas on a small example with only four enterprises and 5 dollars; i.e.,

$$\max \; [f_1(x_1) + f_2(x_2) + f_3(x_3) + f_4(x_4)] \qquad (1)$$
$$\text{subject to} \;\; x_1 + x_2 + x_3 + x_4 = 5$$
$$x_i \geqslant 0, \;\; \text{integers} \; (i = 1, ..., 4) \;.$$

The boundary conditions are $f_i(0) = 0$ for all i, and the return functions are listed in Table 3.1.

Table 3.1

x	$f_1(x)$	$f_2(x)$	$f_3(x)$	$f_4(x)$
1	11	0	2	20
2	12	5	10	21
3	13	10	30	22
4	14	15	32	23
5	15	20	40	24

Since each variable x_i can take 6 possible values $(0,1,2,3,4,5)$, a brute-force (brainless) approach would require the examination of 6^4 possibilities.

Define $F_k(x)$ to be the maximum return from the first k enterprises using x dollars. Here we are interested in $F_4(5)$.

$F_1(x)$ is then the maximum return from the 1st enterprise. $F_1(x) = f_1(x)$, since the function f_1 is monotonically increasing. For $F_2(x)$, we have to decide how much x_2 is. The remaining amount $x-x_2$ is then spent on the first enterprise. Thus

$$F_2(x) = \max_{0 \leqslant x_2 \leqslant x} [f_2(x_2) + F_1(x-x_2)] \qquad (2)$$

If we know the values of $F_2(x)$ for all x, we can set

$$F_3(x) = \max_{0 \leqslant x_3 \leqslant x} [f_3(x_3) + F_2(x-x_3)] \qquad (3)$$

and then

$$F_4(x) = \max_{0 \leqslant x_4 \leqslant x} [f_4(x_4) + F_3(x-x_4)]. \qquad (4)$$

In (1), the values of x_i are to be determined simultaneously and substituted into $f_i(x_i)$. Here, the values of $x_1, x_2, \ldots$, are determined sequentially and substituted into $F_i(x)$. Equation (2) could be written as

$$F_2(x) = \max_{0 \leqslant x_2 \leqslant x} [f_2(x_2) + f_1(x-x_2)],$$

and from the point of view of computation, they are just the same.

The real difference comes in (3). We do not have to know precisely how $F_2(x-x_3)$ is achieved. All we have to know is the number which is the return. The same is true when we consider (4). The calculation can be put in a table as shown in Table 3.2.

Table 3.2

x	$F_1(x)$	$x_1(x)$	$F_2(x)$	$x_2(x)$	$F_3(x)$	$x_3(x)$	$F_4(x)$	$x_4(x)$
1	11	1	11	0	11	0	20	1
2	12	2	12	0	13	1	31	1
3	13	3	16	2	30	3	33	1
4	14	4	21	3	41	3	50	1
5	15	5	26	4	43	4	61	1

We proceed, column by column from left to right. In order to calculate a new column, say $F_3(x)$, we only need $F_2(x)$ and $f_3(x)$ as shown in (3).

When the table is complete, we get $F_4(5) = 61$ and $x_4 = 1$. This means

$$F_3(x-x_4) = F_3(5-1) = F_3(4) = 41 \text{ with } x_3 = 3,$$

$$F_2(x-x_4-x_3) = F_2(5-1-3) = F_2(1) = 11 \text{ with } x_2 = 0,$$

and $$F_1(x-x_4-x_3-x_2) = F_1(5-1-3) = F_1(1) = 11 \text{ with } x_1 = 1 .$$

So the optimum solution is $x_1 = 1$, $x_2 = 0$, $x_3 = 3$ and $x_4 = 1$.

Note that for $F_3(x)$, we need $x+1$ additions and x comparisons:

$$F_3(x) = \max \begin{cases} f_3(0) & + & F_2(x-0) \\ f_3(1) & + & F_2(x-1) \\ & \bullet & \\ & \bullet & \\ & \bullet & \\ f_3(x) & + & F_2(0) \end{cases}$$

When the total amount of money available is b dollars and there are n enterprises, then there are nb entries for $F_i(x)$ to be filled. For each i, there are

$$\sum_{x=1}^{b} (x+1) = b(b+3)/2 \text{ additions}$$

and $$\sum_{x=1}^{b} x = b(b+1)/2 \text{ comparisons.}$$

So there are roughly nb^2 operations. Normally the functions $f_i(x_i)$ can be approximated by piecewise linear functions and we only have to consider the critical values of x_i.

§3.2 KNAPSACK PROBLEMS

The problem of minimizing or maximizing a linear function subject to linear constraints is called a linear program. For example, we may want to minimize

$$z = \sum_j c_j x_j \quad (j = 1, ..., n) \tag{1}$$

$$\text{subject to } \sum a_{ij} x_j \geqslant b_i \quad (i = 1, ..., m) \tag{2}$$

$$x_j \geqslant 0 \tag{3}$$

where x_j are unknown variables and a_{ij}, b_i and c_j are given constants. When the variables x_j are restricted to be integers in addition to being nonnegative, the program is called an integer program. A great many combinatorial optimization problems can be formulated as integer programs. Books and papers have been written on linear and integer programs. These subjects are commonly referred to as mathematical programming.

We cannot treat these general problems here. Instead, we shall consider the simplest kind of integer programs; namely, an integer program with only one constraint in (2). This is commonly known as the knapsack problem.

The name "knapsack problem" arises from the following hypothetical situation. Consider a hiker who is going to carry a knapsack with him on his trip. To fill the knapsack he must choose among many items, each of which has a weight and a value to him. Certainly, he would like to carry with him the maximum amount of value with total weight less than a prescribed amount.

Let w_j be the weight of the jth item, v_j be the value of the jth item, x_j be the number of items of type j that the hiker carries with him, and let b denote the total weight limitation. Then the problem becomes

$$\max \ \sum v_j x_j \qquad (v_j \geqslant 0, j = 1, ..., n)$$

$$\text{subject to} \ \sum w_j x_j \leqslant b \quad (w_j \geqslant 0, b > 0, j = 1, ..., n)$$

$$x_j \geqslant 0, \text{ integers .}$$

In order to solve this problem, we shall introduce a new function $F_k(y)$. Define

$$F_k(y) = \max \sum_{j=1}^{k} v_j x_j \ (0 \leqslant k \leqslant n),$$

with

$$\sum_{j=1}^{k} w_j x_j \leqslant y \quad (0 \leqslant y \leqslant b),$$

i.e., $F_k(y)$ is the maximum value obtained by using only the first k items when the total weight limitation is y. Thus

$$F_0(y) = 0 \text{ for all y } (0 \leqslant y \leqslant b), \text{ since no items are chosen}$$

and

$$F_k(0) = 0 \text{ for all k } (0 \leqslant k \leqslant n), \text{ since the total weight limitation is zero.}$$

Then $F_1(y) = \left\lfloor y/w_1 \right\rfloor v_1$, since we want to put in as many of the first items as possible. For a general $F_k(y)$ we have the following recursive relation:

$$F_k(y) = \max \ \{F_{k-1}(y), F_k(y-w_k)+v_k\} \qquad (4)$$

The reason is simply this: when the first k items are chosen to obtain $F_k(y)$, either the kth item is used at least once or not at all. If it is not used, then $F_k(y)$ is the same as $F_{k-1}(y)$. If it is used *at least once*, then the total weight limitation is reduced to $y - w_k$. Obviously we must make the best use of the weight limitation $y - w_k$. The optimum value when the first k items are allowed is, by definition $F_k(y-w_k)$. Note that we used $F_k(y-w_k)$ instead of $F_{k-1}(y-w_k)$ because the kth item may be used more than once. We can prepare a table with n by b entries where each entry is the value $F_k(y)$ $(k=1,...,n; y=1,...,b)$. Using the recursive relation (1), we can calculate $F_k(y)$ in the order of $F_1(1),F_1(2),...,F_1(b)$; $F_2(1),...,F_2(b);...;F_n(1),...,F_n(b)$. In the recursive relation (4) we define F_k (negative number) $= -\infty$.

Example 3

Assume that we have four items, the total weight limitation is 10, and $v_1 = 1$, $v_2 = 3$, $v_3 = 5$, $v_4 = 9$, $w_1 = 2$, $w_2 = 3$, $w_3 = 4$, and $w_4 = 7$. Using (4), we start with the first row from left to right and then the second row from left to right, etc. The result is shown in Table 3.3.

Table 3.3. Values of $F_k(y)$

k \ y	1	2	3	4	5	6	7	8	9	10
1	0	1	1	2	2	3	3	4	4	5
2	0	1	3	3	4	6	6	7	9	9
3	0	1	3	5	5	6	8	10	10	11
4	0	1	3	5	5	6	9	10	10	12

Note that in a table such as Table 3.3, we get the values for $F_k(y)$ but we do not give the values of x_j's that yield the values for $F_k(y)$. (This is just like knowing the shortest distance of a shortest path without the knowledge of the intermediate nodes.) To find the x_j's that yield the values for $F_k(y)$, we need another table of n by b entries, where each entry is the maximum index of x_j that is used in $F_k(y)$. We define the entry in the kth row and y^{th} column

$$i(k,y) = \text{the maximum index of x's used in } F_k(y).$$

Thus if $i(k,y) = j$, this means $x_j \geq 1$, or the jth item is used in $F_k(y)$ and $x_q = 0$ for all $q > j$.

In calculating the entries for $F_k(y)$, we also record the corresponding value $i(k,y)$ in the second table. The boundary conditions for $i(k,y)$ are:

$$i(1,y) = 0 \quad \text{if } F_1(y) = 0$$

$$i(1,y) = 1 \quad \text{if } F_1(y) \neq 0.$$

In general, we set

$$i(k,y) = \begin{cases} i(k-1,y) & \text{if } F_{k-1}(y) > F_k(y-w_k) + v_k, \\[2em] k & \text{if } F_{k-1}(y) \leqslant F_k(y-w_k) + v_k. \end{cases} \tag{4'}$$

To see why (4') makes sense, we first refer back to (4). If $F_{k-1}(y) > F_k(y-w_k) + v_k$, then this implies that $x_k = 0$ in $F_k(y)$. So we simply copy down the maximum index that make up $F_{k-1}(y)$ as the maximum index for $F_k(y)$. This is the first line in the RHS of (4').

If $F_{k-1}(y) \leqslant F_k(y-w_k) + v_k$, then this implies that $x_k \geqslant 1$ in $F_k(y)$ and we simply write down k. This is the second line in the RHS of (4'). Thus the table of $i(k,y)$ is recorded as the table for $F_k(y)$ is calculated. When both the tables for $F_k(y)$ and $i(k,y)$ are completed, we can easily trace the values of x's that yield a value of $F_k(y)$.

If $i(k,y) = q$, then this implies that $x_q \geqslant 1$ in $F_k(y)$. Since the qth item is used at least once in $F_k(y)$, the total weight limitation is reduced to $y-w_q$, and we look at the entry $i(k, y-w_q)$.

If $i(k, y-w_q) = q$, then this implies that $x_q \geqslant 1$ in $F_k(y-w_q)$ (or $x_q \geqslant 2$ in $F_k(y)$).

If $i(k, y-w_q) = p$, then this implies that $x_p \geqslant 1$ in $F_k(y-w_q)$ (or $x_q = 1$, $x_p \geqslant 1$ in $F_k(y)$).

Note that the tables for $F_k(y)$ and $i(k,y)$ are calculated from left to right and row by row just as we read an English text. To trace the values of x's that yield the value of a particular $F_k(y)$, we start from $i(k,y)$ and go from right to left and look for $i(k,y')$ where $y' < y$ and $y = y' + w_q$ if $i(k,y) = q$. The result of $i(k,y)$ is listed in Table 3.4.

Table 3.4. Values of $i(k,y)$

k \ y	1	2	3	4	5	6	7	8	9	10
1	0	1	1	1	1	1	1	1	1	1
2	0	1	2	2	2	2	2	2	2	2
3	0	1	2	3	3	3	3	3	3	3
4	0	1	2	3	3	3	4	3	4	4

Note that in computing $\Gamma_4(10)$ we have actually computed all values $F_k(y)$ for $1 \leqslant k \leqslant 4$ and $0 \leqslant y \leqslant 10$. From Table 3.3, we see that $F_4(10) = 12$. From Table 3.4, the corresponding value is 4; that is, the fourth item is used at least once. Therefore we look for

$$i(4, 10-w_4) = i(4, 10-7) = i(4, 3) = 2 ,$$

which means that the second item is used at least once. Then we have

$$i(4, 3-w_2) = i(4,0) = 0 ,$$

which means that we have all the x_j we needed in making up $F_4(10) = 12$. One important feature of this computation is that when we are computing $F_k(y)$ $(0 \leqslant y \leqslant b)$ we need only $F_{k-1}(y)$ $(0 \leqslant y \leqslant b)$. Hence we need not keep the entire table and can erase an entry in a row as soon as the entry beneath it is computed. This saves a tremendous amount of memory space in a computer. The same is true in computing the second table, and we need only the last row to determine the values of the x_j's.

Another thing that should be noted is the value of $i(4,8) = 3$; i.e., when the total weight limitation is 8 we do not use the fourth item, which has the greatest value per pound.

We have mentioned that the knapsack problem is the simplest integer program where x_j are restricted to be nonnegative integers and only one additional constraint is present. Now we shall study the knapsack problem by first allowing x_j to be any nonnegative real value. This will give us some insight on how the integer restriction affects our optimization.

If x_j's are not restricted to integers, then the problem can be easily solved by first selecting

$$\max_j \quad \frac{v_j}{w_j} = \frac{v_r}{w_r}$$

i.e., the rth item is the item with maximum value per pound. The knapsack is then filled with the rth item with $x_r = b/w_r$. The trouble with this approach is that the x_r may not be integral. Let $\rho_j = v_j/w_j$ and reorder the subscripts of the items so that

$$\rho_1 > \rho_2 \geqslant \rho_3 \ldots \geqslant \rho_n,$$

where ρ_j denotes the value per pound of the item j. Intuitively we would fill the knapsack with the first item and then with whatever the weight allowance left, fill it with the second item, etc. This intuitive approach usually gives very good results but it does not always give the optimum solution due to integer restrictions. One thing which is intuitively clear is that if b is large compared to w_1, then $x_1 > 0$ in the optimum solution. To see this, let us assume that $x_1 = 0$ in the optimum solution. Then the maximum value will certainly not exceed $\rho_2 b$.

However, if we try to fill the knapsack with only the first item, we can get a value

$$v_1 \left\lfloor \frac{b}{w_1} \right\rfloor \geqslant v_1 \left(\frac{b}{w_1} - \frac{w_1}{w_1} \right) = v_1 \cdot \frac{b-w_1}{w_1} = \rho_1 w_1 \frac{b-w_1}{w_1} = \rho_1 (b-w_1) \ . \qquad (5)$$

To find the value b which yields

$$v_1 \left\lfloor \frac{b}{w_1} \right\rfloor > \rho_1 (b - w_1) \geqslant \rho_2 b,$$

we solve the equation

$$\rho_1 (b-w_1) = \rho_2 b \quad \text{or} \quad b = \frac{\rho_1}{\rho_1 - \rho_2} \ w_1 \ ,$$

i.e., for

$$b \geqslant \frac{\rho_1}{\rho_1 - \rho_2} \ w_1 \ , \quad \text{we have} \quad \rho_1 (b-w_1) \geqslant \rho_2 b$$

In other words, for b sufficiently large, we have $x_1 \geqslant 1$ in the optimum solution. This means that

$$F_n (b) = v_1 + F_n (b-w_1) \quad \text{for } b > \rho_1 w_1 / (\rho_1 - \rho_2) \ . \qquad (6)$$

Define $\theta(b) = \rho_1 b - F_n(b)$; here $\theta(b)$ represents the difference in the optimum value of the objective functions without and with the integer restrictions. Then

$$\theta(b-w_1) = \rho_1 (b-w_1) - F_n (b-w_1)$$
$$= \rho_1 b - \rho_1 w_1 - (F_n (b) - v_1) \text{ [from (6) and for sufficiently large b.]}$$
$$= \rho_1 b - F_n (b)$$
$$= \theta(b) \ .$$

This shows that the function $\theta(b)$ is periodic in nature with period w_1 for b sufficiently large. The difference function $\theta(b)$ is well defined whether $b \lessgtr \rho_1 w_1 / (\rho_1 - \rho_2)$. We can get a recursive relation for the function $\theta(b)$ as follows.

Obviously $\theta(b) = 0$ if w_1 divides b evenly, since the knapsack is filled with the first item having the greatest value per pound. When b (mod w_1) $\neq 0$, we may have to use some x_j other than x_1. Since

$$\theta(b) = \rho_1 b - F_n (b) \ ,$$

the maximum value of $F_n(b)$ gives the minimum value for $\theta(b)$. In other words, we want to choose x_j such that the loss due to integer restriction is minimized.

The loss due to selecting x_j ($j \neq 1$) is $(\rho_1 - \rho_j)w_j$ and the weight limitation is reduced to $b - w_j$. The selection of x_j is obtained by minimizing with respect to all j, i.e.

$$\theta(b) = \min_j \ \{\theta(b-w_j) + (\rho_1-\rho_j)w_j\} \qquad (7)$$

Expression (7) then gives a recursive formulation in which $\theta(b)$ can be calculated for all b. Since $\theta(0) = 0$ and we can proceed from smaller values of b to larger values of b using (7).

Example 4

$$v_1 = 18, \qquad v_2 = 14, \qquad v_3 = 8, \qquad v_4 = 4, \qquad v_5 = 0,$$

$$w_1 = 15, \qquad w_2 = 12, \qquad w_3 = 7, \qquad w_4 = 4, \qquad w_5 = 1,$$

$$\rho_1 = 1.2, \qquad \rho_2 = 1.167, \qquad \rho_3 = 1.143, \qquad \rho_4 = 1, \qquad \rho_5 = 0.$$

Now

$$\frac{\rho_1}{\rho_1-\rho_2} \ w_1 = \frac{(18/15)}{(18/15)-(14/12)} \bullet 15 = 540.$$

Thus if the weight limitation b exceeds 540, the optimum solution definitely has $x_1 \neq 0$. In other words, we could keep subtracting w_1 from b as long as the resulting difference is still greater than 540. The number of times that w_1 is subtracted is a lower bound on the value of x_1. For example, if $b = 1000$ then $x_1 \geq 30$ in the optimum solution, since $1000 - 30\,w_1 = 550$ which is greater than 540.

Note that the estimate 540 is sufficient but not necessary. As we shall see later, the optimum solution for $b = 1000$ is actually $x_1 = 65$, $x_2 = 2$, and $x_5 = 1$.

To get the exact nature of the periodic solution for the knapsack problem, we shall calculate $\theta(b)$ for all values of b starting with $b = 0,1,2,...$, using (7). The result is tabulated in Table 3.5. There are four columns in Table 3.5: the first column is the values of b, the second column is the corresponding optimum solution (which is not shown), the third column is $\Sigma w_i x_i$ (not shown), and the fourth column is $\theta(b)$. If we check the values of $\theta(b)$ in the fourth column, we shall see that $\theta(b) = \theta(b + 15)$ for $b \geq 26$. (This shows that the estimate $b \geq 540$ is too conservative.) From (7), we can see that as soon as $\theta(b)$ falls into a cycle, it will be periodic from that point on.

Let us discuss how we can use Table 3.5 for all possible values of b. Consider $b = 56$. Since

Table 3.5

Values of b	Solutions	$\Sigma w_j x_j$	$\theta(b)$
0			
1			
•			
•			
•			
25			
26			1.2
•			•
•			•
•			•
40			2.0
41			1.2
•			•
•			•
•			•
55			2.0

} $\theta(b)$ are the

same for the

} two intervals

$$b - 2w_1 = 56 - 2\times 15 = 26 \, ,$$

we find the optimum solution for $b = 26$ in the second column in Table 3.5 which turns out to be $x_1 = 1$, $x_3 = 1$, and $x_4 = 1$. Then we know the optimum solution for $b = 56$ is $x_1 = 3$, $x_3 = 1$, and $x_4 = 1$. (Note that the solutions for $b = 56$ and $b = 26$ differ only in the values of x_1.)

Actually we could condense Table 3.5 into Table 3.6. There are again four columns in Table 3.6. The first column is $b(\bmod w_1)$, the second column lists the w_j ($j \neq 1$) in the optimum periodic solution. The third column shows the value of

$$\sum_{j=2}^{n} w_j x_j$$

and the fourth column is the value of $\theta(b)$.

Let us consider the first and the third columns of Table 3.6. They are almost the same except for $b(\bmod 15) = 3$, 6, 9, and 10. For all the other values of b, say $b(\bmod 15) = 5$, we know that the optimum solution is $x_4 = 1$, $x_5 = 1$ as shown in the second column plus the appropriate amount of x_1, i.e.

Table 3.6

$b(\text{mod } w_1)$	$(x_j\text{'s})$ **Periodic Solution**	$\sum\limits_{j=2}^{n} w_j x_j$	θ **value**
0	0	0	0
1	1	1	1.2
2	1,1	2	2.4
3	4,7,7	18	1.6
4	4	4	0.8
5	1,4	5	2.0
6	7,7,7	21	1.2
7	7	7	0.4
8	1,7	8	1.6
9	12,12	24	0.8
10	1,12,12	25	2.0
11	4,7	11	1.2
12	12	12	0.4
13	1,12	13	1.6
14	7,7	14	0.8

$$b = x_1 \bullet w_1 + w_4 + w_5 \ .$$

Thus, the row $b(\text{mod } w_1) = 5$ gives optimum solutions to all possible b which can be expressed as a multiple of w_1 plus 5. For b = 18, 21, 24, and 25, the optimum solutions are shown in the second column. Thus we know the optimum solution for $b(\text{mod } 15) = 18$, 21, 24, and 25, since we simply add the appropriate amount of x_1. The only values of b not covered by Table 3.6 are b = 3, 6, 9, and 10, which could be calculated separately.

§3.3 TWO-DIMENSIONAL KNAPSACK PROBLEMS

In the last section, items are to be put into a knapsack where the only constraint is the weight constraint. In other words, items are restricted by one parameter - the weight. This version of a knapsack problem can be referred to as a one-dimensional knapsack problem. In this section, we consider a two-dimensional version of the knapsack problem where each item is restricted by two parameters, say the length and the width.

To formulate this version of the knapsack problem, we consider the problem of cutting a large board into small rectangles of given sizes.

Assume that we are given a large rectangular board and that we would like to cut the large board into small rectangles that will be sold at the market. If we know the prices of various small rectangles at the market, how should we cut the large board so that we get the maximum profit? A restricted one dimensional version of this problem (also called a stock-cutting problem) is related to a knapsack problem. Here, each item is characterized by two parameters, the length and the width, and the knapsack is equivalent to the large board. In computer science, each item may be a job which requires a certain amount of time and a certain amount of memory space, and we would like to finish all the jobs within the memory capacity of the computer and within a 24 hour period.

If a small rectangular board represents a job of given time and space, then the rectangle cannot be rotated to fit the size limitation of the large board. If we were really cutting a large sheet of glass, the orientation of the small rectangle with respect to the large sheet is irrelevant. If rotation of the rectangle is allowed, it is equivalent to having two kinds of rectangles with the same price (each with a given orientation). From now on, we shall assume that the rotation of small rectangles are not allowed. The stock-cutting problem allows the large board to be cut in an arbitrary manner.

This version of stock-cutting is still too complicated, and we shall treat a more restricted way of cutting. This restricted problem allows the large board to be cut as follows:

(i)   by horizontal lines all the way across the board followed by vertical cuttings on each of the horizontal strips as shown in Figure 3.4(a).

(ii) by vertical lines all the way across the board followed by horizontal cuttings on each of the vertical strips as shown in Figure 3.4(b).

The patterns in 3.4(a) and (b) are called two-stage cutting since these patterns can be achieved first by cutting along one coordinate axis and then by cutting along the other axis on the resulting pieces. The cutting pattern shown in Figure 3.4(c) is not allowed since it cannot be achieved by recursively cutting a larger rectangle into two rectangles. Figure 3.4(d) is not allowed since it requires more than two cutting stages.

Suppose that we are given the values v_i of n rectangles, where l_i is the (horizontal) length of the ith rectangle and w_i the (vertical) width of the ith rectangle. We shall cut the large board in two stages such that the total value of the resulting rectangles is a maximum. If a resulting rectangle is not exactly $l_i \times w_i$ for any i, we shall assume that the rectangle has value equal to the maximum of the values of all rectangles that can fit inside it. In other words, we need not trim the rectangle down to the exact size of $l_i \times w_i$.

Example 5

Let the large board be of size L = 14, W = 11 and the small rectangles be

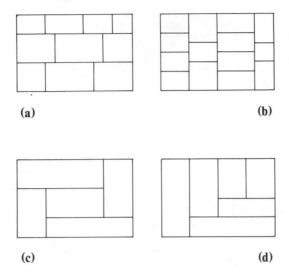

(a)   (b)

(c)   (d)

Figure 3.4

$$v_1 = \$6 \qquad l_1 = 7 \qquad w_1 = 2$$
$$v_2 = \$7 \qquad l_2 = 5 \qquad w_2 = 3$$
$$v_3 = \$9 \qquad l_3 = 4 \qquad w_3 = 5 \ .$$

One way of cutting by horizontal lines and then vertical lines is shown in Figure 3.5(a) with a total profit of $63, while another way of cutting by vertical lines and then horizontal lines is shown in Figure 3.5(b) with a total profit of $64.

Note that the cutting in Figure 3.5(b) cannot be achieved in two stages, a third trimming stage is needed. However, we do not do a trimming stage and simply leave the 5×5 and 4×6 rectangles as they are with a value of $9.

To get the optimum pattern of cutting horizontally and then vertically, we consider the problem of cutting a board of length 14 disregarding the width restriction. This is a one-dimensional knapsack problem, namely:

$$\max \ 6x_1 + 7x_2 + 9x_3 \tag{1}$$

$$\text{subject to} \ 7x_1 + 5x_2 + 4x_3 \leqslant 14$$

where x_i denotes the number of the ith small rectangles produced. If the large board is of width 2, then only the first rectangle can be produced. If the large board is of width 3, only the first and the second rectangles can be produced. Here, we define

$$F_k(x) = \max \sum_{i=1}^{k} v_i x_i$$

$$\text{subject to} \quad \sum_{i=1}^{k} l_i x_i \leqslant x \tag{2}$$

$$x_i \geqslant 0 \text{ integers} \ .$$

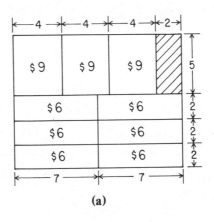

(a)

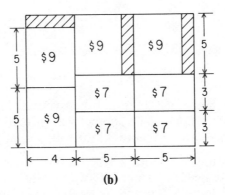

(b)

Figure 3.5

Problem (2) can be solved by the knapsack algorithm of the last section. The result of this computation is shown in Table 3.7(a).

Note that $F_1(14) = 12$, $F_2(14) = 14$, and $F_3(14) = 27$.

This means a board of 14 by 2 can have a value of \$12,

and   a board of 14 by 3 can have a value of \$14,

and   a board of 14 by 5 can have a value of \$27.

Table 3.7. Values of $F_k(x)$ and $G_k(y)$

(a)

x	1	2	3	4	5	6	7	8	9	10	11	12	13	14
$F_1(x)$	0	0	0	0	0	0	6	6	6	6	6	6	6	12
$F_2(x)$	0	0	0	0	7	7	7	7	7	14	14	14	14	14
$F_3(x)$	0	0	0	9	9	9	9	18	18	18	18	27	27	27

(b)

y	1	2	3	4	5	6	7	8	9	10	11
$G_1(y)$	0	12	12	24	24	36	36	48	48	60	60
$G_2(y)$	0	12	14	24	26	36	38	48	50	60	62
$G_3(y)$	0	12	14	24	27	36	39	48	51	60	63

The question now becomes "How many of these strips worth \$12, \$14, and \$27 should be produced?" This is again a one-dimensional knapsack problem, namely:

$$\text{max}\ \ 12y_1 + 14y_2 + 27y_3$$
$$\text{subject to}\ \ 2y_1 + 3y_2 + 5y_3 \leqslant 11 \tag{3}$$
$$y_i \geqslant 0 \text{ integers }.$$

Here y_i represents the number of the ith strips produced. (In operations research, the prices \$12, \$14, and \$27 can be interpreted as shadow prices for the width.)

We can solve problem (3) by

$$\text{defining}\ G_k(y) = \sum_{i=1}^{k} \pi_1 y_i$$
$$\text{subject to}\ \ \sum_{i=1}^{k} w_i y_i \leqslant y \tag{4}$$
$$y_i \geqslant 0\ \text{ integers }.$$

where $(\pi_1, \pi_2, \pi_3) = (12, 14, 27)$.

The result of computation of (4) is shown in Table 3.7(b) and the pattern that achieves \$63 is shown in Figure 3.5(a).

If the original large board has $L = 13$, $W = 11$, then we should use (π_1, π_2, π_3) as $(6, 14, 27)$ in (4).

In general, we would have

$$w_1 < w_2 < \cdots < w_n .$$

Then $F_k(x)$ is the maximum value that can be obtained in a strip with width less than or equal to w_k. We then solve (4) with $\pi_i = F_i(L)$, where L is the length of the large board being cut.

We can obtain the optimum pattern of cutting vertically and then horizontally in a similar manner. Here we first reorder the rectangles according to their lengths.

$$
\begin{array}{lll}
v_1' = \$9 & l_1' = 4 & w_1' = 5 \\
v_2' = \$7 & l_2' = 5 & w_2' = 3 \\
v_3' = \$6 & l_3' = 7 & w_3' = 2 .
\end{array}
$$

The one dimensional problem becomes

$$\max \quad 9x_1' + 7x_2' + 6x_3'$$

$$\text{subject to} \quad 5x_1' + 3x_2' + 2x_3' \leq 11 \tag{5}$$

$$x_i' \geq 0 \text{ integers}$$

where x_i' is the number of the ith rectangles in a vertical strip.

Problem (5) can be solved by defining

$$F_k'(y) = \max \quad \sum_{i=1}^{k} v_i' x_i'$$

$$\text{subject to} \quad \sum_{i=1}^{k} w_i' x_i' \leq y \leq 11 \tag{6}$$

$$x_i' \geq 0 \text{ integers} .$$

The result of (6) is shown in Table 3.8(a). Also in Table 3.8(a), we see that a vertical strip of length 4×11, 5×11, 7×11 are worth \$18, \$23, and \$31, respectively. Thus, the problem now becomes

$$\max \quad 18y_1' + 23y_2' + 31y_3'$$

$$\text{subject to} \quad 4y_1' + 5y_2' + 7y_3' \leq 14 \tag{7}$$

$$y_i' \geq 0 \text{ integer} .$$

Here y_i' denotes the number of the ith vertical strips that are produced. Again (7) can be solved by defining

$$G_k'(x) = \sum_{i=1}^{k} \pi_i' \, y_i'$$

$$\text{subject to } \sum_{i=1}^{k} l_i' y_i' \leqslant x \qquad \qquad (8)$$

$$y_i' \geqslant 0 \text{ integers} .$$

The result of (8) is shown in Table 3.8(b) and the pattern that achieves the $64 is shown in Figure 3.5(b).

Table 3.8. Values of F_k' (y) and G_k' (x)
(a)

y	1	2	3	4	5	6	7	8	9	10	11
$F_1'(y)$	0	0	0	0	9	9	9	9	9	18	18
$F_2'(y)$	0	0	7	7	9	14	14	16	21	21	23
$F_3'(y)$	0	6	7	12	13	18	19	24	25	30	31

(b)

x	1	2	3	4	5	6	7	8	9	10	11	12	13	14
$G_1'(x)$	0	0	0	18	18	18	18	36	36	36	36	54	54	54
$G_2'(x)$	0	0	0	18	23	23	23	36	41	46	46	54	54	64
$G_3'(x)$	0	0	0	18	23	23	31	36	41	46	49	54	54	64

§3.4 MINIMUM-COST ALPHABETIC TREES

This example may look very artificial at first, but it has real applications (see Chapter 5). Given an ordered sequence of positive numbers, say

$$4, 1, 2, 3,$$

we shall put three pairs of parentheses around them and add them

$$((4+1) + (2+3)) = ((5) + (5)) = (10).$$

Note that three intermediate sums are generated, namely 5, 5, and 10. The total of these three numbers is $5 + 5 + 10 = 20$. If we put the parentheses somewhat differently and add them, we have

$$(4 + ((1+2) + 3)) = (4 + ((3) + 3)) = (4 + (6)) = (10) .$$

Now, the intermediate sums generated are 3, 6, and 10. The total sum of these three numbers is $3 + 6 + 10 = 19$.

This example shows that the total sum of intermediate sums depends on how we put the parentheses around the sequence of numbers. So here is the general question.

Given a sequence of n positive numbers, we are to put $n - 1$ pairs of parentheses around the n numbers such that the total sum of the $n - 1$ intermediate sums is minimized.

The problem has a graphical formulation, and can be drawn as a tree.

In the tree, we write the weight of a father to be the sum of the weights of his two sons. Two nodes can have the same father only if they are adjacent. To any way of putting parentheses around a sequence of n terminal nodes, there corresponds a unique tree, and vice versa. The tree is called an alphabetic tree. The cost of an alphabetic tree is the sum of weights of all the circular nodes in the tree. Thus, the tree in Figure 3.6(a) costs $20 = 10 + 5 + 5$ and the tree in Figure 3.6(b) costs $19 = 10 + 6 + 3$. For a given sequence of terminal nodes, an alphabetic tree with minimum cost is called an optimum alphabetic tree.

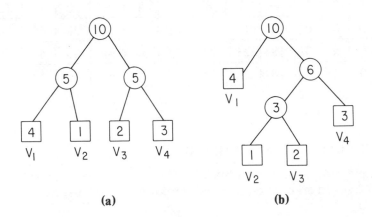

(a)   (b)

Figure 3.6

Consider a slightly larger example with seven terminal nodes in the sequence. One way of adding parentheses may yield the tree configuration in Figure 3.7.

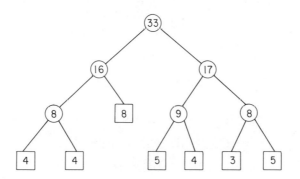

Figure 3.7

Again, we make the same sort of observation as we did before.

(1)   If the tree in Figure 3.7 is optimum, then the subtree with root weight 17 must be an optimum tree for the sequence ⑤ ④ ③ ⑤ . If there exists a better way of grouping the four terminal nodes ⑤ ④ ③ ⑤ , then we could replace the subtree in Figure 3.7 by the better arrangement. This would contradict that the original tree with seven terminal nodes is optimum. Just like all subpaths of an optimum path must be optimum, the situation here is that all subtrees of an optimum tree are optimum.

(2)   In the shortest path problem, we want to know which direction to go. The sequence of directions successively determines the path. Here, we would like to know how the sequence of terminal nodes is successively partitioned. If we know that the first partition is three nodes in the left subtree and four nodes in the right subtree, and then we can ask how the left subtree is partitioned. Thus knowing the successive partition is equivalent to knowing the tree. We shall write (3,4) to denote the partition of three nodes in the left subtree and four nodes in the right subtree. The initial partition of the seven nodes may be any one of the following: (1,6), (2,5), (3,4), (4,3), (5,2), and (6,1). In Figure 3.8, we have a (3,4) partition. For the three-terminal-node subtree on the left, the partition can be (1,2) or (2,1). For the four-node subtree on the right, the partition can be (1,3), (2,2), or (3,1). Knowing the optimum partitioning is equivalent to knowing the optimum tree.

(3)   In the shortest path problem, we worked from the right to the left. Now, we work from the bottom to the top. The cost of a tree containing one terminal node is zero by definition.

The cost of an optimum tree consisting of two terminal nodes is simply the sum of two weights. In general, let C_{ik} denote the cost of the optimum tree with the sequence of terminal nodes $V_i, V_{i+1}, ..., V_k$, and $W_{ik} = w_i + w_{i+1} + ... + w_k$. Then we have the following formula which can be proved by induction:

$$C_{ik} = \min_{j} \ [C_{ij} + C_{j+1,k}] + W_{ik} \qquad (i \leqslant j < k) \qquad (1)$$

$$C_{ii} = 0 \qquad \text{for all } i \ .$$

For example, the cost of the optimum tree with three terminal nodes ④ ④ ⑧ is

$$C_{13} = \min[(C_{11}+C_{23}), \ (C_{12}+C_{33})] + W_{13}$$
$$= \min[(0+12), \ (8+0)] + 16 = 24 \ .$$

We can use the formula to calculate the cost of optimum trees for every triple of nodes

$$(4,4,8), \ (4,8,5), \ (8,5,4), \ (5,4,3), \text{ and } (4,3,5).$$

Once we know the cost of every triple of nodes, it is easy to calculate the cost for every four nodes. For example, the cost of the tree with ④ ④ ⑧ ⑤ is

$$\min[(C_{11}+C_{24}), \ (C_{12}+C_{34}), \ (C_{13}+C_{44})] + W_{14}$$

$$= \min[(0+29),(8+13),(24+0)] + 21$$
$$= (8+13) + 21$$
$$= 42 \ .$$

The cost of every optimum subtree is tabulated in Figure 3.8.

The minimization in (1) is to find the root of the binary tree. Knuth [12] noted that if a leave is added to the right of an optimum alphabetic binary tree with n leaves, then the root of the optimum alphabetic tree with $n+1$ leaves is the same or moves to the right. This fact enables us to cut down the amount of work to search for the root. The algorithm is $O(n^2)$.

In a more general problem, the function W_{ik} in (1) may not be the sum of weights of leaves. Nevertheless, we can still have an $O(n^2)$ algorithm to obtain the minimum C_{ik} in (1). This result is proved by Dr. F.F. Yao [16].

The function W_{ik} is called the increment function in [16]. If the increment function satisfies the following conditions (2) and (3), then the cost function C_{ik} also satisfies the similar conditions.

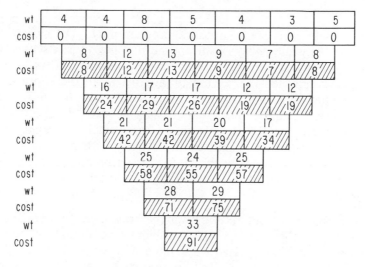

wt	4	4	8	5	4	3	5
cost	0	0	0	0	0	0	0

wt	8	12	13	9	7	8
cost	8	12	13	9	7	8

wt	16	17	17	12	12
cost	24	29	26	19	19

wt	21	21	20	17
cost	42	42	39	34

wt	25	24	25
cost	58	55	57

wt	28	29
cost	71	75

wt	33
cost	91

Figure 3.8

$$W_{pr} + W_{qs} \leqslant W_{qr} + W_{ps} \qquad \text{for } p \leqslant q \leqslant r \leqslant s \qquad (2)$$

$$W_{qr} \leqslant W_{ps} \qquad \text{for } p \leqslant q \leqslant r \leqslant s \qquad (3)$$

In otherwords, (2) and (3) imply that cost functions C_{ik} satisfies (4) and (5)

$$C_{pr} + C_{qs} \leqslant C_{qr} + C_{ps} \qquad \text{for } p \leqslant q \leqslant r \leqslant s \qquad (4)$$

$$C_{qr} \leqslant C_{ps} \qquad (5)$$

Note that the minimization in (1) is to find the index j such that the minimum is achieved. The index j is certainly a function of i and k once the increment function is defined.

If the increment functions W_{ik} satisfies (2) and (3), and the cost function satisfies (4) and (5), then we can show that the index j satisfies the condition (6)

$$j(i,k) \leqslant j(i,k+1) \leqslant j(i+1,k+1) \qquad \text{for } i \leqslant k . \qquad (6)$$

Note (6) is a more general way of saying that the root of the optimum alphabetic tree will stay at the same place or move to the right if more leaves were added to the right.

Based on (6), we can have an $0(n^2)$ algorithm to find the minimum C_{ik} in (1).

§3.5 SUMMARY

We have seen some examples of dynamic programming. The slogan of dynamic programming is "Any sub-policy of an optimum policy must itself be optimum." To solve a problem using dynamic programming, we usually first solve all the subproblems. This is called the bottom up approach. In the shortest-path problem and the money-allocation problem, the subproblems are loosely connected, and not too much repetition of computation is needed. In the minimum cost alphabetic tree problem, the subproblems are very much integrated, and we have to calculate all the sequential pairs, all the sequential triples, all the sequential quadruples, and so forth. Even so, the saving of computation achieved by moving from a brute force approach to dynamic programming is from $0(2^n)$ to $0(n^3)$ or $0(n^4)$ in most cases.

Not all problems of optimization can be solved by the dynamic programming approach. In the shortest path problem, we define optimality as the minimum sum of arc lengths. Had we defined optimality as the minimum value of the number which is the sum of all arc lengths modulo 10 dynamic programming cannot be used without modification. The following is one characteristic of problems which might be solved by dynamic programming. The objective function of the whole problem is the sum of the objective functions of the subproblems.

No one has ever stated a precise characterization of problems which can or cannot be solved by dynamic programming.

EXERCISES

1. In Example 1, we obtain the shortest paths from all nodes to T_j. Modify the formulation such that we will get the shortest paths from S_i to all the nodes in the network.

2. How many additions and comparisons are needed in Example 1?

3. Can the knapsack problem be solved by the same technique if we want to maximize $\sum v_j x_j^2$ subject to $\sum w_j x_j^2 \leqslant b$, $x_j \geqslant 0$ integers?

4. Solve Example 1 with the additional requirement that each change in the direction of the shortest path is equivalent to adding five units in the total length. (Hint: Introduce a new parameter with every node to indicate the direction of the path leaving the node.)

5. The problem of producing given numbers of rectangular boards with the minimum number of large boards of standard sizes can be formulated as a large linear program. See [6], [9].

6. The minimum-cost alphabetic tree was first solved by Gilbert and Moore [5] as a problem in encoding. Compare the dynamic programming technique with that of Hu-Tucker's algorithm in Chapter 5.

7. Use the dynamic programming approach to find the longest path in the acyclic network.

8. Consider the multiplication of a sequence of matrices

$$M = M_1 \times M_2 \times ... \times M_n$$

Use dynamic programming to find the optimum order of multiplying the matrices such that the total number of operations is minimized (the number of operations of multiplying two matrices of dimensions $r \times s$ and $s \times t$ is $r \times s \times t$). (see Chapter 7)

9. Use dynamic programming to solve the shortest path (mod 10) problem in Figure 3.3.

CHAPTER 3

BIBLIOGRAPHIC NOTES AND SUGGESTED READING

There are several books on dynamic programming; see, for example, [1], [2], [4], [14], [15]. Two general survey papers [3] and [10] are also highly recommended. The sections on knapsack problems are based on the papers: [6], [7], [8], [9], [11]. The section on minimum-cost alphabetic trees is based on [5], [12], [13].

1. R. Bellman, "Dynamic Programming", Princeton University Press, Princeton, N.J., 1957.

2. R. Bellman and S. E. Dreyfus, "Applied Dynamic Programming", Princeton University Press, Princeton, N.J., 1962.

3. K. Brown, "Dynamic Programming in Computer Science", Carnegie-Mellon University, Feb. 1979.

4. S. E. Dreyfus and A. M. Law, "The Art and Theory of Dynamic Programming", Academic Press, 1977.

5. E. N. Gilbert and E. F. Moore, "Variable-length Binary Encoding", Bell Systems Tech. J. 38 (1959), pp. 933-968.

6. P. C. Gilmore, "Cutting Stock, Linear Programming, Knapsack, Dynamic Programming and Integer Programming, Some Interconnections", IBM Research Report RC6528, May 1977.

7. P. C. Gilmore and R. E. Gomory, "The Theory and Computation of Knapsack Functions", J. ORSA 14(6) (1966), pp. 1045-1074.

8. P. C. Gilmore and R. E. Gomory, "A Linear Programming Approach to the Cutting Stock Problem", Part I, J. ORSA 9 (1961), pp. 849-859, Part II 11 (1963), pp. 863-887.

9. P. C. Gilmore and R. E. Gomory, "Many Stage Cutting Stock Problems of Two and More Dimensions", J. ORSA 13 (1965), pp. 94-120.

10. M. Held and R. M. Karp, "Finite-State Process and Dynamic Programming", SIAM J. 15 (1967), pp. 693-718.

11. T. C. Hu, "Integer Programming and Network Flows", Addison-Wesley, 1969.

12. D. E. Knuth, "Optimum Binary Search Trees", Acta Information 1 (1971), pp. 14-25.

13. D. E. Knuth, "Sorting and Searching", Addison-Wesley, 1973.

14. G. L. Nemhauser, "Introduction to Dynamic Programming", John Wiley & Sons, 1966.

15. M. L. Puterman (ed.), "Dynamic Programing and Its Application", Academic Press, 1977.

16. F. F. Yao, "Efficient Dynamic Programming Using Quadrangle Inequalities", Proceedings of the 12th Annual ACM Symposium on Theory of Computing, April, 1980, pp. 429-435.

ANSWERS TO EXERCISES - CHAPTER 3

1. Define $S(V_j)$ to be the shortest distance from a starting node to the node V_j. For example,
    $$S(B_2) = \min \{[S(A_1) + 4], [S(A_2) + 3]\} \ .$$
    The boundary conditions are $S(A_1) = 4$, $S(A_2) = 5$, etc.

3. The approach in Example 2 still works but we cannot have a simple recursion like (1) in § 3.2.

4. Define $T(V_j,d)$ to be the shortest distance from V_j to a terminal node T where d is a parameter having the value 0 or 1. The value 0 means that the path is leaving V_j in a downward direction. Thus
    $$T(B_3,0) = 2 + \min \{T(C_3,0),[5 + T(C_3,1)]\}$$
    $$T(B_3,1) = 4 + \min \{T(C_2,1),[5 + T(C_2,0)]\}$$

5. (For readers familiar with linear programming.) We can consider any way of cutting a large board an activity. Then the problem becomes one to minimize the total number of activities subject to the constraint that the number of rectangles produced must be greater than the required amount. For a given basis, we have shadow prices for the rectangles and we use the two stage dynamic programming to produce the best activity under the given shadow prices.

9. We can define
    $$S_k^i = \min \ (\text{cost} + i) \ (\text{mod } 10)$$
    starting at the node k.
    Then the recursion takes the form
    $$S_k^i = \min\left[S_{k+1}^{i+1} \ (\text{mod } 10), \ S_{k+1}^{i+9} \ (\text{mod } 10)\right]$$
    The boundary condition is
    $$S_9^i = S_t^i = i \ .$$
    Defining $i = 0,1,...,9$, we have
    $$S_8^0 = 1, \ S_8^1 = 0, \ S_8^2 = 1,...,S_8^9 = 0 \ .$$
    $$S_7^0 = 0, \ S_7^1 = 1, \ S_7^2 = 0,...,S_7^4 = 1 \ .$$
    Finally, $S_0^0 = S_s^0 = 1 \ .$

CHAPTER 4. BACKTRACK

Never burn your bridges after crossing — you may have to backtrack someday.

§4.1 INTRODUCTION

In many combinatorial problems, we search for all possible configurations satisfying certain requirements. For example, we may want all the patterns of putting eight queens on a chessboard so that no queen can attack another queen. Or we may want all the nonnegative integer solutions satisfying certain constraints. One way to solve such problems is to generate all possible configurations one-by-one. This technique, commonly known as exhaustive search, usually requires the examination of so many cases that it is not practical even for a very fast computer. In most applications, there are special structures in the problems, and we do not have to try all possible solutions. One technique of implicitly searching all possible solutions in a systematic manner is called *backtrack*. Like dynamic programming, this is a general technique which may not be competitive with tailor-made algorithms for specific problems. However, due to its general applicability, backtrack has been widely accepted by computer scientists.

We shall first illustrate the idea of backtracking by an example.

Example 1

We want to put four queens on a 4×4 chessboard so that no queen can attack another queen. Since there are 16 positions on a 4×4 chessboard, an exhaustive search would try $\binom{16}{4}$ = 1820 possible configurations. Because each row can have at most one queen, we can consider the solution as a sequence (x_1,x_2,x_3,x_4) where x_i indicates the position of the queen in the ith row. There are $4^4 = 256$ of these configurations. Some configurations satisfy the requirement and others do not. Backtrack is a systematic way of listing all the configurations satisfying the requirements.

The first job in backtracking is to set up a one-to-one correspondence between the configurations and the sequences (or vectors). In this example, it is very easy. There are four positions in each row and four rows in the board; and we can describe the pattern of the queens on the board by a vector with four components (x_1,x_2,x_3,x_4), where each variable x_i can assume the values 1,2,3,4. The values 1,2,3, and 4 correspond to the four positions in each row. For example, the pattern in Figure 4.1 could be characterized by the vector $(x_1,x_2,x_3,x_4) = (2,4,\_,1)$.

In order to list all the solutions, we need the idea of lexicographically

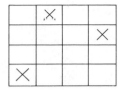

Figure 4.1

ordering. A vector $(x_1,x_2,...,x_n)$ is *lexicographically positive* if its leftmost nonzero component is positive. Thus the vector $(0,0,1,-10,-2,100)$ is lexicographically positive. A vector $(x_1,x_2,...,x_n)$ is *lexicographically smaller* than a vector $(y_1,y_2,...,y_n)$ if and only if the vector $(y_1-x_1,y_2-x_2,...,y_n-x_n)$ is lexicographically positive. For example, the vector $(0,0,1,-10,-2,100)$ is lexicographically smaller than $(0,0,1,-1,-100,-100)$.

The algorithm of backtrack is to enumerate the vectors starting from the lexicographically smallest vector.

In our 4×4 chessboard problem, the smallest vector is $(x_1,x_2,x_3,x_4) = (1,1,1,1)$, but it does not satisfy the constraint of no queen being able to attack another queen. If we enumerate the vectors $(1,1,1,1),(1,1,1,2),...,(4,4,4,4)$, we will find that most of the vectors do not satisfy the constraint. We can organize the search as a decision tree as shown in Figure 4.2.

A decision tree is a rooted tree with the root representing the state that no decision is made. There are many nodes at different levels in the decision tree, each node represents a state where partial decisions have been made.

In Figure 4.2, the node V_A is the root of the decision tree and is said to be at the zeroth level. The four nodes V_B, V_C, V_D, and V_E (directly below V_A) are at the first level. Nodes like V_F, V_G, ... are said to be at the second level, and V_Q is at the third level, and V_Z at the fourth level. The nodes at the first level denote that the value of x_1 has been fixed. The four nodes at the first level indicate that there are four possible choices for the value of x_1. V_B denotes $x_1 = 1$ and V_D denotes $x_1 = 3$. Each node of the first level has four nodes below it indicating the four possible choices for the value of x_2. Thus V_B has four nodes, V_F, V_G, V_H, and V_I where V_H represents the state $x_1 = 1$ and $x_2 = 3$. Not all of the nodes at level two are drawn in Figure 4.2. There should be 16 nodes at level two, 64 nodes at level three, and 256 nodes at level four.

It is customary to denote the nodes in a tree by *father-son* relationship. The node V_A is called the *father* of V_B, V_C, V_D, and V_E. The node V_Z is a *grandson* of

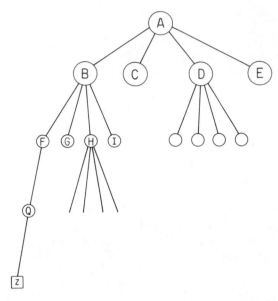

Figure 4.2

V_F, etc. Each node (except those at level four) has exactly four sons and is represented by a circular node. The nodes at level four have no children and are represented by squares, they are called the *leaves*.

A circular node represents a vector with some components unassigned. A square node represents a vector with all its components assigned. For example, the node V_Z represents the vector $(1,1,1,1)$. A vector satisfying all the requirements is called a *feasible* vector, otherwise, an *infeasible* vector.

Two leaves with the same father represent two vectors which differ in only one component. Two leaves with the same grandfather represent two vectors differ in at most two components. On the other hand, a node at the first level denotes a vector with one value fixed, the rest of the components are still open to choices. A vector with some components open to choices is called a *partial vector*. A partial vector V_x is shorter than a partial vector V_y if the number of fixed components in V_x is less than that of V_y. In terms of the decision tree, nodes at higher levels represent shorter partial vectors. The root is at the highest level and represents a vector with none of its components fixed.

In terms of a decision tree, the backtrack algorithm is to traverse the tree in a depth-first-search manner, starting from the root. (See DFS in section 1.7.) From a given node, we always traverse the leftmost arc if that arc has not been traversed previously. If all arcs going down from a node V_y have been traversed, we back up one level to the father of V_y, say V_x and check if all arcs going down from V_x have been examined.

For example, the node V_H in Figure 4.2, denotes a partial vector $(1,3,\_,\_)$ as shown in Figure 4.3. Since none of the choices for x_3 can be feasible vectors corresponding to patterns of nonattacking queens, all the children of V_H represent infeasible vectors, and we can back up to V_B and pick the path leading to V_I. Assume that the path from V_B to V_F and V_G have been examined before.

Note that picking the leftmost path is picking the smallest value of an unassigned component.

In the beginning, we want the lexicographically smallest vector, we set $x_1 = 1$, which means that we put a queen at the upper left corner. After x_1 is fixed at 1, we try to set x_2 as small as possible. x_2 cannot be 1 or 2, so the smallest value x_2 can assume is 3. Now we have the pattern in Figure 4.3.

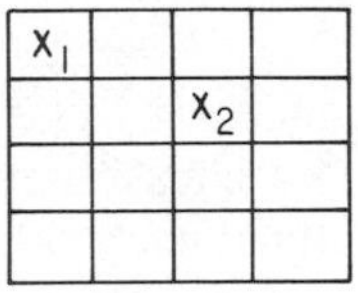

Figure 4.3

Having set $(x_1,x_2,\_,\_) = (1,3,\_,\_)$, we try to set x_3 as small as possible. Now since x_3 cannot be any of the values 1,2,3, or 4, we *backtrack* to increase the value of x_2. So we set $x_2 = 4$, and then set $x_3 = 2$. This is shown in Figure 4.4.

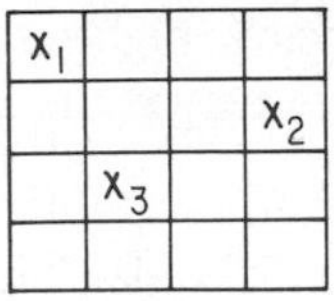

Figure 4.4

Having set $(x_1,x_2,x_3,\_) = (1,4,2,\_)$, we find that x_4 cannot be assigned. So we have to backtrack to increase the value of x_3. But x_3 cannot be increased, so we backtrack to increase x_2. But x_2 is already at the maximum value, so we backtrack to increase the value of x_1, and x_1 is set to be 2. Once $x_1 = 2$, we can set $x_2 = 4$, $x_3 = 1$, and $x_4 = 3$, which gives one solution of four queens

$(x_1, x_2, x_3, x_4) = (2, 4, 1, 3)$ as shown in Figure 4.5.

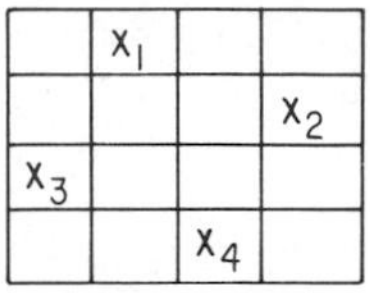

Figure 4.5

Let us digest what we have done in the preceding example. We have considered each pattern of the 4×4 chessboard as a vector; the first component is the position of the queen in the first row. Then we systematically search for all feasible vectors lexicographically.

In general, we want all sequences $(x_1, x_2, ..., x_n)$ which satisfy some property $P_n(x_1, x_2, ..., x_n)$. For example, in 4×4 chessboards, the property $P_4(x_1, x_2, x_3, x_4)$ is that none of the four queens can attack each other while $P_2(x_1, x_2)$ means the two queens on the board cannot attack each other. Here if P_4 is satisfied then P_2 is satisfied, and if P_2 is not satisfied then no possible extension of the partial vector $(x_1, x_2, \_, \_)$ can make P_4 satisfied. Putting this in general terms, we have

$$P_{k+1}(x_{1, x_2}, ..., x_k, x_{k+1}) \rightarrow P_k(x_1, x_2, ..., x_k) \quad \text{for } 0 \leqslant k < n .$$

Let us consider the backtrack algorithm in general, assuming that x_i can be picked from a set X_i. The implicit assumption is that all the choices in a set X_i are linearly ordered. Once the values of $x_1, x_2, ..., x_{k-1}$ are fixed, we select among the set X_k, the smallest value x_k which might lead to a feasible vector, i.e.
$$P_k(x_1, x_2, ..., x_{k-1}, x_k) \text{ is satisfied.}$$

We shall denote the subset (of X_k) which represents feasible choices for x_k by S_k. Since X_k is ordered, all the choices in S_k are also ordered. In our example, x_2 can be chosen from the set $X_2 = \{1, 2, 3, 4\}$, but if x_1 is fixed at 1, then $S_2 = \{3, 4\}$.

The general backtrack algorithm can now be stated formally.

Step 0.   Set up one-to-one correspondence between sequences $(x_1, x_2, ..., x_n)$ and the possible configurations. The possible choices for x_i belong to the set X_i. If $x_1, x_2, ..., x_{k-1}$ are fixed, the subset of X_k containing the possible choices of x_k is denoted by S_k.

We start by examining S_k ($k = 1, 2, ..., n$) sequentially.

Step 1.   If S_k is not empty, set x_k to be the smallest value in S_k which has not been tried previously. If $k < n$, increase k by 1 and repeat the step. If $k=n$, record the vector $(x_1, x_2, ..., x_n)$ as a feasible vector. (If we want all feasible vectors, decrease k by 1 and repeat this step. Otherwise, stop.)

Step 2.   If S_k is empty and $k=1$, no more feasible vector exists, stop. If S_k is empty and $k \neq 1$, decrease k by 1 and return to Step 1.

Let us now apply this backtrack algorithm to another example.

Example 2

Find all the positive integer solutions (x_1, x_2, x_3) satisfying

$$3x_1 + 4x_2 + x_3 \leq 10 \tag{1a}$$

$$1 \leq x_i \leq 3, \text{ integers}. \tag{1b}$$

Here the sequence is (x_1, x_2, x_3) and $X_i = \{1, 2, 3\}$ for all i since each variable can assume the value 1,2,3.

We draw the decision tree in Figure 4.6.

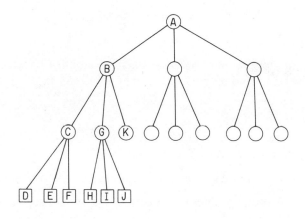

Figure 4.6

Not all the nodes in the decision tree are drawn in Figure 4.6, and the nodes will be visited in the order of V_A, V_B, V_C, ... in the backtrack algorithm. Here $P_3(x_1, x_2, x_3)$ corresponds to satisfying constraints $3x_1 + 4x_2 + x_3 \leq 10$ and $1 \leq x_i \leq 3$.

$P_2(x_1,x_2)$ corresponds to the satisfaction of

$$3x_1 + 4x_2 \leqslant 10$$

$$1 \leqslant x_i \leqslant 3, \text{ integers, } i = 1,2 \ .$$

The nodes V_D, V_E, V_F correspond to the vectors

$$(1,1,1)$$

$$(1,1,2)$$

$$(1,1,3)$$

and the node V_B corresponds to the partial vector

$$(1,\_,\_) \ .$$

Originally, x_2 has three choices, but once x_1 is fixed at 1, then $S_2 = \{1\}$. Thus V_G represents an infeasible vector; i.e., $P_2(x_1,x_2) = P_2(1,x_2)$ is already violated for $x_2 \geqslant 2$. Thus $S_3 = \varnothing$; i.e., all V_H, V_I, V_J correspond to infeasible vectors. Similarly, the node V_K is an infeasible vector and so are all its children.

Here, once we find a partial vector that does not satisfy the requirements, it makes no sense to extend the partial vector. Essentially, we have assumed that

$$P_k(x_1,...,x_k) \text{ false} \rightarrow P_{k+1}(x_1,...,x_k,x_{k+1}) \text{ false}.$$

We shall call the phenomenon that

$$P_k \text{ false} \rightarrow P_{k+1} \text{ false},$$

the *domino phenomenon.*

Note that the domino phenomenon must be true for backtrack to work. For example, if we want to find all positive integer solutions (x_1,x_2,x_3) satisfying

$$3x_1 + 4x_2 - x_3 \leqslant 10$$

$$1 \leqslant x_i \leqslant 3, \text{ integers .}$$

The $P_2(1,2)$ false does not imply $P_3(1,2,1)$ false.

This is one of the points often overlooked by people using backtrack.

To handle the above problem, we can ask for sequences (x_1,x_2,x_3') satisfying

$$3x_1 + 4x_2 + x_3' \leqslant 13$$

$$1 \leqslant x_1,x_2 \leqslant 3, \ 0 \leqslant x_3' \leqslant 2$$

and then let $x_3 = 3 - x_3'$.

§4.2 ESTIMATING THE EFFICIENCY OF BACKTRACK

Before we solve a large-scale problem on a computer, we usually estimate the running time of the algorithm. The estimation can be done in many ways. If the algorithm is $O(n^3)$ in the worst case and a small example for n = 10 takes 5 minutes, then we estimate that for n = 100, the algorithm will take $5 \times 100^3/10^3 = 5000$ minutes.

In backtrack, the algorithm is usually exponential in the worst case but performs much better on the average. So the above way of estimation is too pessimistic.

One way to estimate the amount of work of backtrack is to count the number of nodes in the decision tree. In the four-queen problem, $|X_i| = 4$ and we could use $|X_i|$ to estimate the number of nodes in the tree to be

$$1 + 4 + 4 \times 4 + 4 \times 4 \times 4 + 4 \times 4 \times 4 \times 4 = 341.$$

But this is very unrealistic. When x_1 is set at 1, x_2 has only two choices, not 4 choices. And if $x_1 = 1$, $x_2 = 3$, $S_3 = \emptyset$. So a more realistic way is to count the number of nodes based on $|S_i|$. But this is not a simple job because the $|S_i|$ are not known in advance. To count exactly the number of feasible solutions is equivalent to running the algorithm completely, which we have tried to avoid.

To estimate the number of nodes in a decision tree for a large example, we can use the Monte Carlo approach. Roughly speaking, the Monte Carlo approach is to traverse the decision tree, selecting the value of x_i randomly from S_i (instead of the smallest value in S_i). When a computation path is completed, we assume that all the computation paths (those we did not travel) are exactly the same as the one path we chose randomly.

So the Monte Carlo approach to backtrack is:

Step 0.   Set up one-to-one correspondence between sequences $(x_1, x_2, ..., x_n)$ and the possible configurations.

Step 1.   Set the unassigned value x_k of the sequence from S_k randomly. Increase k by 1. (If $k \geqslant n$, go to step 3.)

Step 2.   If S_{k+1} is not empty, return to Step 1. If S_{k+1} is empty, go to Step 3.

Step 3.   Count the number of nodes in the tree assuming that at each node, the computation path which was not chosen is exactly the same as the computation path that was chosen.

To illustrate the idea, let us again use the 4×4 chessboard. Assume that x_1 is chosen randomly to be 1 from four possible values (1,2,3,4), and x_2 is chosen randomly to be 4 from two possible values (3,4), then x_3 is set to be 2 since it is the only choice. Then we imagine that the decision tree looks like Figure 4.7.

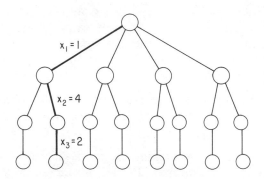

Figure 4.7

The particular computation path is drawn in heavy lines. If we had chosen $x_2 = 3$, then $S_3 = \varnothing$. Since we have not chosen $x_2 = 3$, we assume that part of the tree is exactly like $x_2 = 4$. Similarly, we assume that the four subtrees under the root are exactly the same. Using this approach, we have

$$1 + 4 + 4 \times 2 + 4 \times 2 = 21 \text{ nodes in Figure 4.7.}$$

Had we set $x_2 = 3$, we would estimate the decision tree to be like that in Figure 4.8. And we would conclude that there are 13 nodes.

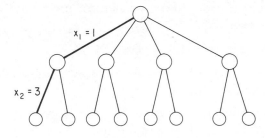

Figure 4.8

If we set $x_1 = 2$, we would imagine that the decision tree has 17 nodes and looks like the tree in Figure 4.9.

The real decision tree for the 4×4 chessboard problem looks like Figure 4.10.

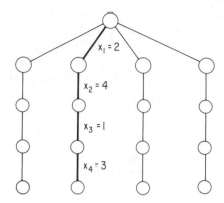

Figure 4.9

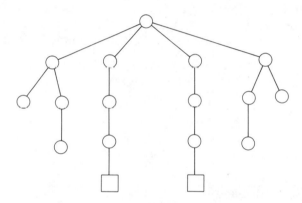

Figure 4.10

Although the real decision tree in Figure 4.10 is not like any of the trees we imagined in Figures 4.7, 4.8, or 4.9, the number of nodes in Figure 4.10 could be estimated rather accurately by several experiments. Assume that we get Figure 4.7 twice, Figure. 4.8 once and Figure 4.9 once. Then we estimate the number of nodes to be

$$(2 \times 21 + 1 \times 13 + 1 \times 17) \div 4 = 18$$

while the decision tree has 17 nodes.

§4.3 BRANCH AND BOUND

We shall discuss a special variation of backtrack known as branch and bound. In backtrack, a partial vector and all its children are excluded from the search if the partial vector already violates the constraints. If we associate infeasible vectors with high cost and feasible vectors with zero cost, then we are searching for a minimum cost vector. In many cases, it is natural to associate a cost with a partial vector and the cost structure satisfies the following relationship:

$$\text{cost of } (x_1, x_2, ..., x_{k-1}) \;\leqslant\; \text{cost of } (x_1, x_2, ..., x_{k-1}, x_k) \qquad (1)$$

for all possible values of x_k.

In other words, the cost of a father is always less than or equal to the cost of its son in the decision tree (compare this with the domino phenomenon, in § 4.1).

In such a case, if we have found a square node V_X with cost B, then we shall not branch from another circular node V_Y whose cost exceeds B, since all the children of V_Y will be of higher cost than B.

This is the central idea in branch and bound. We do not *branch* from a circular node whose cost is higher than the cost of the minimum cost solution found so far. Of course, the *bound* is updated if a better solution is found.

Thus, we traverse the decision tree by DFS and record the least cost solution V_X. When the cost of a partial vector V_Y exceeds the cost of V_X, all the children of V_Y are excluded. If a better solution V_Z is found, then its cost becomes the new bound.

For a maximatization problem, we do exactly the opposite. We do not *branch* from a circular node whose value is *less* than the value of the maximum-value solution.

Let us use branch-and-bound to solve the knapsack problem discussed in Chapter 3.

$$\begin{aligned} \max \quad & v_1x_1 + v_2x_2 + v_3x_3 + v_4x_4 \\ \text{subject to} \quad & w_1x_1 + w_2x_2 + w_3x_3 + w_4x_4 \leqslant b \\ & x_i \geqslant 0, \text{ integers} \end{aligned} \qquad (2)$$

i.e., maximizing the total value subject to the constraint that the total weight limitation be less than or equal to b and all variables are integers. (Usually, v_i and w_i are all positive.) A particular instance is

$$\begin{aligned} \max \quad & x_1 + 3x_2 + 5x_3 + 9x_4 \\ \text{subject to} \quad & 2x_1 + 3x_2 + 4x_3 + 7x_4 \leqslant 10 \\ & x_i \geqslant 0, \text{ integers .} \end{aligned} \qquad (3)$$

There are several points worth noting before we use the branch-and-bound algorithm to solve the knapsack problem.

1. We shall reorder the variables such that

$$\frac{v_i}{w_i} \geqslant \frac{v_{i+1}}{w_{i+1}} \tag{4}$$

i.e., we shall maximize

$$9x_1 + 5x_2 + 3x_3 + x_4$$

$$\text{subject to} \quad 7x_1 + 4x_2 + 3x_3 + 2x_4 \leqslant 10 \tag{5}$$

$$x_i \geqslant 0, \quad \text{integers}$$

(the reason will be discussed later).

2. We do not branch from a node if the weight limitation is violated. Since we are maximizing instead of minimizing, we do not branch from a node if its value is less than the value of a feasible solution found so far.

3. It is natural to assign the weight of a node $(x_1, x_2, ..., x_k, \_, ..., \_)$ to be $\sum_{i=1}^{k} w_i x_i$ so that if a node does not satisfy the weight limitation, neither do its children. How do we set the value of a node $(x_1, x_2, ..., x_k, \_, ..., \_)$? The value is set to be

$$\sum_{i=1}^{k} v_i x_i + \left(b - \sum_{i=1}^{k} w_i x_i \right) v_{k+1}/w_{k+1} \quad \text{if } b - \sum_{i=1}^{k} w_i x_i \geqslant w_j \quad \text{for some } j > k \text{ (6a)}$$

or

$$\sum_{i=1}^{k} v_i x_i \quad \text{if } b - \sum_{i=1}^{k} w_i x_i < w_j \quad \text{for all } j > k \quad \text{(6b)}$$

The value in (6a) consists of two parts, the first part is the value of all those variables already assigned. These variables take $\Sigma w_i x_i$ in weight and there is only $b - \Sigma w_i x_i$ left. Since variables are ordered according to (4), the maximum value that could possibly be achieved in the leftover weight limitation is $\left(b - \sum_{i=1}^{k} w_i x_i \right) v_{k+1}/w_{k+1}$ provided that x_{k+1} does not have to be an integer. If every node's value is set by (6a), the value of a node is an upper bound on the value of all his children. If the father's value is less than or equal to the value of the current best feasible solution, then all his children can be disregarded. When

$$\left(b - \sum_{i=1}^{k} w_i x_i\right) < w_j \quad \text{for all } j > k$$

no more item could be put into the knapsack, and we just record

$$\sum_{i=1}^{k} v_i x_i$$

as the node's value and the node is a leaf.

We draw a decision tree for the knapsack problem in Figure 4.11. The value of a node based on (6) is written inside a node in the top, while the total weight is written below. And we do not branch from a node if

(i)   its total weight exceeds the limitation b

or

(ii)   its value is less than or equal to the value of the current best feasible vector.

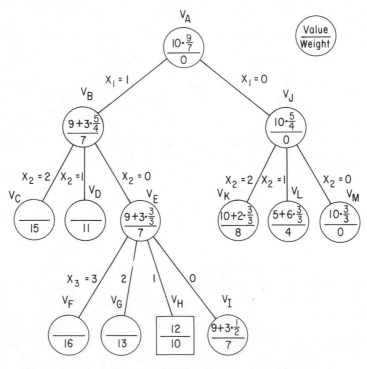

Figure 4.11

Note that for problem (5)

$$X_1 = \{0,1\}, \ X_2 = \{0,1,2\}, \ X_3 = \{0,1,2,3\}, \ X_4 = \{0,1,2,3,4,5\} \ .$$

Instead of assigning x_k to be the smallest value in S_k, we shall assign x_k to be the largest value in S_k.

The order of visiting the nodes in the decision tree is $V_A, V_B, ..., V_M$.

Since the weight limitation is exceeded at V_C, we do not branch from it. The same reason holds for V_D, V_G. At V_H, we get the first bound, the value of a feasible solution. We do not branch again from V_H because the total weight of the solution equals the weight limitation. (In general, we do not branch from a node if (6b) is used.)

We do not branch from V_I, V_K, V_L, and V_M because their values are the same or less than the current bound - 12.

Let us discuss the three points we made previously.

1. The reason that we reorder the variables is to have the first item be the most valuable item in terms of its value per unit weight.

As the values of the internal nodes are set by (6a), the value of a father is equal to or greater than that of its children.

2. In this problem, a node has a value and a weight, and we are trying to find the node with maximum value and with its weight less than the weight limitation. The weight of a node at the level k is defined to be $\sum_{i=1}^{k} w_i x_i$, so that if a node exceeds the limitation, his son's weight will also exceed. If we define the value of a node to be $\sum_{i=1}^{k} v_i x_i$, then the value of a son may be greater than its father; and if the father's value is not competitive with the current best solution, its children may, and the subtree rooted at the father cannot be excluded. To avoid this, we define the value of a node by (6).

3. Since the variables are ordered according to (4), filling the knapsack with item i is always better than filling the knapsack with item $i+1$ if x_i is allowed to be a continuous variable.

§4.4 GAME-TREE

In games like tic-tac-toe, nim, checkers, we can model the different stages of the game by a rooted tree. Instead of considering all the possible situations of a game, we can predict the outcomes of the game using the idea of branch-and-bound.

Let us define a *modified* version of nim for example. The game is played by two players who alternately take chips from a given pile. Each player must take at least one chip, and at most three chips in his turn. The winner is the player who takes all the chips from the pile, i.e., who empties the pile. The amount of payoff is the number of chips the winner takes in his last turn.

Assume the pile contains n chips in the beginning. The first player can have three choices, i.e., take one, two, or three chips; and the second player also has three choices. So we can model the entire game by a ternary tree as shown in Figure 4.12, where we assume that there are six chips in the pile in the beginning.

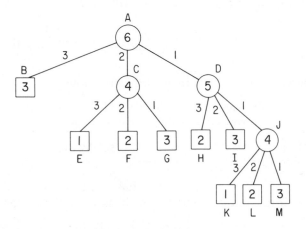

Figure 4.12

In Figure 4.12, we write the number of chips in the pile inside the node, so that the root contains six chips. We write the number of chips taken by the players beside the arcs so that node B at the first level shows that there are 3 chips left if the first player takes 3 chips, and node C shows 4 chips left if the first player takes 2 chips, etc. Obviously, the game will end immediately if the pile contains three chips or less. Thus a node with a number 3 or less is drawn as a square.

In order to avoid confusion, we always think in terms of the first player and regard the payoff as the amount the first player receives at the end of the game. If the second player wins, then the payoff is negative. Thus the first player wishes to maximize the payoff while the second player wishes to minimize the payoff. The players will be called the Max and the Min from now on. When it is the Max player's turn, we draw the node as ⌂ and when it is the Min player's turn, we draw ∪. We now redraw the game as shown in Figure 4.13 where the *number inside the node indicates the amount of payoff.* (We will explain later how we obtain the numbers inside the internal nodes such as A, C, D.)

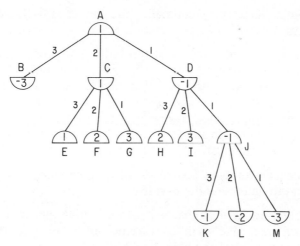

Figure 4.13

In the beginning, we only know the payoff inside terminal nodes.

The questions are: i) who is the winner if both players play optimally? ii) how much is the payoff?

It is easier to settle these questions by looking at the nodes of the lowest level and working back towards the root.

Consider the node J where there are four chips left in the pile, and it is the Max player's turn. Obviously, Max is not going to take 1 chip so as to lose 3 dollars, Max should take 3 chips so as to lose 1 dollar. Thus, if the game should become stage J, the payoff will be -1, and we can write -1 inside node J.

At node D, it is the Min player's turn, and he would definitely take 1 chip since

$$\min(H, I, J) = \min(2, 3, -1) = -1 .$$

Thus we can write -1 inside node D.

By the same reasoning, the Min player would take 3 chips at node C, since

$$\min(E, F, G) = \min(1, 2, 3) = 1 .$$

Thus we can write 1 inside node C.

Now at node A, the Max player would take 2 chips since

$$\max(B, C, D) = \max(-3, 1, -1) = 1 ,$$

so we can write 1 inside node A.

Thus, if both players play optimally, the payoff is 1. In other words, the Max player always wins.

In a more complicated game, it is too tedious to work from all the leaves corresponding to all the possible ways the game might end. We would like to work from the root and know the payoff of the game without searching all the possible branches of the tree. The assumption is that both players will play optimally. In other words, both players will play most conservatively assuming his opponent is very smart. (In the real world, the strategies against a good player and a poor player are different.)

We shall use Depth First Search for the game tree, and use the idea of branch-and-bound to determine the payoff.

The main feature here is that we can use both upper and lower cut-off values in a game tree. We shall use "value" of a node to mean the payoff corresponding to that stage of the game.

Consider a node Q in Figure 4.14 where it is the Max's turn and we have already evaluated a leftson R of Q where the value is α.

Once we know R has the value α, then the value of Q must be greater than or equal to α. The node Q may have many other sons with different values. If these values are less than α, Max will take R with value α. So the value of Q is at least α, and α is the lower cut-off value for Q. Once we know that Q has a lower cut-off value α, all the children of Q will also have the lower cut-off value α. Consider S which is a son of Q. Suppose all the children of S have values less than α so that the node S has a value less than α. Then Max at Q will definitely take R. In other words, only children of S that may have values greater than α need to be evaluated.

We can summarize the result by saying:

If the value of a Max son is α, then α is a lower cut-off value on the value of Max.

If Max has a lower cut-off value α, then all Max's children have lower cut-off value α.

We draw this symbolically in Figure 4.15 where the arrows indicate how the value α propogates through the rest of the game tree.

Similarly, if a Min son has a value β, then β becomes the upper cut-off value for the value of Min. Also all the children of Min will have the upper cut-off value β. This is shown symbolically in Figure 4.16.

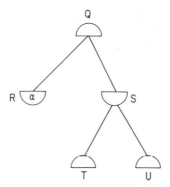

Figure 4.14

In Figure 4.15, if we can establish the fact that the node S has a value less than or equal to α, then we need not search the subtree with S as the root. This is called α-cutoff. In Figure 4.16, if we can establish that the node S has a value greater than or equal to β, then we need not search the subtree with S as the root. This is called β-cutoff. In the literature, we also use the terminology α-β pruning.

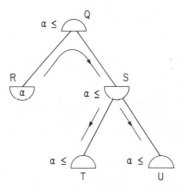

Figure 4.15

We shall first evaluate a game tree without using α-β pruning. This game tree is shown in Figure 4.17 where the values of terminal nodes are given in the beginning. The values of all internal nodes are obtained by working upwards, and finally the root of the tree has a value 1; i.e., the Max will win by one dollar if both players play optimally.

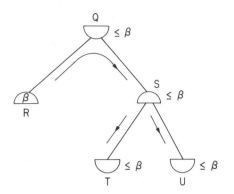

Figure 4.16

Let us now evaluate exactly the same game tree using α-β pruning. We start from the root A in Figure 4.18, then B, C, D, in depth-first-search manner. At D, we see that its leftson has a value of 2 and its rightson has value 1. Since D is a Min node, we can write 1 inside D.

Once D has value 1, then the lower cut-off value of C is 1, and E has a lower cut-off value 1 also. The leftson of E is 1 and the value 1 becomes an upper cut-off value on E. Now E has lower and upper cut-off values, both 1, so we can write 1 inside E.   Here we can determine the value of E without looking at the rightson. Thus we leave the value of its rightson blank. Note that the real value of E is -3 in Figure 4.17 but we can write E as 1 since it will not affect the value of C. And we are interested in the correct value of the *root only*.

The value of C is $\max(D,E) = \max(1,1) = 1$. This value of C now becomes the upper cut-off value of B and all its children, F, G, H, etc.

The value of $G = \min(3,2) = 2$, which is greater than the current upper cut-off value 1.

We shall write 2 inside G which is a lower cut-off value for F. (If we write 1 inside G, we get the same value at B.) Now F has lower cut-off value 2, and upper cut-off value 1 so that the value of F is determined without looking at H or its children.

We shall write $F = 2$. (Whenever the lower cut-off value exceeds the upper cut-off value, we use the lower cut-off value if the node is Max's and use the upper cut-off value if the node is Min's).

Now the value of $B = \min(C,F) = \min(1,2) = 1$. (Note that we could write $F = 1$ and the final value of B would be the same.)

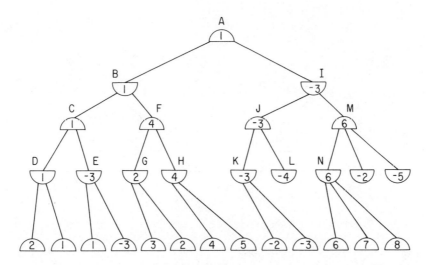

Figure 4.17

The value of B is a lower cut-off value of A and all its children I, J, K, L, M, etc.

Now the values of the children of K are upper cut-off values for K, so we have $1 \leqslant K \leqslant -2$.

We shall use -2 as the value of K since K is a Min node.

The value of K $(= -2)$ is again a lower cut-off value for J and since J has a lower cut-off value 1, we maintain the greater lower cut-off value 1.

The value at J $= \max(K,L) = \max(-2,-4) = -2$. Since the value of J is an upper cut-off value for I, we have at I, $1 \leqslant I \leqslant -2$. We use -2 for I since I is a Min node. Now the value of A is determined. The value of A $= \max(B,I) = \max(1,-2) = 1$. Note that the value of A is determined without looking at M or any of its children.

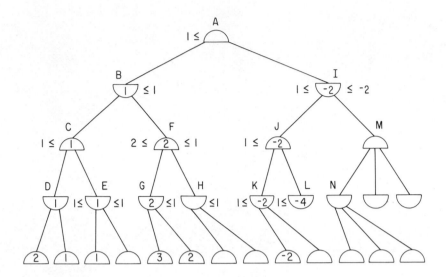

Figure 4.18

EXERCISES

1. Construct a five-city travelling salesman example using the branch-and-bound technique.

2. Use the α-β pruning technique to solve the tic-tac-toe game.

3. A game of Nim consists of 3 piles of chips in the beginning. A player can take up to 3 chips in each pile (but not from different piles). What is the value of the game if the three piles have two, three, and five chips in the beginning?

4. Use the backtrack technique to find the minimum number of queens in a chessboard such that every unoccupied position is under attack by at least one queen.

5. The partition of a positive integer is to write the integer as the sum of k other positive integers. For example,

$$12 = 1 + 1 + 3 + 3 + 4 = 1 + 2 + 2 + 2 + 5 \, .$$

Generate all possible partitions of the integer 6 into exactly four other integers.

CHAPTER 4

BIBLIOGRAPHIC NOTES AND SUGGESTED READING

It is hard to trace the origin of backtracking. Some earlier papers on this subject are Golomb and Baumert [3], Hall and Knuth [4], Lehmer [8], and Walker [13]. For most people in operations research, this technique is commonly called branch-and-bound since the technique is used mainly for optimization problems. One of the earliest papers to use branch-and-bound to solve the traveling salesman problem is due to Little, Murty, Sweeney, and Karel [9]. For general discussions on backtracking and branch-and-bound, see the books by Garfinkel and Nemhauser [2], Horowitz and Sahni [5], Nijenhuis and Wilf [10], Reingold, Nievergelt and Deo [11], and Wells [14].

For estimating the efficiency of backtracking, see Knuth [6]. For the analysis of alpha-beta pruning, see Baudet [1], and Knuth and Moore [7]. The recursive version of backtracking on graphs can be found in Tarjan [12].

1.   G. M. Baudet, "An Analysis of the Full Alpha-Beta Pruning Algorithm", Proceedings of the 10th Annual ACM Symposium on Theory of Computing, May 1978, pp. 296-313.

2.   R. S. Garfinkel and G. L. Nemhauser, "Integer Programming", John Wiley & Sons, 1972.

3.   S. W. Golomb and L. D. Baumert, "Backtrack Programming", J. ACM, 12 (1965), pp. 516-524.

4.   M. H. Hall and D. E. Knuth, "Combinatorial Analysis and Computers", Am. Math. Monthly 72, part II (1965), pp. 21-28.

5.   E. Horowitz and S. Sahni, "Fundamentals of Computer Algorithms", Computer Science Press, 1978.

6.   D. E. Knuth, "Estimating the Efficiency of Backtrack Programs", Math. Computations 29 (129) (1975), pp. 121-136.

7.   D. E. Knuth and R. W. Moore, "An Analysis of Alpha-Beta Pruning", Artificial Intelligence 6 (4) (1975), pp. 293-326.

8.   D. H. Lehmer, "The Machine Tools of Combinatorics", in Applied Combinatorial Math., edited by E. F. Beckenback, Wiley, 1964, pp. 5-31.

9.   J. D. C. Little, K. G. Murty, D. W. Sweeney, and C. Karel, "An Algorithm for the Traveling Salesman Problem", ORSA 11 (1963), pp. 972-989.

10.   A. Nijenhuis and H. S. Wilf, "Combinatorial Algorithm", Academic Press, 1975.

11.   E. M. Reingold, J. Nievergelt, and Deo, "Combinatorial Algorithms", Prentice Hall, 1977.

12.   R. E. Tarjan, "Depth-First Search and Linear Graph Algorithms", SIAM J. Computing 1 (1972), pp. 146-160.

13.   R. J. Walker, "An Enumerative Technique for a Class of Combinatorial Problems", Proceedings of Symposia in Applied Mathematics, Vol. X, AMS, 1960.

14.   M. B. Wells, "Elements of Combinatorial Computing", Pergamon Press, 1971.

CHAPTER 5. BINARY TREES

Make your binary decisions in life carefully.

§5.1 INTRODUCTION

A *binary tree* consists of a *root* and two disjoint binary subtrees; either of which, or both, could be empty. In this chapter, a binary tree consists of at least one node, the root.

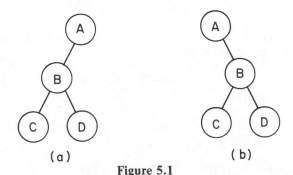

(a)   (b)

Figure 5.1

In Figure 5.1(a), V_A is the root of the binary tree and the right subtree is empty. The left subtree of V_A consists of a binary tree with V_B as the root and two single nodes V_C and V_D as its two subtrees.

Note that the two binary trees in Figure 5.1(a) and (b) are different since one has a right subtree empty while the other has the left subtree empty.

In most of this chapter, we shall deal with extended binary trees. An *extended binary tree* is obtained from a binary tree by adding square nodes to a binary tree whenever a null subtree was present. Thus, the binary trees in Figure 5.1 become the extended binary trees in Figure. 5.2.

In an extended binary tree, a circular node (also called an internal node) has two sons and a square node (also called an external node) has no sons. From now on, we shall use the term "binary tree" to mean an "extended binary tree".

If we consider the arcs of a binary tree as *directed downward*, then there is a directed path from the root to every node (circular or square). The number of arcs in the path to a node, V_i, is called the path length of V_i. The path length is denoted by l_i. Thus $l_B = 1$, $l_E = 3$ in Figure 5.2(a). The path length, l_i, of a node is also referred to as the level of the node. The root is defined to be at the level zero and is considered to be the highest level.

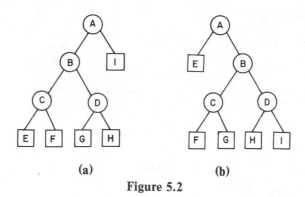

(a)   (b)

Figure 5.2

A node V_i is an *ancestor* of a node V_j if there is a directed path from V_i to V_j (V_j is a *descendent* of V_i). And if the path consists of only one arc, we use father and son instead. In Figure 5.2(a), V_A is the ancestor of every node. V_C is the father of V_E and V_F, with V_E being the left son. The node V_G is an descendent of V_B but not of V_C.

A computer program can be represented by a binary tree. An internal node represents an intermediate stage of computation where a decision is made which leads to two possible computational paths. An external node represents a solution or a final result. For example, a loop which increases the value of a parameter n until n equals 100 can be represented by the binary tree in Figure 5.3.

The root of the binary tree represents the start of the computer program and each leaf is a possible outcome (corresponding to certain input data). The path length of a leaf is then an indication of the time to reach that particular result. If we add up the path lengths of all the leaves, divide by the number of leaves, then it is an average of how long the computer program runs. The *external path length* of a tree is defined to be the sum (taken over all external nodes) of the path length of the external nodes of the tree. Thus, the external path length of the tree in Figure 5.2(a) is

$$l_E + l_F + l_G + l_H + l_I = 3 + 3 + 3 + 3 + 1 = 13 .$$

In other applications, we may want the *internal path length* of the tree where the sum of path length is taken over all internal nodes. Thus, the internal path length of the tree in Figure 5.2(a) is

$$l_A + l_B + l_C + l_D = 0 + 1 + 2 + 2 = 5 .$$

Let I denote the internal path length and E denote the external path length. It is easy to verify by induction that

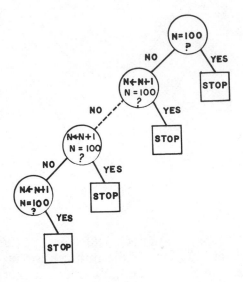

Figure 5.3

$$E = I + 2(n-1) \tag{1}$$

where n is the number of leaves in the binary tree.

§5.2 HUFFMAN'S TREE

Consider the binary trees in Figure 5.4 where the four leaves are labeled A, B, C, D and the left arcs are labeled zero and the right arcs are labeled one.

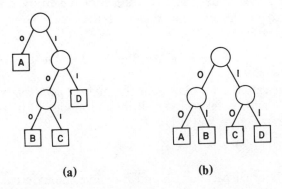

(a)   (b)

Figure 5.4

We can regard the trees in Figure 5.4 as representations of the letters A, B, C, D by binary sequences. Such a representation is called an encoding. A letter is represented by the binary digits associated with the arcs which form the path to the letter. Thus in Figure 5.4(a) the letters and their corresponding binary sequences are

A	0
B	100
C	101
D	11

A sequence such as 100011 of zero's and one's can be uniquely decoded as follows: Starting from the left, we delete the subsequence which corresponds to a letter. In other words, we mark off the left part as soon as its correspondence to a letter is known. Thus, the sequence

$$1\ 0\ 0\ 0\ 1\ 1$$

corresponds to

$$100\quad 0\quad 11$$

$$B\quad A\quad D$$

Note that in the encoding of the letters A, B, C, D, no code of one letter is a prefix of another. This property is called the prefix property and it is why we use the extended binary tree and represent the letters by the leaves instead of the internal nodes. When an encoding has the prefix property, we do not need spaces between binary digits in decoding.

Different binary trees correspond to different ways of encoding. Thus the tree in Figure 5.4(b) represents the following encoding:

A	00
B	01
C	10
D	11

The same message "BAD" would be represented by

$$01\quad 00\quad 11$$

$$B\quad A\quad D$$

Here every letter is represented by exactly two digits while previously some letters were represented by one digit and others by three digits.

We want to have a system such that we need the minimum number of digits, on the average, to transmit messages. Thus letters used frequently should be represented by short sequences and letters seldom used should be represented by long sequences.

Thus we associate a positive weight w_i with every letter V_i which indicates the relative frequency, and define the weighted path length of a tree to be

$$\Sigma w_i l_i$$

If the letters A, B, C, D have weights 4, 1, 2, 3 respectively, then the weighted path length of the tree in Figure 5.4(a) is

$$w_A \bullet 1 + w_B \bullet 3 + w_C \bullet 3 + w_D \bullet 2$$
$$= 4 \bullet 1 + 1 \bullet 3 + 2 \bullet 3 + 3 \bullet 2$$
$$= 19.$$

While the weighted path length of the tree in Figure 5.4(b) is

$$w_A \bullet 2 + w_B \bullet 2 + w_C \bullet 2 + w_D \bullet 2$$
$$= 4 \bullet 2 + 1 \bullet 2 + 2 \bullet 2 + 3 \bullet 2$$
$$= 20 .$$

We shall refer to the "weighted path length" as the cost, since the weighted path length is, in a sense, the cost of the encoding.

For given weights of the leaves, a binary tree with minimum cost is called an *optimum binary tree*. Th algorithm which constructed an optimum binary tree is due to Huffman [9] and people usually refer to the optimum binary tree as *Huffman's tree*.

Now we shall describe the Huffman algorithm. Let the weights of the n leaves be $w_1, w_2, ..., w_n$ where

$$w_1 \leqslant w_2 \leqslant ... \leqslant w_n .$$

Replace the two smallest nodes by a node with weight $w_1 + w_2$ and do this recursively for the n−1 weights

$$(w_1 + w_2), w_3, ..., w_n .$$

The final single node with weight $(w_1 + w_2 + ... + w_n)$ is the root of the binary tree.

If we apply the algorithm to the set of weights 4, 1, 2, 3, we first combine the two smallest weights 1 and 2 and obtain a set of three weights

$$4, 3, 3 \ .$$

Then the two smallest weights 3 and 3 are combined, and we have two weights

$$4, 6$$

and so the final tree looks like Figure 5.5.

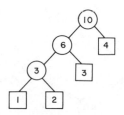

Figure 5.5

Note that we have written the weight of a node inside the node and the sum of the weights of the $n-1$ internal nodes

$$\text{③} + \text{⑥} + \text{⑩} = 19$$

is the weighted path length of the tree, a fact which can be proved in general.

Lemma 1 The sum of the weights of the $n-1$ internal nodes is equal to the cost of the binary tree.

Proof. By induction.

A larger numerical example with combined weights underlined is shown on page 168.

The resulting Huffman tree is shown in Figure 5.6.

We can easily prove the validity of Huffman's algorithm as follows. Given any binary tree, there must be an internal node of maximum path length. If this internal node V_i has two sons V_a and V_b which are not the smallest nodes, we could interchange the positions of w_1 and w_2 with the current two sons of V_i without increasing the cost of the tree. In the resulting tree, we have essentially $n-1$ leaves with weights

$$(w_1 + w_2), w_3, ..., w_n$$

2,	2,	2,	3,	4,	6,	6,	7,	9,	12,	13
	4,	2,	3,	4,	6,	6,	7,	9,	12,	13
	4,		5,	4,	6,	6,	7,	9,	12,	13
			5,	8,	6,	6,	7,	9,	12,	13
				8,	11,	6,	7,	9,	12,	13
				8,	11,		13,	9,	12,	13
					11,		13,	17,	12,	13
							13,	17,	23,	13
								17,	23,	26
									40,	26
										66

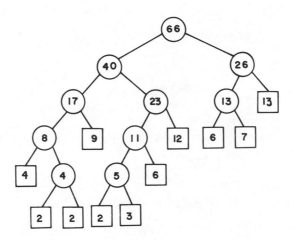

Figure 5.6

The proof is therefore completed by induction.

If we stop the Huffman construction after creating m internal nodes (m < n−1), then the result is a *forest*. (A forest is just a set of trees.) We shall call the forest an m-sum forest if it is obtained after creating m internal nodes.

We can define the cost of a forest as $\Sigma w_i l_i$ where l_i is the path length of every node in its trees. For example, the 4-sum forest of the leaves in Figure 5.6 is shown in Figure 5.7.

The cost of the 4-sum forest is

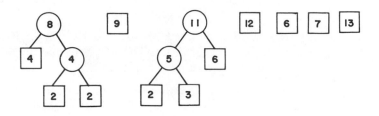

Figure 5.7

$$2 \bullet 2 + 2 \bullet 2 + 4 \bullet 1 + 2 \bullet 2 + 3 \bullet 2 + 6 \bullet 1 = 28$$

which is also equal to the sum of the weights of circular nodes created so far

$$④ + ⑧ + ⑤ + ⑪ = 28$$

Lemma 2 The Huffman algorithm gives the minimum cost m-sum forest for $1 \leqslant m \leqslant n-1$.

Proof. The proof is by induction on m. It is clear that Huffman's algorithm gives an optimum 1-sum forest. Assume that the lemma is true for k-sum forests and we now try to construct an optimum $(k+1)$-sum forest.

In this $(k+1)$-sum forest, there must be an internal node V_i of maximum path length. If the two sons of V_i do not have the smallest weights w_1 and w_2, then we can interchange the two sons of V_i with the nodes w_1 and w_2 without increasing the cost of the forest. Hence this new $(k+1)$-sum forest, which combines w_1 and w_2, is also optimum. Clearly, this $(k+1)$-sum forest can be optimum if and only if the k sum forest on the weights

$$(w_1 + w_2), w_3, ..., w_t$$

is optimum. However, by induction, the Huffman algorithm generates the optimum k-sum forest. Q.E.D.

We can define t-ary trees analogously to binary trees, where every internal node has exactly t sons and every square node has no sons.

It is easy to see that the Huffman construction of combining the t smallest nodes will give an optimum t-ary tree.

There is no explicit formula which gives the cost (of an optimum binary tree) as a function of the weights of the leaves. Consider two sets of nodes, both sets have the same number of nodes and the same total weight. For example, the sets (A) and (B) both have four nodes and total weight 20.

$$(A) \quad 1, 3, 6, 10$$

$$(B) \quad 2, 5, 5, 8$$

If we build Huffman's tree on (A), denoted by T_A, and Huffman's tree on (B), denoted by T_B, which tree has the higher cost? The following lemma decides this issue. We shall use $|T_A|$ to denote the cost of the tree T_A.

Lemma 3 (Extreme Set Lemma). Let T denote the optimum tree built on a set of nodes with weight w_i and T_u be the optimum tree built on a set of nodes with weight w_i'. If the following conditions are satisfied, then the cost of T is less than or equal to the cost of T_u.

(i) $\displaystyle\sum_{i=1}^{n} w_i = \sum_{i=1}^{n} w_i'$

(ii) $w_1 \leqslant w_2 \leqslant ... \leqslant w_n$ and $w_1' \leqslant w_2' \leqslant ... \leqslant w_n'$

(iii) $w_i + \delta_i = w_i'$ $(i=1,...,k-1)$ and $w_i - \delta_i = w_i'$ $(i=k,...,n)$.

$\qquad (\delta_j \geqslant 0, j=1,...,n)$.

Roughly speaking this lemma says that if the total weight of two sets are the same, the set with more extreme weights will give a tree of less or equal cost.

Proof. Assume that in the minimum cost tree, the path length for w_j' is l_j' $(j=1,...,n)$ then it follows from (ii) that

$$l_1' \geqslant l_2' \geqslant ... \geqslant l_n' . \tag{1}$$

It follows from (i) and (iii) that

$$\sum_{j=1}^{k-1} \delta_j - \sum_{j=k}^{n} \delta_j = 0$$

and $\qquad \displaystyle\sum_{j=1}^{k-1} \delta_j - \sum_{j=k}^{m} \delta_j > 0 \qquad (m < n) \tag{2}$

Now $|T_u| = w_1' l_1' + w_2' l_2' + ... + w_k' l_k' + ... + w_n' l_n'$

$\qquad = (w_1 + \delta_1) l_1' + ... + (w_k - \delta_k) l_k' + ... + (w_n - \delta_n) l_n'$

$\qquad = \displaystyle\sum_{j=1}^{n} w_j l_j' + [\delta_1 l_1' + \delta_2 l_2' + ... + \delta_{k-1} l_{k-1}' - \delta_k l_k' - ... - \delta_n l_n']$

$\qquad = \displaystyle\sum_{j=1}^{n} w_j l_j' + l_n' [\delta_1 + \delta_2 + ... + \delta_{k-1} - \delta_k - ... - \delta_n]$

$\qquad\qquad + (l_{n-1}' - l_n')[\delta_1 + \delta_2 + ... + \delta_{k-1} - \delta_k - ... - \delta_{n-1}]$

$\vdots$

$$+ (l_1' - l_2') \delta_1$$

$$= \sum_{j=1}^{n} w_j l_j' + s'$$

$$= |T''| + s' \qquad \text{where } s' \geqslant 0 .$$

$$\geqslant |T|$$

Intuitively, the proof of this lemma is to remove the leaves w_i' from the tree T_u and attach the leaves w_i to the corresponding places. This will create a tree T" cheaper than T_u. Since T is the optimum tree for w_i, $|T| \leqslant |T''| \leqslant |T_u|$.

§5.3 ALPHABETIC TREES

In section 5.2, we showed that a binary tree can be used as an encoding, and the best encoding is the Huffman tree. The intuitive idea behind Huffman's algorithm is to assign short binary sequences to letters often used and to assign long binary sequences to letters rarely used. Thus, we combine the two letters with the smallest weights (weights correspond to frequencies of usage). In English, the two least-used letters are Q and Z, and they will have the same father in Huffman's tree.

Sometimes, we put additional restrictions on the encoding. We may require that the alphabetic order of letters corresponds to the numerical binary order of the codes. In other words, when we scan the bottom of the tree from left to right, the letters (leaves) must occur in alphabetic order. Such a tree is called an *alphabetic tree* for the ordered sequence of leaves. For a binary tree, if left arcs are assigned digit 0 and right arcs 1, we can associate a number $n(V_j)$ with each leaf V_j which is a decimal point followed by the sequence of digits associated with the arcs in the order on the path from the root to V_j. An alphabetic tree then has a sequence of assigned numbers that satisfies

$$n(V_i) < n(V_{i+1})$$

where the order of leaves from left to right are $V_1, V_2, ..., V_n$.

We can define t-ary alphabetic trees in an analogous way.

Note that Huffman's tree does not satisfy the alphabetic constraint since Q and Z are not adjacent in the alphabetic order of letters.

An alphabetic tree corresponds to a computer search procedure for a word in a dictionary. When we look for a word, we may check if it is before or after m. If before m, we may check if it is before or after f. After the first letter of

m. If before m, we may check if it is before or after f. After the first letter of the word is found, we repeat the same procedure for the second letter, etc. The entire search procedure can be represented by an alphabetic tree as shown in Figure 5.8.

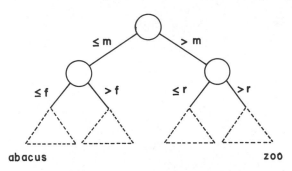

Figure 5.8

Think how hard it would be to find a word in a dictionary if the words were listed randomly!

When all words have the same weight, then the optimum search is to always bisect the number of words. For leaves with unequal weights, we can use the same approach and try to partition the sequence of nodes such that the total weight on the left and right subtrees are approximately equal, and then apply this partition recursively for each of the subtrees. Unfortunately, this intuitive approach does not work, as seen in the following example.

Example 1

(Counterexample to equal weight partition). Consider the four leaves V_A, V_B, V_C, V_D with weights 4, 1, 2, 3.

Following the intuitive approach, we should assign the leaves V_A and V_B to the left subtree and V_C and V_D to the right subtree. This would be given an alphabetic tree as shown in Figure 5.4(b) with cost equaling 20. However, the alphabetic tree in Figure 5.4(a) costs 19.

The reader should note that Huffman's construction of the four nodes V_A, V_B, V_C and V_D in Figure 5.4(a) happens to satisfy the alphabetic ordering. This is not true in general. If the weights of the nodes are $w_A = 1$, $w_B = 4$, $w_C = 3$, $w_D = 2$, then the Huffman tree will not satisfy the alphabetic constraint.

Since we are only allowed to combine letters when they are adjacent, a natural approach would be to combine the adjacent pair with minimum weight and then do this recursively for the remaining n−1 letters with the father having the sum of its sons' weights. Unfortunately, this approach does not work as seen in Example 2.

Example 2

(Counterexample to minimum adjacent pair approach). Consider the four leaves V_A, V_B, V_C and V_D with weights 4, 2, 3, 4.   The minimum adjacent pair is (V_B, V_C) with total weight 5, but the optimum alphabetic tree is shown in Figure 5.9 where V_B and V_C do not have a common father.

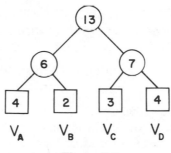

Figure 5.9

For example, we may want to construct an optimum alphabetic tree with 26 leaves corresponding to the letters of the alphabet, but there is no easy way to know if the letter H should be combined with G or with I. In 1959, Gilbert and Moore [3] used the dynamic programming approach to construct an optimum alphabetic tree. Their algorithm is $0(n^3)$ in time and $0(n^2)$ in space. This is the algorithm presented in section 3.4. Knuth [12] improved their bounds to $0(n^2)$ in time. The algorithm that will be described in §5.4 is due to Hu and Tucker [8] with $0(n \log n)$ time and $0(n)$ space.

§5.4 HU-TUCKER ALGORITHM

In the alphabetic tree problem, the order of the leaves $V_1,V_2,...,V_n$ is given together with their weights $w_1,w_2,...,w_n$. These sequences are called the *node sequence* and the *weight sequence* respectively.

If we combine V_i and V_j, then their father is denoted by V_{ij} and its weight is w_{ij}. If V_{ij} and V_k are combined, their father is denoted by $V_{ij,k}$. In this notion, a single subscript denotes a leaf and double or triple subscript denotes a circular node.

If no confusion should arise, we shall use w_i to mean the node V_i with the weight w_i. Thus, the phrase "combine (or merge) w_i and w_j to form w_{ij}" means

"Combine the nodes V_i and V_j with weights w_i and w_j, forming a node V_{ij} with weight w_{ij}."

Consider any algorithm that will construct an optimum alphabetic tree from a node sequence represented by a sequence of n squares with weights written inside the squares. Let us say we combine w_i and w_j. Then their father w_{ij} is a circle with the combined weight written inside the circle. Now we have n−2 squares and 1 circle and we make another combination. This process of combination is repeated n−1 times and the original sequence of n squares is combined into a circle which is the root of the alphabetic tree.

Unfortunately, there is no algorithm that will construct an alphabetic tree as we describe above. The Hu-Tucker algorithm first constructs a tree which is *not* alphabetic and then transforms the tree into an optimum alphabetic tree.

To describe this unusual algorithm, we need to introduce some new concepts.

Two nodes in a node sequence are called a *compatible pair* if they are adjacent or if all nodes between them are circular nodes. Thus in Figure 5.10 the nodes joined by solid lines are compatible pairs and the nodes joined by dotted lines are not compatible.

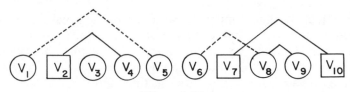

Figure 5.10

If V_2 and V_4 are combined first to become V_{24}, then V_1 and V_5 will become compatible in the new sequence.

When a pair of nodes w_i and w_j are combined, their father's weight $w_{ij} = w_i + w_j$ is called the weight of the pair. A pair with minimum weight is called a *minimum* pair. In a node sequence, there may be many pairs of equal weight. To break the ties, we shall use the following rule. For two pairs with equal weight, the one having the leftmost node is considered to be of less weight. If both pairs have the same leftmost nodes, i.e., "w_a and w_i" and "w_a and w_j", then the pair with the right son at the leftmost position is of less weight. In other words, the one with the smallest subscript is of less weight, and further ties are broken by the second smallest subscript.

Using this tie-breaking rule, we shall write $w_i \leqslant w_j$ to mean $w_i < w_j$, or $w_i = w_j$ with V_i on the left of V_j in the node sequence. When we compare two weights in a node sequence, there is *no equality* from now on. If all nodes are of equal weight, then we have $w_1 \leqslant w_2 \leqslant \ldots \leqslant w_n$.

Among all compatible pairs in the node sequence, the one with minimum weight is called the *minimum compatible* pair.

The Hu-Tucker algorithm constructs an alphabetic tree minimizing $\Sigma w_i l_i$ by the following steps.

(1)   Combination:

Given a sequence of n nodes with weights $w_1, w_2, \ldots, w_n$, we produce a sequence of n−1 nodes by combining the minimum compatible pair, replacing the left son by his father, and removing the right son from the node sequence. In Figures 5.11 and 5.12 we place the father directly above the left son. The procedure of merging weights is continued until only one weight is left. The corresponding tree is denoted by T'.

(Actually, we need not scan the whole sequence to find the minimum compatible pair. We can simply combine the so-called local minimum compatible pair which will be discussed later.)

(2)   Level Assignment:

From the root of T' in Step (1), we find the level number l_i of every leaf V_i. (Remember that the node with the largest l_i is at the bottom of the tree.)

(3)   Reconstruction:

When the level numbers $l_1, l_2, \ldots, l_n$ of all leaves are known from (2), we scan the sequence from left to right and locate the leftmost maximum level number, say $l_i = q$. Then $l_{i+1} = q$ also. (The level sequence $l_1, l_2, \ldots, l_n$ has the property that the maximum level numbers are always adjacent.) We create a father of the pair with level q and assign the father with the level q−1. In other words, we replace the level sequence

$$l_1, \ l_2, \ \ldots, \ l_{i-1}, \ q, \ q, \ l_{i+2}, \ \ldots, \ l_n$$

by

$$l_1, \ l_2, \ \ldots, \ l_{i-1}, \ (q-1), \ l_{i+2}, \ \ldots, \ l_n.$$

Then we repeat the same process of combining maximum-level adjacent pairs to the new level sequence of n−1 numbers. Finally, we create the root with level zero.

Actually, we do not have to find the maximum level number in the whole level sequence. The following *stack algorithm* will successively construct an alphabetic tree. We first put $l_1, l_2, \ldots, l_n$ in a queue, with l_1 in the front of the queue. Then we remove l_i one at a time and put them into a stack, which is empty at the beginning.

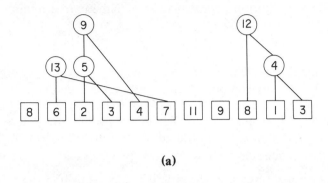

(a)

(b)

Figure 5.11

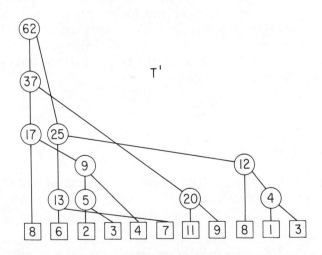

Figure 5.12

Step 0.   The stack is empty, $l_1, l_2, ..., l_n$ in the queue.

Step 1.   If there are less than two elements in the stack, go to Step 2. Otherwise, check to see if the top two elements of the stack are equal in value. Go to Step 2 if they are different and go to Step 3 if they are equal.

Step 2.   Remove the element in the front of the queue and put it on the top of the stack. Return to Step 1.

Step 3.   Let l_j be the top element of the stack and l_{j-1} be the element just below l_j. Replace l_{j-1} and l_j by $(l_j - 1)$. Stop if $l_j - 1$ equals zero. Otherwise, return to Step 1. (This means that the node V_{j-1} and V_j are combined and their father $V_{j-1,j}$ receives the level $l_j - 1$.)

(This reconstruction phase will be illustrated later.)

In the weight sequence shown in Figure 5.11(a), the minimum compatible pair is ① ③ and the next minimum compatible pairs are ② ③, ⑤ ④, ⑧ ④, and ⑥ ⑦ . Note that the last compatible pair ⑥ ⑦ is separated by a circular node ⑨. The resulting weight sequence after all the above combinations is shown in Figure 5.11(b). Note in Figure 5.11(b), the minimum compatible pair is ⑧   ⑨ since they are separated only by circular node ⑬ .

If we continue to apply this algorithm for the weight sequence in Figure 5.11(a), then we obtain the tree T' in Figure 5.12.

If we trace the path from the root in T' to every leaf we find the level numbers of the leaves are (from left to right)

weight w_i	⑧	⑥	②	③	④	⑦	⑪	⑨	⑧	⑪	③
level l_i	3	3	5	5	4	3	3	3	3	4	4

In the reconstruction phase, we will first combine ② ③ since they are at the lowest level. Their father ⑤ is then at the level 4 and we shall combine ⑤ and ④ since they are now the leftmost pair at the lowest level 4, and also combine ⑪ ③ which are both at the level 4.

After these combinations, every remaining node is at level 3 and they can be combined pair by pair from the left to right, and finally, we would get the tree T'_N in Figure 5.13a. Note that every leaf of T'_N has the same level number as T', but in T'_N, ⑥ ⑦ do not have a common father as they did in T'.

Here, we did not use the stack algorithm to reconstruct the tree, but simply looked for the maximum level numbers successively. If we had used the stack algorithm, then the successive contents of the stack would be as shown in Figure 5.13b.

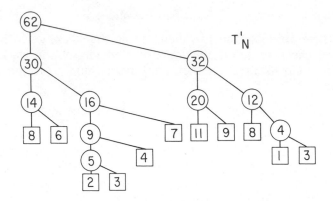

Figure 5.13a

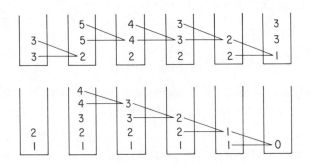

Figure 5.13b

(The reader should compare Figure 5.13a with Figure 5.13b and construct a proof himself that the stack algorithm works.)

The reader should do several numerical examples using the Hu-Tucker algorithm before going to the next section. (The reader can test his skill by solving the problem in § 3.3.)

In the combination phase, in order to combine the minimum compatible pair, we have to scan the entire weight sequence from left to right. Actually, this is not necessary. It is sufficient to combine the so-called *local minimum compatible pair*. The minimum compatible pair is a compatible pair with the smallest weight in the whole weight sequence, while a local minimum compatible pair is a compatible pair with its weight less than its neighboring compatible pairs.

A pair of nodes (w_b, w_c) is a *local minimum compatible pair* (l.m.c.p.) when the following are true:

$$w_a \geqslant w_c \quad \text{for all nodes } V_a \text{ compatible with } V_b$$

and
$$w_b \leqslant w_d \quad \text{for all nodes } V_d \text{ compatible with } V_c \ .$$

Note that when all nodes are square nodes, the pair (w_{j-1}, w_j) is an l.m.c.p. if

$$w_{j-2} > w_j$$
$$w_{j-1} \leqslant w_{j+1} \ .$$

For example, in Figure 5.11(a), the pair ② ③ is a local minimum compatible pair (l.m.c.p.) while ① ③ is the minimum compatible pair (m.c.p.). As soon as we spot an l.m.c.p., we could combine the pair *without* scanning the rest of the weight sequence. Similarly in Figure 5.11(b), as soon as we spot ⑧ ⑨ satisfying the condition of l.m.c.p., we could combine them without checking what is to the right of ① . (In this particular case, ⑧ ⑨ happens to be the m.c.p. as well.)

Since there are many l.m.c.p.'s in a weight sequence, should we combine the leftmost one first? Would the order in which we combine these l.m.c.p.'s make a difference?

In general, we can combine any l.m.c.p. until there is only one node left. The order of merging l.m.c.p. makes no difference. In fact, the tree obtained will always be the unique T'. We shall now prove the following lemma.

Lemma 4 Let V_a be an arbitrary node in a node sequence consisting of circular and square nodes, and w_i be the weight of the smallest node V_i compatible to V_a. If any l.m.c.p. is combined in the node sequence, and a new node V_d becomes compatible to V_a, then $w_i \leqslant w_d$. In particular, an l.m.c.p. in a node sequence will remain as an l.m.c.p. as other l.m.c.p.'s are successively combined.

Note that this Lemma implies that the tree obtained by arbitrarily combining l.m.c.p. in a node sequence is unique.

Proof. Let us focus on an arbitrary node V_a and assume w_i is the weight of the smallest node compatible to V_a.

Let the l.m.c.p. combined be (V_b, V_c) where V_a is closer to V_b. Then there is no square node between V_a and V_b, and at least V_b or V_c must be a square; otherwise the merger of (V_b, V_c) will not introduce new nodes (besides V_{bc}) compatible to V_a (see Figure 5.14).

Note that w_i could be on either side of V_a. The node w_i must be a circle if it is on the right side of V_a. Let V_d be a new node which becomes compatible to V_a after (V_b, V_c) is merged. (V_d could be a square or a circle.)

Then V_d must be compatible to V_c in the original sequence and by the local minimality of (V_b, V_c), $w_b \leqslant w_d$.

Figure 5.14

But $w_i \leqslant w_b$ as V_b is compatible to V_a in the original sequence and w_i is the smallest compatible weight by assumption. Thus $w_i \leqslant w_b \leqslant w_d$.

Since we have proven that the weight of the smallest node compatible to any node cannot decrease, then any l.m.c.p. (V_x,V_y) will remain as an l.m.c.p. even after other l.m.c.p. mergers, since V_x will remain the smallest node compatible to V_y and vice versa.

As every l.m.c.p. will eventually be combined, the order of combining l.m.c.p. is irrelevant, and the tree obtained by combining l.m.c.p. is unique.

§5.5 FEASIBILITY AND OPTIMALITY

In this section, we shall prove that the Hu-Tucker algorithm works. Remember that the algorithm consists of three steps:

(1)   combining l.m.c.p. to get the tree T'

(2)   getting the level number l_i of every leaf of T'

(3)   constructing an alphabetic tree T'_N using the l_i obtained in (2).

Thus, the algorithm has to satisfy three conditions:

(1)   The level numbers l_i of T' obtained in the level assignment are realizable by an alphabetic tree T'_N ("feasibility").

(2)   The tree T' must be optimum within a class of trees including all alphabetic trees ("optimality").

(3)   The optimality of T' must imply the optimality of T'_N

Since both trees have the same l_i's and the cost is defined to be $\Sigma w_i l_i$, the two trees cost the same, and condition (3) is satisfied.

To prove feasibility, we introduce a class C of trees and will show later that any tree in this class can be transformed into an alphabetic tree of equal cost.

Let T be a tree built from a given node sequence. We can decide if T belongs to the class C by the following steps.

(i)   Obtain the level number of every node in T.

(ii)   Do all combinations in T again, but in the following order. Reconstruct the tree T by combining nodes at the lowest level first, then the next-to-lowest level and so on. In other words, reconstruct the tree T from the bottom up. For nodes on the same level, the order of combination can be in any order as long as the restriction in (iii) is satisfied (but we must combine all nodes at a given level before we can combine nodes at the next higher level).

(iii)   In the level-by-level construction described in (ii), every combination must be a compatible pair in its node sequence.

If there exists a way of reconstructing T satisfying (i) (ii) (iii) then T belongs to the class C.

For example, the tree in Figure 5.15 is in this class, because the tree in Figure 5.15 could be constructed by merging (V_d, V_e) first, then (V_c, V_f), (V_{de}, V_{cf}), (V_a, V_b), and finally $(V_{ab}, V_{de,cf})$.

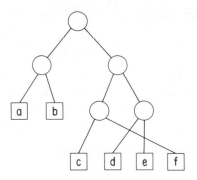

Figure 5.15

Note that we could construct the tree T in Figure 5.15 by merging (V_a, V_b) first and then merging (V_d, V_e), (V_c, V_f). The important thing is not how the tree T *was* constructed but how it can be *reconstructed* by merging compatible pairs, level-by-level from the bottom up.

For example, the tree in Figure 5.16 is not in C since there is no way to reconstruct the tree level-by-level from the bottom up.

The tree T in Figure 5.16 could be constructed by merging compatible pairs (V_c, V_d), (V_b, V_e), (V_a, V_f) and then (V_{af}, V_{cd}) and $(V_{af,cd}, V_{be})$. Here $l_a = l_c = l_d = l_f = 3$ and $l_b = l_e = 2$. According to the level-by-level construction, we should merge V_a, V_c, V_d, V_f first. We can merge compatible pairs (V_c, V_d) first but then (V_a, V_f) will still be separated by square nodes V_b, V_e.

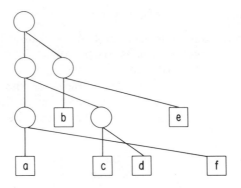

Figure 5.16

The level sequence of an alphabetic tree obviously admits a level-by-level construction. Hence the class C includes all alphabetic trees. The *first step* of the Hu-Tucker algorithm need not be a suitable first step for such a level-by-level *construction.*

For example, in Figure 5.12, we could merge ① ③ first in constructing the tree T′, although ① ③ is not at the lowest level. But once T′ is formed, there is a way of reconstructing T′ level-by-level from the bottom using only compatible pairs. Hence T′ belongs to the class C. (The proof appears later.) This level-by-level construction of a tree T is denoted by C(T).

Theorem 1 The level sequence of leaves of any tree T in C is realizable by an alphabetic tree.

Proof. A level sequence is realizable if the lowest level nodes occur in even-length consecutive blocks, and after replacing consecutive pairs on the lowest level from left to right by their fathers, the same condition holds while this process is iterated to the top.

Since every node has a brother, the number of nodes at a level k must be even. If the nodes occur in even-length blocks, then they can be merged two at a time from left to right in each block, and the process can be repeated recursively for the nodes at level k−1.

If the nodes at the level k do not occur in even-length blocks, then there must be a pair of nodes V_a, V_d which is separated by a leaf, V_b say, at a higher level than k; i.e., $l_b < l_a$.

This means that (V_a, V_d) is not compatible and contradicts the assumption that the tree T is in C.   Q.E.D.

We shall use the notation

$V_i < V_j$ to mean V_i is formed before V_j (equality indicates they are the same node)

$V_i \sim V_j$ to mean V_i and V_j are compatible. Note that if $V_i \sim V_j$ and both of them are circular nodes, then they are compatible to precisely the same set of nodes.

If a circular node V_{bc} is formed *before* a circular node V_{ad}, and V_{bc} has a son which lies between two sons of V_{ad}, then we say the node V_{ad} *crosses* over V_{bc}. We denote the crossing relationship by

$$V_{bc} \lesssim V_{ad}$$

Note that the notation indicates that V_{ad} is formed after V_{bc} and that V_{bc} and V_{ad} become compatible after both of them are formed. For example, in Figure 5.15, we have $V_{de} \lesssim V_{cf}$.

We shall now prove that the Hu-Tucker algorithm for constructing T' by combining l.m.c.p. successively, satisfies the following Lemma.

Lemma 5 In the construction of T' by the Hu-Tucker algorithm, if $V_{bc} \lesssim V_{ad}$ (V_{bc} is crossed over in the formation of V_{ad}), then

(i) $w_{bc} < w_{ad}$ (weight of V_{bc} < weight of V_{ad}),

(ii) $V_{bc,i} \leqslant V_{ad,j}$ (V_{bc} merges before or with V_{ad}),

(iii) $w_{bc,i} \leqslant w_{ad,j}$ (the weight of the node formed by the merger of V_{bc} is less than or equal to that formed by the merger of V_{ad}),

(iv) $l_{bc} \geqslant l_{ad}$ (the path length of V_{bc} is no less than that of V_{ad}).

Proof. Without loss of generality, we assume that V_b is to the left of V_c and V_a is to the left of V_d. In order to have V_{ad} cross over V_{bc}, the node sequence must be (V_a, V_b, V_c, V_d), (V_b, V_a, V_c, V_d), or (V_a, V_b, V_d, V_c). Thus we shall assume that the node sequence is V_a, V_b, V_c, V_d. The same argument will apply for other node sequences. If there are nodes interspersed between the four nodes, they must be circular nodes, and they will not affect the argument.

(i) $V_b \sim V_a$ implies $w_a > w_c$ (From Lemma 4, V_c will remain as the smallest node compatible to V_b, and V_b will remain as the smallest node compatible to V_c.)

$V_c \sim V_d$ implies $w_b \leqslant w_d$

since (V_b, V_c) is a l.m.c.p.

$$w_b + w_c \leqslant w_c + w_d < w_a + w_d \text{ (as } w_b \leqslant w_d \text{ \& } w_c < w_a)$$

or $w_{bc} < w_{ad}$.   This proves (i).

But both w_{bc} and w_{ad} are circular nodes, so they are compatible to precisely the same set of nodes from this point on. The fact that $w_{bc} < w_{ad}$ requires w_{bc} be combined first with another node, say w_i. Thus $V_{bc,i} < V_{ad,j}$. (If w_{bc} is combined with w_{ad}, then $V_{bc,i} = V_{ad,j}$.) This proves (ii).

Since V_{bc} and V_{ad} are compatible to precisely the same set of nodes, and from Lemma 4, the weight of the smallest node compatible to V_{bc} or V_{ad} cannot decrease. This means $w_i \leqslant w_j$, and since $w_{bc} < w_{ad}$, we have (iii).

Statements (ii) and (iii) mean that V_{bc} merges first before V_{ad} does, and V_{bc}'s father has smaller weight. It follows similarly that its father also merges first and its grandfather has smaller weight. Iteration of this statement implies that V_{bc}'s kth merger precedes that of V_{ad}, so that if the level of V_{ad} is l_{ad}, the level of V_{bc} is at least that large.

This proves (iv).

Theorem 2 The level numbers of leaves of T' can be realized by an alphabetic tree.

Proof. If the nodes of T' at any level always occur in even-length blocks, then T' can be made alphabetic as in the proof of Theorem 1.

If the nodes at the level k do not occur in even-length blocks, then there must be a pair of nodes (V_a, V_d) which is separated by a leaf V_b at a level higher than k; i.e., $l_b < l_a$. We shall show this will lead to a contradiction.

In the tree T', the node V_b must be merged with another node V_c before V_a and V_d are merged. So V_{bc} is crossed over by V_{ad}. By Lemma 5, $l_{bc} \geqslant l_{ad}$ or $l_b \geqslant l_a$. (Note that this argument also shows T' is in C.)   **Q.E.D.**

Having proved the feasibility, we now turn to the question of optimality.

First, we introduce the notion of a generalized initial sequence. A generalized initial sequence S* is a sequence of circular and square nodes. A binary tree built on S* is a binary tree with circular and square nodes at its leaves. Since all circular nodes are crossable, the relative positions of all the circular nodes between two square nodes are irrelevant. A sequence S of squares is a special case of S*. The cost of a binary tree built on S* is again defined to be $\Sigma w_i l_i$ where w_i are the weights of circular and square nodes and l_i are their level numbers.

Given a sequence S*, the set of circular nodes between two square nodes can be combined without any order restriction. We shall call the set of circular nodes a Huffman's set. Given two circular nodes V_a and V_b in the same Huffman's set and $w_a < w_b$, then the level numbers in the optimum tree built on S* must have $l_a \geqslant l_b$. Thus, we can generalize Lemma 3 (Extreme Set Lemma) to the case of an optimum binary tree built on S*.

Lemma 6 (Extreme Set Lemma). Let T denote the optimum binary tree built on a generalized initial sequence S* where w_i are weights of circular nodes which form a Huffman's set. Let T_u denote the optimum normalized binary tree built on the same sequence S* except the weight w_i are replaced by w_i'. If the following conditions are satisfied, then the cost of T is less than or equal to the cost of T_u.

(i) $\displaystyle\sum_{i=1}^{n} w_i = \sum_{i=1}^{n} w_i'$

(ii) $w_1 \leqslant w_2 \leqslant ... \leqslant w_n$; $w_1' \leqslant w_2' \leqslant ... \leqslant w_n'$

(iii) $w_i + \delta_i = w_i'$ $(i = 1,...,k-1)$

and $w_i - \delta_i = w_i'$ $(i = k,...,n)$

$\delta_j \geqslant 0$ $(j = 1,...,n)$

Proof. Same as Lemma 3.

This lemma, as well as Lemma 3, has not been stated in the literature and should be useful on many occasions.

We have introduced a class C of trees which can be constructed by merging compatible pairs and form level-by-level upward. We have also shown that this class C includes alphabetic trees as well as the tree T' constructed by the Hu-Tucker algorithm. Then it was shown that T' can be transformed into an alphabetic tree of equal cost.

Now we have to prove that T' is optimum within the class C. To do this, we introduce a class C* which includes C and then shows that T' is optimum in the class C*. The class C* is a natural generalization of the class C. A tree T built on a generalized sequence S* belongs to the class C* if there exists a way of reconstructing T by merging compatible pairs level-by-level from the bottom up. The only difference between C* and C is that the trees in C* are built on S* while the trees in C are built on S. The class C* obviously includes the class C as S is a special case of S*. Since we are to prove that T' is an optimum tree in the class C*, we are not concerned whether every tree (built on S*) in C* can be transformed into an alphabetic tree of the same cost.

The class C* of trees built on S* can also be characterized as follows:

(i)   every combination is a compatible pair in its node sequence S* ,

(ii)   if V_b and V_c are two nodes in the generalized initial sequence S* with at least one of the two nodes being a square node, and $V_{bc} \lesssim V_{ad}$ where V_a and V_d are also nodes in S* then $l_{bc} \geqslant l_{ad}$.

Note that the condition (ii) is equivalent to the level-by-level construction, and that Lemma 4 and Lemma 5 are true for a generalized initial sequence S*. Thus the class C* of trees includes alphabetic trees as well as T' built on S*.

Theorem 3 Given a generalized initial sequence S*, there is an optimum tree in C* built on S* whose combinations are all l.m.c.p.'s.

Proof. The proof is by induction on the number of nodes in S*. Assume that the theorem is true for a generalized initial sequence of n−1 nodes or less. Now consider the case of n nodes in S*.

If there is no optimum tree in the class C* whose first pair is l.m.c.p., then pick the optimum tree T° whose first pair has the total weight as small as possible, say (V_b, V_c). After (V_b, V_c) is combined in S*, then there are n−1 nodes in S*, and by the induction hypothesis, the rest of the mergers can all be chosen to be l.m.c.p.'s. The situation is shown in Figure 5.17.

Figure 5.17

Assume that both V_b and V_c are square nodes and

$\quad\quad$ V_a is the smallest node compatible to V_b and on its left

$\quad\quad$ V_d is the smallest node compatible to V_c and on its right

$\quad\quad$ V_x is the smallest node compatible to V_a and on its left

V_y is the smallest node compatible V_d and on its right.

(If some of the nodes are not squares, the proof is similar.)

Consider now the second merger which by assumption is an l.m.c.p.. There are four conceivable cases:

(i)   The second pair is of the form (V_{bc}, V_d) or (V_a, V_{bc}). Since (V_b, V_c) is not l.m.c.p., we must have either $w_a \leqslant w_c$ or $w_b > w_d$. Suppose $w_b > w_d$. (The case $w_a \leqslant w_c$ is similar.) Let the second pair be (V_{bc}, V_d), then the combinations (V_b, V_{cd}) would create a cheaper tree contradicting that $T°$ is optimum. Let the second pair be (V_a, V_{bc}). Since $V_c \sim V_d$, then $V_{bc} \sim V_d$ and V_d would be compatible to any node which is compatible to V_{bc}. But $w_b + w_c > w_b > w_d$ so the pair (V_a, V_{bc}) is of greater weight than that of (V_a, V_d) contradicting that (V_a, V_{bc}) is an l.m.c.p..

(ii)   The second pair is (V_r, V_s), an l.m.c.p. in the sequence S^*, and the merger (V_r, V_s) does not cross over V_{bc}. In this case, we could merge (V_r, V_s) first, obtain a generalized sequence of n−1 nodes. Then we can do the rest of the combinations in l.m.c.p. by the induction hypothesis.

(iii)   It is (V_d, V_y) where (V_d, V_y) was not l.m.c.p. in the original sequence S^* but becomes an l.m.c.p. after (V_b, V_c) is combined. Since (V_d, V_y) was not l.m.c.p. in S^*, we have

$$w_c < w_y \tag{1}$$

As (V_d, V_y) is l.m.c.p. after (V_b, V_c) is combined, we have

$$w_a > w_y . \tag{2}$$

There are two subcases:

    (a) $w_b < w_d$. From (1) and (2) we have $w_c < w_y < w_a$ which would imply (V_b, V_c) is l.m.c.p., a contradiction.

    (b) $w_b > w_d$. From (1), we see (V_c, V_d) is l.m.c.p.. Furthermore, (V_c, V_d), (V_b, V_y) is a more extreme set. (Lemma 6)

(iv)   The second pair is (V_a, V_d) which crosses over V_{bc}. There are four subcases:

    (a) $w_a > w_c$, $w_b < w_d$, then (V_b, V_c) is l.m.c.p., a contradiction.

(b) $w_a > w_c$, $w_b > w_d$, then the set w_{ab}, w_{cd} is a more extreme set than w_{bc}, w_{ad} and $w_c + w_d < w_b + w_c$ contradicting that the weight of the first pair is smallest.

(c) $w_a < w_c$ and $w_b < w_d$, then $w_a + w_b < w_b + w_c$, the same contradiction as (b).

(d) $w_a < w_c$, $w_b > w_d$, the set (w_{ab}, w_{cd}) costs the same as (w_{bc}, w_{ad}) due to $l_{bc} \geq l_{ad}$. And $w_a + w_b < w_b + w_c$ contradicts that the weight of the first pair is minimum.

In summary, we have introduced a class C of trees (built on S) which is a subclass of the class C* of trees built on S*. The class C includes alphabetic trees as well as T′ constructed by the Hu-Tucker algorithm. We have showed that T′ can be transformed into an alphabetic tree T_N of equal cost. To prove the optimality of the Hu-Tucker algorithm, we show that there exists an optimum tree (in C*) which is built by merging l.m.c.p. in S*. Since merging l.m.c.p. gives the unique tree T′, the tree T′ is an optimum tree in C* and in its subclass C.

§5.6 GARSIA AND WACHS ALGORITHM

In the combination phase of the Hu-Tucker algorithm, we successively combine l.m.c.p. while the pair in consideration could be separated by many circular nodes. The Garsia and Wachs algorithm eliminates the distinction between circular and square nodes and arranges the weight sequence such that the l.m.c.p. is always an adjacent pair. As we have mentioned in §5.4, in a sequence of square nodes, an adjacent pair (w_{j-1}, w_j) is an l.m.c.p. if and only if

$$w_{j-2} > w_j$$

and $\quad\quad w_{j-1} \leq w_{j+1}$

Now we state the Garsia-Wachs implementation.

Let $w_1, w_2, ..., w_{j-1}, w_j, w_{j+1}, ..., w_n$ be the weight sequence.

(i)   Find the leftmost minimal adjacent pair, $w_{j-1} + w_j$.

(ii)   Combine w_{j-1} and w_j as a single node with weight $w_j^* = w_{j-1} + w_j$.

(iii)   Move w_j^* to the left, skipping over all nodes with weight less than or equal to w_j^*. Obtain the new working sequence of $n-1$ nodes

$$w_1, ..., w_i, w_j^*, w_{i+1}, ..., w_{j-2}, w_{j+1}, ..., w_n$$

where $w_i > w_j^* \geq \max(w_{i+1}, ..., w_{j-2})$.

Repeat the process until we get only one node in the node sequence. This is the tree T′ in the Hu-Tucker algorithm. The rest of the algorithm is the same as Hu-Tucker.

If we apply this implementation to the weight sequence in Figure 5.11(a), we have the successive steps shown in Figure 5.18.

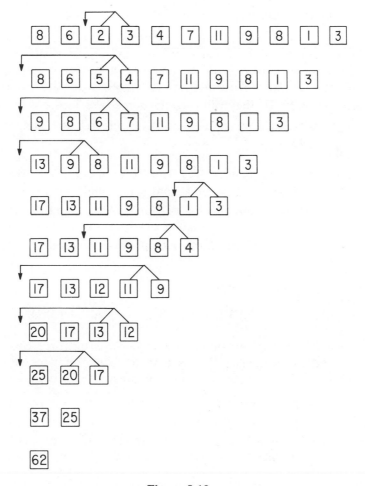

Figure 5.18

Note each of these combinations is the leftmost l.m.c.p. in the Hu-Tucker algorithm. If we scanned (from left to right) for an l.m.c.p. in the weight sequence, we would make precisely these combinations.

To show that the two algorithms will obtain the same tree T', consider the following two sequences (A) and (B).

(A) $w_1, w_2, \ldots, w_i, w_j^*, w_{i+1}, \ldots, w_{j-2}, w_{j+1}, \ldots, w_n$

(all nodes are squares).

(B) $w_1, w_2, \ldots, w_i, w_{i+1}, \ldots, w_{j-2}, w_j^*, w_{j+1}, \ldots, w_n$

(all square nodes except w_j^* which is circular node).

Note that (A) consists of $n-1$ squares and is derived from a sequence of n squares after one combination of Garsia-Wachs; and (B) consists of $n-2$ squares and one circle, and is derived from the same sequence of n squares after one combination of Hu-Tucker. We will show that if we apply the Hu-Tucker algorithm to both (A) and (B), they will give the same tree T', i.e. all combinations will be identical. (If a node w_p combines with w_j^* of (A), the same node w_p will combine with w_j^* in (B)).

Now consider two sequences (A$'$) and (B$'$) where (A$'$) consists of $n-2$ squares and (B$'$) consists $n-3$ squares and one circle. The sequence (A$'$) is derived from (A) after one combination of Garsia-Wachs, and the sequence (B$'$) is derived from (A) after one combination of Hu-Tucker. Again, we can show that applying the Hu-Tucker algorithm to sequences (A$'$) and (B$'$) will give the same tree T'.

Similarly, we can obtain many sequences

$$(A), (B), \quad (A'), (B'), \quad (A''), (B''), \quad \ldots, \quad (A^{n-2}), (B^{n-2})$$

where the sequence (A$''$) is derived from a sequence after three combinations of Garsia-Wachs, and the sequence (B$''$) is derived from the same sequence after two combinations of Garsia-Wachs and one combination of Hu-Tucker.

Essentially, we can show that the tree constructed by any number of combinations of Garsia-Wachs followed by l.m.c.p. will be the tree T' as defined in the Hu-Tucker algorithm. In particular, the sequences (A), (A$'$), ..., (A^{n-2}) are the sequences generated by the Garsia-Wachs algorithm.

To show that (A) and (B) will give the same tree T', we can make three observations about the merging of l.m.c.p. in the sequence (B).

Observation 1. In the subsequence of nodes $w_1, \ldots, w_i, w_{i+1}, \ldots, w_{j-2}$, a node cannot be merged before a node to its right is merged. This is because $w_{j-1} + w_j \ (= w_j^*)$ is the leftmost minimal adjacent pair.

Observation 2. When w_j^* is merged, $w_{i+1}, \ldots, w_{j-2}$ have all been merged (or merged with w_j^*). If this is not true, let w_l be the rightmost node among $w_{i+1},...,w_{j-2}$ which has not been merged. From observation 1, all the nodes between w_l and w_j^* have been merged and w_l is compatible to any node compatible to the circular node w_j^* in (B) and $w_l \leqslant w_j^*$. Hence w_j^* cannot form an l.m.c.p. with another node.

Observation 3. When an l.m.c.p. is between a node in $w_1,...,w_i$ and a node in $w_{i+1},...,w_n$, then w_j^* has been merged. Let the l.m.c.p. be (w_x,w_y) where w_x is either a node in $w_1,...,w_i$ or a sum of at least two nodes in $w_1,...,w_i$. Since $w_j^* = w_{j-1} + w_j$ is the leftmost minimal adjacent pair

$$w_1 + w_2 > w_2 + w_3 > ... > w_{i-1} + w_i$$

or

$$w_1 > w_3 > w_5 > ...$$

$$w_2 > w_4 > w_6 > ...$$

Thus one of the two adjacent nodes is larger than w_i. Thus $w_x > w_i \geqslant w_j^*$. Let w_y be the right node. From observation 1, when w_y is merged, all the nodes between w_y and w_j^* have been merged and $w_y \sim w_j^*$. But $w_x > w_i > w_j^*$, this contradicts that (w_x,w_y) is l.m.c.p. if w_j^* has not been merged.

From the above three observations, we can now consider the sequences (A) and (B). Before w_j^* in either (A) or (B) is merged, from observation 3, the two sequences (A) and (B) can do exactly the same combinations since $w_1,...,w_i$ are not involved and w_j^* is a circular node in (B). From observation 2, when w_j^* is merged in (B), all the nodes between w_i and w_{j+1} are circular nodes. So the square node w_j^* in (A) and the circular node w_j^* in (B) are compatible to the same set of nodes. After w_j^* is merged, sequences (A) and (B) result in the same node sequence.

§5.7 REGULAR COST FUNCTIONS

We have given two algorithms for constructing optimum trees: the Huffman algorithm for the non-alphabetic case and the Hu-Tucker algorithm for the alphabetic case. The cost of a tree is defined to be $\Sigma w_i l_i$. In the problem of coding, the cost function is equivalent to the average rate of transmitting information. In file-searching, the cost function is a measure of the average number of steps to locate a file. If we are not concerned with the average but with the worst case, then the cost function should be defined as

$$\max_i \quad w_i l_i$$

On the other hand, if the cost of accessing a record V_i is not linear, but exponential in the path length, then it makes sense to minimize

$$\sum w_i t^{l_i}$$

where t is a constant.

When the cost function is not $\sum w_i l_i$, do we need a new algorithm to construct optimum binary trees? The answer is "no". We can modify Huffman's algorithm and the Hu-Tucker algorithm slightly to cover many different cost functions.

We shall define the class of functions which includes the cost function $\sum w_i l_i$. Any function belonging to this class can be handled by the modified Huffman algorithm and the modified Hu-Tucker algorithm.

Example 3

Given $(w_1, w_2, ..., w_5) = (4,2,3,4,7)$, find an optimum alphabetic tree minimizing
$$\max_i \; w_i(2^{l_i})$$
.

Solution: Find the minimum weight compatible pair ② ③ and replace the two nodes by their father with weight

$$2 \cdot \max(2,3) = 6$$

Find the minimum weight compatible pair in the node sequence

④ ⑥④ ⑦

and replace ④ ④ by their father with weight

$$2 \cdot \max(4,4) = 8 \; .$$

Continuing in this fashion, we get the tree T' in Figure 5.19. Note that the weight of a pair (w_a, w_b) is defined to be

$$2 \cdot \max(w_a, w_b) \; .$$

As in the Hu-Tucker algorithm, we can transform the tree T' into an alphabetic tree T'_N as shown in Figure 5.20.

Here the difference is in assigning the weight of a father formed by merging two compatible nodes. In other words,

$$w_{ij} = f(w_i, w_j) \; . \tag{1}$$

We shall denote the value of the cost function of T by |T| and consider the properties that the cost function must satisfy.

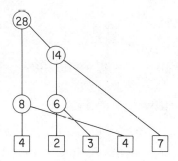

Figure 5.19

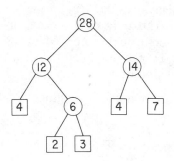

Figure 5.20

Properties of regular cost functions

P1 $|T|$ cannot increase, if any of its weights are replaced by a smaller weight.

P2   For all w_a, w_b, and w_x

$$f(w_a, w_b) = f(w_b, w_a)$$

$$w_a \leqslant f(w_a, w_x)$$

and $w_a \leqslant w_b \iff f(w_a, w_x) \leqslant f(w_b, w_x)$

P3   If $w_b \leqslant w_c$ and $l_b \geqslant l_c$, then interchanging V_b and V_c cannot decrease the cost of the tree.

P4   Let T be a tree with n nodes and in which V_a and V_b are merged. And let T^* be the tree of n−1 nodes resulting from the merger with the father of V_a and V_b having the weight $f(w_a, w_b)$. Then there exists a function

$\theta(w_a, w_b)$ such that

$$|T| = \theta(w_a, w_b) + |T^*| \ .$$

P5   The functions $f(w_a, w_b)$ and $\theta(w_a, w_b)$ in P4 must satisfy the following conditions if $w_b \leqslant w_c$:

$$f[f(w_a, w_b), \ w_c] \leqslant f[f(w_a, w_c), \ w_b]$$

$$\theta(w_a, w_b) + \theta[f(w_a, w_b), w_c] \leqslant \theta(w_a, w_c) + \theta[f(w_a, w_c), w_b]$$

Roughly speaking, properties P2-P5 insure that the two smallest nodes of a three-node tree or a four-node tree should be combined if the two nodes are compatible. The function $|T|$ is called a regular function if there exists f and θ such that P1 to P5 are satisfied. All the examples mentioned before have *regular cost functions*.

It is easy to verify whether a cost function satisfies the properties. If it does, then we can essentially use the Hu-Tucker algorithm in constructing the optimum alphabetic tree. The only difference is in assigning the weight of a father during merging of a compatible pair. When the alphabetic constraint is not present, the tree formed by the modified Huffman algorithm is an optimum binary tree for the cost function.

The following are some examples of regular cost functions.

1. $\Theta(w_x, w_y) = w_x + w_y = f(w_x, w_y)$

$|T| = \Sigma w_i l_i$ (Hu-Tucker) $|T|$ of a single node $= 0$

2. $\Theta(w_x, w_y) = 0, f(w_x, w_y) = t(w_x + w_y), t \geqslant 1$

$|T| = w(\text{root}) = \sum_i t^{l_i} w_i$ (power summation)

$|T|$ of a single node $=$ the weight of the node.

3. $\Theta(w_x, w_y) = 0, f(w_x, w_y) = t \bullet \max(w_x, w_y)$

$|T| = w(\text{root}) = \max_i t^{l_i} w_i$ (min$-$max)

$|T|$ of a single node $=$ the weight of the node

4. $\Theta(w_x, w_y) = 0$ and let g be any function, for which $g(x) > x$, and increasing for all relevant x in the range of the problem.

$$f(w_x, w_y) = \max\ (g(w_x), g(w_y))$$

$|T|$ of a single node $=$ the weight of the node

$$|T| = \max_i g^{\cdot^{l_i}} (w_i)\ \ (\text{min}-\text{max})$$

In all these cases, verification of the regular cost functions are trivial.

§5.8 T-ARY TREE AND OTHER RESULTS

Consider a weight sequence $w_1, w_2, ..., w_{j-1}, w_j, ..., w_n$ where

$$w_1 > w_2 > w_3 > ... > w_{j-1} \leqslant w_j \leqslant w_{j+1} ... \leqslant w_n \qquad (1)$$

In other words, the weights are first decreasing and then increasing. Such a weight sequence is called a *valley sequence*. As two special cases of a valley sequence, we have

$$w_1 > w_2 > ... > w_n \qquad (2a)$$

or $\qquad\qquad w_1 \leqslant w_2 \leqslant ... \leqslant w_n \qquad\qquad\qquad\quad (2b)$

Lemma 7 If the weight sequence is a valley sequence, then the cost of the optimum alphabetic tree is the same as the cost of the optimum tree without the alphabetic constraint.

Proof. Assume that the weight sequence is like (1) and the l.m.c.p. is $w_{j-1} + w_j$ (or $w_{j-2} + w_{j-1}$). Then $w_{j-1,j}^*$ is a circular node and the next minimum weight pair may be one of the following five pairs:

$$w_{j-2} + w_{j+1}$$

$$w_{j-3} + w_{j-2}$$

$$w_{j+1} + w_{j+2}$$

$$w_{j-2} + w_{j-1,j}^*$$

$$w_{j-1,j}^* + w_{j+1}$$

In any case, the node constructed, call it w_A, is a circular node.

In general, let $w_A \leqslant w_B \leqslant ... \leqslant w_G$ be circular nodes created, while on the left, we have

$$w_1 > w_2 > ... > w_{j-2}$$

and on the right, we have

$$w_{j+1} \leqslant ... \leqslant w_n\ .$$

Then the next l.m.c.p. (the only one) is one of the following six pairs:

$$w_A + w_B$$

$$w_{j-2} + w_{j+1}$$

$$w_{j-3} + w_{j-2}$$

$$w_{j+1} + w_{j+2}$$

$$w_{j-2} + w_A$$

$$w_A + w_{j+1} \ .$$

So the next circular node created w_H is again compatible to all the circular nodes created so far.

In other words, the minimum weight compatible pair is always the minimum weight pair. Since $|T'| = |T_N'|$, the cost of the optimum alphabetic tree is the same as Huffman's tree. For other cost functions, the argument is the same.

Lemma 8 There exists a Huffman tree with

$$w_1 \leqslant w_2 \leqslant ... \leqslant w_n$$

$$l_1 \geqslant l_2 \geqslant ... \geqslant l_n$$

and the nodes from the left to right are $w_1, w_2, ..., w_n$.

Proof. We can first sort the weights of leaves into an increasing sequence and then put them in alphabetic order from left to right. The weight sequence is then a special case of a valley sequence, so from Lemma 7, the optimum alphabetic tree costs the same as Huffman's tree. Furthermore, if the path lengths do not satisfy

$$l_1 \geqslant l_2 \geqslant ... \geqslant l_n$$

we can interchange the nodes with a decrease in cost contradicting that the original binary tree is optimum.   Q.E.D.

We now consider the question: which of our results generalize to ternary or k-ary tree? In a k-ary tree, all internal nodes will have k "sons". The following example shows that the Hu-Tucker algorithm which replaces minimal compatible triple nodes, w_a, w_b and w_c by $w_a + w_b + w_c$ does not minimize $\Sigma w_i l_i$.

The Hu-Tucker tree has level sequence $(2,2,2,2,2,2,1)$ with cost 66, as shown in Figure 5.21; but the tree in Figure 5.22 has cost 62.

We can define minimum compatible triple (m.c.t.) just as we define minimum compatible pair (m.c.p.). But for local minimality, there are various

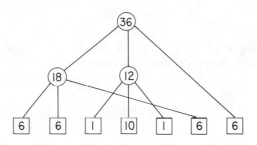

Figure 5.21

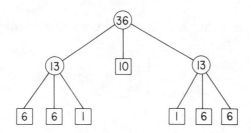

Figure 5.22

definitions for triples. We define a weak local minimum compatible triple (w.l.m.c.t.) to be (w_a, w_b, w_c) such that any one of the three nodes is the smallest one compatible to the other two.

For "minimax" cost functions, such as that of Example 3 of section 5.7 it can be shown that there is a "class C" construction all of whose merges are w.l.m.c.t.'s. Furthermore, by use of the following trick and a tie-breaking rule, one can insure that such w.l.m.c.t.'s do not overlap, and can therefore show that an optimal tree can be constructed by the ternary analogue of the Hu-Tucker algorithm.

Since in the merge step of Example 3, the algorithm gives the new node a weight t times the maximum weight of its offspring, there is no change in the tree cost if the weight of the other offspring are increased to that maximum. Again merging a w.l.m.c.t. cannot decrease the minimum compatible triple. The Hu-Tucker type algorithm therefore works for the ternary min-max problem.

Whether there is a method of handling the ternary case in greater generality remains an open question.

EXERCISES

1.   If the encoding is the one shown in Figure 5.4(a), what does the sequence 0111111 mean? Translate this into the encoding system 5.4(b).

2.   Prove Lemma 6.

3.   Construct an optimum alphabetic tree based on the following sequences of weights:

   (i)   3, 4, 5, 6, 4, 2

   (ii)   2, 6, 3, 5, 4, 4

   (iii)   6, 4, 3, 2, 2, 5.

4.   Given a set of weights 2, 3, 4, 4, 5, 6 construct a binary tree such that

$$\max_{i} w_i \left(\frac{1}{2}\right)^{l_i} \text{ is minimized.}$$

5.   Construct an alphabetic binary tree such that

$$\max_{i} w_i t^{l_i} \text{ is minimized}$$

Consider the case (i) $t \geqslant 1$, (ii) $t < 1$.

CHAPTER 5

BIBLIOGRAPHIC NOTES AND SUGGESTED READING

The algorithm for constructing optimum binary trees was discovered by Huffman [9]. Glassey and Kary [2] showed that the same algorithm can be used for other cases of binary trees. Most of these papers treat the subject of binary trees as a problem in coding.

Using dynamic programming techniques, Gilbert and Moore [3] construct optimum alphabetic trees. Their algorithm is $0(n^3)$ in speed and $0(n^2)$ in memory space.

By modifying the dynamic programming procedure, Knuth [12] reduces the Gilbert and Moore algorithm to $0(n^2)$ in speed but still $0(n^2)$ in space. The algorithm for constructing optimum alphabetic trees was due to Hu and Tucker [8] which requires $0(n)$ space. Knuth [13] gives an excellent description of the Hu-Tucker algorithm and shows how to implement the Hu-Tucker algorithm in $0(n \log n)$ speed. So the current bound is $0(n \log n)$ in speed and $0(n)$ in space. The same bound is achieved in Garsia and Wachs [1]. The proof of equivalence of the two algorithms follows from the suggestions of Mr. Y. S. Kuo.

The proof of the Hu-Tucker algorithm [1], [4], [8] remains long and tedious. The current proof in this chapter is a modification of the proof in [5] which also generalizes both the Huffman tree and the Hu-Tucker tree to different cost functions. Other papers relating to optimum alphabetic trees are [6], [7], [10].

For papers dealing with optimum prefix codes, see [11], [14].

1. A. M. Garsia and M. L. Wachs, "A New Algorithm for Minimal Binary Search Trees", SIAM J. Computing 6 (1977), pp. 622-642.

2. C. R. Glassey and R. M. Karp, "On the Optimality of Huffman Trees", ORC 74-21, Univ. of California, Berkeley, 1974.

3. E. N. Gilbert and E. F. Moore, "Variable Length Binary Encodings", Bell System Tech. J. 38 (1959), pp. 933-968.

4. T. C. Hu, "A New Proof of T-C Algorithms", SIAM J. on Appl. Math. 25 (1973), pp. 83-94.

5. T. C. Hu, D. J. Kleitman, and J. K. Tamaki, "Binary Trees Optimum under Various Criteria", to appear in SIAM on Appl. Math. 37(2) (1979), pp. 246-256.

6. T. C. Hu and K. C. Tan, "Path Length of Binary Search Trees", M.R.C. Report 1111, Univ. of Wisconsin, Nov. 1970.

7. T. C. Hu and K. C. Tan, "Least Upper Bound on the Cost of Optimum Binary Search Trees", Acta Informatica 1 (1972), pp. 307-310.

8. T. C. Hu and A. C. Tucker, "Optimal Computer-search Trees and Variable-Length Alphabetic Codes", SIAM J. on Appl. Math. 21 (1971), pp. 514-532.

9. D. A. Huffman, "A Method for the Construction of Minimum Redundancy Codes", Proc. IRE 40 (1952), pp. 1098-1101.

10. A. Itai, "Optimal Alphabetic Trees", SIAM J. Computing 5(1) (1976), pp. 9-18.

11. R. M. Karp, "Minimum-Redundancy Code for the Discrete Noiseless Channel", IEEE Trans. Information Theory IT-7 (1961), pp. 27-39.

12. D. E. Knuth, "Optimum Binary Search Trees", Acta Informatica 1 (1971), pp. 14-25.

13. D. E. Knuth, "Searching and Sorting", Addison-Wesley, 1973.

14. Y. Perl, M. R. Garey, and S. Even, "Efficient Generation of Optimal Prefix Code: Equiprobable Words Using Unequal Cost Letters", J. ACM 22(2) (1975), pp. 202-214.

ANSWERS TO EXERCISES - CHAPTER 5

1. ADD, 001100 .

2. Write $w_i + \delta_i = w_i'$, then

$$\sum_i w_i' l_{i'} = \sum_i w_i l_{i'} + s \quad \text{where } s \geqslant 0 \ .$$

3. The level sequences are

    (i)   3, 3, 2, 2, 3, 3

    (ii)   3, 3, 3, 3, 2, 2

    (iii)   2, 3, 3, 3, 3, 2

4. We always combine the two largest weights w_p, w_q and let their father have the weight

$$w_{pq} = \left(\frac{1}{2}\right) \bullet \max(w_p, w_q).$$

5. Let the father have the weight $t \bullet \max(w_i, w_j)$ where w_i, w_j is the largest or the smallest l.m.c.p. Choose the smallest pair if $t \geqslant 1$ and the largest pair if $t < 1$.

    (when $t < 1$, l.m.c.p. means local maximum compatible pair)

CHAPTER 6. HEURISTIC ALGORITHMS

Optimum is hard to achieve; near-optimum is usually good enough.

§6.1 GREEDY ALGORITHMS

In all the previous chapters, we have studied only optimum algorithms - algorithms that give optimum solutions to problems. Some optimum algorithms are efficient, some optimum algorithms are tedious. Many optimum algorithms require such a long time that they cannot be used in practice.

In the real world, most problems have to be solved before a given deadline. Thus people either use a commercial code which is not tailor-made for the problem, or they invent heuristic algorithms - algorithms which intuitively seem to be all right or which do obtain optimum solutions sometimes. Since a heuristic algorithm does not always get the optimum solution, two natural questions are:

1)   When does the heuristic algorithm get the optimum solution?

2)   If the heuristic algorithm fails to obtain the optimum solution, what is the maximum percentage error?

For the first question, we like to characterize the input data and obtain necessary and sufficient conditions for the heuristic algorithm to work. If a heuristic algorithm works for most of the input data or its maximum percentage error is tolerable, we may prefer the heuristic algorithm to an optimum algorithm that' requires a long time.

Most heuristic algorithms are based on human intuition, and these algorithms cannot be easily analyzed. In the game of chess, where the optimum solution is to capture the king, a heuristic algorithm may be to capture as many pieces as possible. However, to capture a pawn of your opponent is like winning a battle and it may force you to lose the war at the end. (Indeed, it is a well-known practice to sacrifice a pawn in order to capture the opponent's king.) So, here is a heuristic algorithm which does not give the optimum solutions.

However, there are problems where doing the best locally will lead to the optimum solutions. For example, in the problem of minimum spanning tree (§ 1.7), we select the shortest arc adjacent to a component which does not form a cycle. The successive application of this step does get the minimum spanning tree at the end.

In the shortest path problem from V_s to V_t as in Figure 6.1, if we always select the shortest arc adjacent to the node we just reached, the result is not always optimum as seen in Figure 6.1. The approach of doing best locally is called a greedy approach, and an algorithm based on such an approach is called a

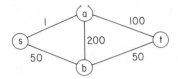

Figure 6.1

greedy algorithm. A greedy algorithm is usually the first heuristic algorithm a person dreams up and it *does* work sometimes. Hence, we shall study such a greedy algorithm in this section.

Consider the daily problem of giving the exact change, say 36 cents. We usually give a quarter, one dime and one penny, and never would give 36 pennies. So let us assume that the objective is to minimize the total number of coins. Then a greedy algorithm would be to give as many as possible of the largest coins and the balance to be paid by as many as possible of the second largest coins, etc. This greedy algorithm, in fact, always gives the optimum solution for our current monetary system. But if we have three kinds of stamps, 1¢, 9¢ and 10¢, say, and the exact postage is 36¢, then the greedy algorithm does not work.

The coin-changing problem and the stamp problem are really the knapsack problem treated in Chapter 3 except maximizing is replaced by minimizing. The dynamic programming approach (Chapter 3) usually takes too long and we would like to study the greedy algorithm here.

To make the coin-changing problem more general, we shall minimize the total weight of the coins in making the change. This problem reduces to the problem of minimizing the total number of coins if all the weights are equal. Let

$$w_1, w_2, ..., w_n \text{ be the weights of the coins}$$

and $\qquad v_1, v_2, ..., v_n$ be the values of the coins .

The problem is to

$$\text{minimize} \quad \sum_{i=1}^{n} w_i x_i$$

$$\text{subject to} \quad \sum v_i x_i = y \tag{1}$$

$$x_i \geqslant 0, \text{ integers}$$

where x_i is the number of the ith coin used, and y is the amount of change.

We shall assume throughout the section that

(i) $w_i > 0$; v_i are positive integers

(ii) $1 = v_1 < v_2 < \cdots < v_n$ (2)

(iii) $\dfrac{w_1}{v_1} \geqslant \dfrac{w_2}{v_2} \geqslant \cdots \geqslant \dfrac{w_n}{v_n}$

Note that (iii) means that the nth coin is the best in the sense that it needs the least weight per unit value.

We define the function $F_k(y)$ as the total weight of the first k kinds of coins in making the change y as calculated by an optimum algorithm, i.e.,

$$F_k(y) = \min \sum_{i=1}^{k} w_i x_i$$

$$\text{subject to } \sum_{i=1}^{k} v_i x_i = y \tag{3}$$

$$x_i \geqslant 0, \text{ integers} .$$

Note that

$$F_{k+1}(y) = \min_{0 \leqslant x_{k+1} \leqslant \left\lfloor y/v_{k+1} \right\rfloor} \left[F_k(y - v_{k+1} x_{k+1}) + w_{k+1} x_{k+1} \right] \tag{4}$$

and $F_1(y) = w_1 \left\lfloor \dfrac{y}{v_1} \right\rfloor = w_1 y$, since $v_1 = 1$.

To see (4), we essentially try each possible value of x_{k+1} which contributes the weight $w_{k+1} x_{k+1}$, and the remaining balance will be paid by the first k kinds of coins optimally.

We define the function $G_k(y)$ as the total weight of the first k kinds of coins in making the change y as calculated by the Greedy algorithm, i.e.,

$$G_{k+1}(y) = w_{k+1} \cdot \left\lfloor \dfrac{y}{v_{k+1}} \right\rfloor + G_k \left(y \ (\text{mod } v_{k+1}) \right) \tag{5}$$

The first term on the R.H.S. is the weight by using the k+1-st coin as much as possible, the second term represents the greedy solution to the remaining balance. In particular,

$$G_1(y) = w_1 \left\lfloor \dfrac{y}{v_1} \right\rfloor = w_1 \cdot y \quad \text{since } v_1 = 1$$

$$G_2(y) = w_2 \left\lfloor \frac{y}{v_2} \right\rfloor + w_1 [y(\text{mod } v_2)] \qquad (6)$$

Because of condition (2)

$$G_1(y) = F_1(y) \qquad \text{for all } y$$

and $\qquad G_2(y) = F_2(y) \qquad$ for all y (due to (ii) & (iii)) .

Example 1

Let $v_1 = 1$, $v_2 = 5$, $v_3 = 14$, $v_4 = 18$, and $w_i = 1$ for all i. Calculate $G_i(y)$

$$G_1(y) = w_1 \left\lfloor \frac{y}{1} \right\rfloor = w_1 y = F_1(y)$$

$$G_2(y) = w_2 \left\lfloor \frac{y}{5} \right\rfloor + w_1 [y(\text{mod } 5)] = F_2(y) \qquad (7)$$

$$G_3(y) = w_3 \left\lfloor \frac{y}{14} \right\rfloor + G_2\big(y(\text{mod } 14)\big)$$

$$G_4(y) = w_4 \left\lfloor \frac{y}{18} \right\rfloor + G_3\big(y(\text{mod } 18)\big)$$

In general $F_i(y) \leqslant G_i(y)$ for $i \geqslant 3$ since it may not be optimum to use the maximum number of i-th coin. We can certainly rename the coins such that assumption (ii) is satisfied. If (iii) is not satisfied and $(w_i/v_i) < (w_{i+1}/v_{i+1})$, then the greedy algorithm does not work for $y = v_i \bullet v_{i+1}$.

Since $G_1(y) = F_1(y)$, $G_2(y) = F_2(y)$ for all y, the question naturally is when will $G_3(y) = F_3(y)$? In general, if $G_k(y) = F_k(y)$ for all y, would the addition of the $(k+1)$-st kind of coin make $G_{k+1}(y) = F_{k+1}(y)$ for all y? This question is answered by the following remarkable theorem which essentially says that if $G_{k+1}(y) = F_{k+1}(y)$ for a particular y, then $G_{k+1}(y) = F_{k+1}(y)$ for all y. (This theorem is due to Magazine, Nemhauser, and Trotter [10].)

Theorem 1 Suppose $G_k(y) = F_k(y)$ for all non-negative integers y and some fixed k. Let $v_{k+1} > v_k$ and

$$v_{k+1} = p\, v_k - \delta, \quad 0 \leqslant \delta < v_k \quad \text{(p is a positive integer)}$$

then the following are equivalent:

(a) $G_{k+1}(y) \leqslant G_k(y)$ for all positive integers y

(b) $G_{k+1}(y) = F_{k+1}(y)$ for all positive integers y

(c) $G_{k+1}(pv_k) = F_{k+1}(pv_k)$

(d) $w_{k+1} + G_k(\delta) \leqslant p\, w_k$

Before we give any proof, let us see what the theorem means.

The condition (a) compares two greedy solutions, one with $k+1$ kinds of coins and one with k kinds of coins.

Condition (b) says that the greedy solution is also the optimum solution for all values of y. Condition (c) says that the greedy solution and the optimum solution agree at one particular value, while condition (d) involves only the greedy solution at one particular value.

Note that it takes only $O(k)$ operations to compute the value of $G(k)$, independent of the value y. So condition (d) needs $O(k)$ time to check if $G_{k+1}(y) = F_{k+1}(y)$ for all y. Because of condition (c), this is referred to as the one-point theorem.

Proof of Theorem 1. We shall prove the equivalence of (a), (b), (c) and (d) by:

(a) implies (b); (b) implies (c); (c) implies (d); and [not (a)] implies [not (d)].

(a) implies (b):

Assume that (a) is true. We have, by the optimality of $F_{k+1}(y)$,

$$F_{k+1}(y) \leqslant G_{k+1}(y) \leqslant G_k(y) \quad \text{for all } y . \tag{8}$$

We consider two cases (i) $x_{k+1} = 0$ in $F_{k+1}(y)$, (ii) $x_{k+1} > 0$ in $F_{k+1}(y)$.

(i)   For a given y, if no $(k+1)$-st coin is used in $F_{k+1}(y)$, then $F_{k+1}(y) = F_k(y)$ and by assumption, $F_k(y) = G_k(y)$, so we have (from (8)),

$$G_k(y) = F_k(y) = F_{k+1}(y) \leqslant G_{k+1}(y) \leqslant G_k(y)$$

or $F_{k+1}(y) = G_{k+1}(y)$ which is (b).

(ii)   Let x_{k+1} be the number of the $(k+1)$-st kind of coin used in $F_{k+1}(y)$, i.e.,

$$F_{k+1}(y) = w_{k+1} \bullet x_{k+1} + F_k(y') \tag{9}$$

where $y' = y - v_{k+1}\, x_{k+1} .$

Then in $F_{k+1}(y')$, no $(k+1)$-st coin is used, hence

$$F_{k+1}(y') = F_k(y') = G_k(y') \qquad (10)$$

Since (8) is true for all values of y, it is true for the particular value [y']. Substituting y' in (8) and combining with (10), we have

$$G_k(y') = F_{k+1}(y') \leqslant G_{k+1}(y') \leqslant G_k(y')$$

or $\qquad F_{k+1}(y') = G_{k+1}(y')$. $\qquad (11)$

Since

$$G_{k+1}(y' + v_{k+1}x_{k+1}) = w_{k+1}x_{k+1} + G_{k+1}(y') ,$$

from (9) and (11), we see that

$$F_{k+1}(y' + v_{k+1}x_{k+1}) = G_{k+1}(y' + v_{k+1}x_{k+1})$$

or $\qquad F_{k+1}(y) = G_{k+1}(y) \quad$ for all y which is (b).

(b) implies (c):

Let y take the particular value pv_k, we have

$$F_{k+1}(pv_k) = G_{k+1}(pv_k) \quad \text{which is (c)}.$$

(c) implies (d):

Since the optimum weight with $k+1$ coins can be no larger than the optimum weight with k coins,

$$F_{k+1}(y) \leqslant F_k(y) = G_k(y) \quad \text{for all y ,}$$

Let $y = pv_k$. Combining with (c), we have

$$G_{k+1}(pv_k) = F_{k+1}(pv_k) \leqslant F_k(pv_k) = G_k(pv_k) \qquad (12)$$

Evaluating both sides of (12), we have

$$w_{k+1} + G_{k+1}(pv_k - v_{k+1}) \leqslant pw_k$$

or $\qquad w_{k+1} + G_{k+1}(\delta) \leqslant pw_k$

or $\qquad w_{k+1} + G_k(\delta) \leqslant pw_k$

$[G_{k+1}(\delta) = G_k(\delta)$ since $\delta < v_k < v_{k+1}]$ which is (d).

[Not (a)] implies [Not (d)]:

Suppose $\bar{y}$ is the smallest integer for which (a) fails. Obviously $\bar{y} > v_{k+1}$. For this $\bar{y}$, we have

$$G_k(\bar{y}) < G_{k+1}(\bar{y}) = w_{k+1} + G_{k+1}(\bar{y} - v_{k+1}) \ .$$

Adding $G_k(\delta)$ to both sides, we have

$$G_k(\delta) + G_k(\bar{y}) < w_{k+1} + G_k(\delta) + G_{k+1}(\bar{y} - v_{k+1}) \tag{13}$$

Since the greedy algorithm is optimum for k coins

$$G_k(\bar{y} + \delta) \leqslant G_k(\delta) + G_k(\bar{y}) \ . \tag{14}$$

Since $\qquad \bar{y} + \delta = (v_{k+1} + \delta) + (\bar{y} - v_{k+1}) = pv_k + (\bar{y} - v_{k+1}),$

$$G_k(\bar{y} + \delta) = pw_k + G_k(\bar{y} - v_{k+1}). \tag{15}$$

Combining (13), (14) and (15), we have

$$pw_k + G_k(\bar{y} - v_{k+1}) - G_{k+1}(\bar{y} - v_{k+1}) < w_{k+1} + G_k(\delta) \ . \tag{16}$$

Since $\bar{y}$ is the smallest integer for which (a) fails, (a) is true for all values $y < \bar{y}$, in particular $\bar{y} - v_{k+1}$. This means $G_{k+1}(\bar{y} - v_{k+1}) \leqslant G_k(\bar{y} - v_{k+1})$. Thus it follows from (16),

$$pw_k < w_{k+1} + G_k(\delta)$$

which is [not (d)] and the proof of Theorem 1 is complete.

Let us apply Theorem 1 to Example 1 where

$$v_1 = 1, \ v_2 = 5, \ v_3 = 14, \ v_4 = 18 \text{ and } w_i = 1 \text{ for all i.}$$

We know

$$G_1(y) = F_1(y) \text{ for all y}$$
$$G_2(y) = F_2(y) \text{ for all y}$$
$$v_3 = 14 = 3 \cdot v_2 - 1 = pv_2 - \delta \quad \text{or } p = 3, \ \delta = 1 \ .$$

Condition (d) of Theorem 1 says

$$w_3 + G_2(\delta) \leqslant pw_2$$

or $\qquad 1 + G_2(1) \leqslant 3 \cdot 1$

or $\qquad 1 + 1 \leqslant 3$, which is true.

Since (d) is satisfied, we know

$$G_3(y) = F_3(y) \text{ for all } y.$$

Now

$$v_4 = 18 = 2 \cdot v_3 - 10 = pv_3 - \delta \quad \text{or} \quad p = 2, \ \delta = 10 \ .$$

Condition (d) now gives

$$w_4 + G_3(\delta) \leqslant pw_3$$

but $\qquad 1 + G_3(10) \leqslant 2 \cdot 1$

or $\qquad 1 + 2 \leqslant 2 \cdot 1 \quad$ so condition (d) is *not* satisfied.

The greedy algorithm fails to give an optimum solution at $pv_3 = 2 \cdot 14 = 28$.

For $y = 28$, $G_4(y)$ gives

$$\left\lfloor \frac{28}{18} \right\rfloor + \left\lfloor \frac{10}{5} \right\rfloor = 3$$

while $F_4(y) = F_3(y)$ gives

$$\left\lfloor \frac{28}{14} \right\rfloor = 2 \ .$$

Note that it takes $O(n^2)$ time to check whether the greedy algorithm produces the optimum solution for n coins.

§6.2 BIN-PACKING

In the last section, we have studied a particular heuristic algorithm known as the greedy algorithm. The greedy algorithm sometimes does give the optimum solution, and we have proven a theorem which characterizes the input data on which the greedy algorithm will work. Now we study another type of heuristic algorithm which always gives near-optimum solutions. We shall try to establish theorems which say, in the worst case the heuristic solution will not deviate too much from the optimum solution. The upper bound on the maximum percentage error gives the problem solver his peace of mind and allows him to decide if he is willing to pay for the time-consuming optimum algorithms.

Assume that we need many rods of different lengths and the local lumber yard has a supply of rods of standard lengths; how many of the standard rods should we order so that we can cut them to fit our needs? This problem is called the one-dimensional stock cutting problem. If we regard the rods of different lengths to be the time of executions of different jobs on a standard processor, then the problem becomes to use minimum number of processors so as to finish all the jobs within a fixed time [standard length of the rod becomes 24 hours for a certain machine].

To fix ideas, we let a_i be the length of the i-th rod. And the demand is denoted by a list $L = (a_1, a_2, ..., a_n)$. The standard rods are denoted by B_j.

This problem is also known as Bin-Packing since we face the same problem by packing boxes into standard-size bins. Here, the only limitation of a bin is its size and a box is characterized only by its size. Although size is characterized by three parameters: length, width, and depth, we shall treat size as a single parameter here. (More than one parameter would be multi-dimensional stock cutting problems, see section 3.3.)

We shall assume that every bin has capacity 1, and there are n items in the list L, $0 < a_i \leqslant 1$ for $1 \leqslant i \leqslant n$. The bins have indices of 1,...,m, where B_1 is called the first bin and B_m always denotes the last nonempty bin.

The sum of a_i packed in a bin B_j is called the *content* of B_j and will be denoted by $c(B_j)$. Note that $1 - c(B_j)$ is the empty space the bin B_j currently has. We shall call $1 - c(B_j)$ the *gap* of B_j.

Given the list $L = (a_1, a_2, ..., a_n)$, one heuristic algorithm is to pack

$$a_1, a_2, ..., a_i \text{ into } B_1 \text{ until } a_{i+1} > 1 - c(B_1),$$

$$a_{i+1}, a_{i+2}, ..., a_j \text{ into } B_2 \text{ until } a_{j+1} > 1 - c(B_2),$$

$\bullet$

$\bullet$

$\bullet$

In general, a_k is packed into B_i as long as B_i has space for a_k and into B_{i+1} if not. Note that in this algorithm, once a bin has no space for the item we try to pack, the bin is never used again; even though later a smaller item may appear in the list and could fit into this bin. This algorithm is called the Next-Fit algorithm (abbreviated as NF).

Let NF(L) be the number of bins needed in the NF algorithm, and L* be the number of bins needed in the optimum algorithm, then the maximum of the ratio

$$R(NF) = \frac{NF(L)}{L^*}$$

indicates the maximum deviation of the heuristic algorithm. Since this ratio depends on the value L*, the real measure of the performance would be when L* → ∞. Thus we use

$$r(NF) = \lim_{k \to \infty} \left[\max_{L^* = k} \frac{NF(L)}{L^*} \right]$$

Let us establish an upper bound on R(NF). Take any bin B_j (j = 1,2,...,m−1), then we have

$$c(B_j) + c(B_{j+1}) > 1 ,$$

otherwise the items in B_{j+1} would be put in B_j. If we sum over all contents of the nonempty bins, we have

$$c(B_1) + c(B_2) + \cdots + c(B_{m-1}) + c(B_m) > \frac{m}{2} \text{ for m even}$$

and $$c(B_1) + c(B_2) + \cdots + c(B_{m-2}) + c(B_{m-1}) > \frac{m-1}{2} \text{ for m odd}$$

Since each bin has capacity one, the optimum packing needs at least

$$L^* > \frac{m-1}{2}$$

or $$m < 2L^* + 1$$

or $$NF(L) < 2L^* + 1 \tag{1}$$

If we let L* → ∞, we have

$$r(NF) \leqslant 2 \tag{2}$$

This bound shows the NF algorithms can use no more than twice the amount of bins that really are required.

Now we shall show a list for which the NF algorithm does achieve this ratio (2). Let the list L consist of items of size $\frac{1}{2}$ and $\frac{1}{2N}$ alternately, i.e.

$$L = \left[\frac{1}{2}, \frac{1}{2N}, \frac{1}{2}, \frac{1}{2N}, \cdots , \frac{1}{2} \right] .$$

total 4N−1 items

Now, the optimum packing would pack two items of size $\frac{1}{2}$ into one bin.

This requires

$$N \text{ bins for } 2N \text{ items of size } \frac{1}{2}$$

and all items of size $\frac{1}{2N}$ would fit into a single bin since

$$(2N-1) \times \frac{1}{2N} < 1 \ .$$

Thus $L^* = N + 1$.

On the other hand, the NF algorithm needs 2N bins as shown in Figure 6.2.

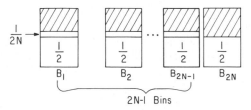

Figure 6.2

Thus we have established that there exists L with arbitrarily large L^* satisfying

$$2L^* - 2 \leqslant NF(L) < 2L^* + 1 \ .$$

This shows $r(NF) \geqslant 2$, so we have $r(NF) = 2$ because of (2).

The 100% error performance of the NF rule usually cannot be tolerated. There are three reasons why the performance is bad:

1.   The NF rule is bad.

2.   We made a decision to put an item a_k in a bin without looking at items appearing later on the list.

This type of algorithm is called an *on-line* algorithm and is used when the items on L are available one at a time, and the assignment has to be made before the next item is available.

3.   The items a_k are of arbitrary size. If the maximum size of the item is restricted, then the performance would be improved as seen in the following theorem.

Theorem 2 If the items on the list L all have size t or less $(0 < t \leqslant 1/2)$, then

$$NF(L) < \frac{L^*}{1-t} + 1 \ . \tag{3}$$

Proof. Since the largest item is of size t or less, then the gap of every bin must be less than t. In other words, $c(B_j) > 1-t$ for all bins except possibly B_m.

Thus
$$\sum_{j=1}^{m-1} c(B_j) > (m-1)(1-t)$$

or
$$L^* > (m-1)(1-t)$$

or
$$NF(L) < \frac{L^*}{1-t} + 1 \qquad\qquad\qquad \text{Q.E.D.}$$

An example can be constructed to show that for a certain list L,

$$NF(L) \geqslant (L^* - 1) \left[\frac{1}{1-t} - \epsilon \right]$$

where ϵ is a positive constant (see Johnson [8]). Since $r(NF) = \dfrac{1}{1-t}$ for upper and lower bounds, the only way to improve performance is to invent new heuristic rules, both on-line and off-line.

One of the on-line rules is called First-Fit (abbreviated as the FF rule). The FF rule assigns each item to the bin with lowest index that has space for the item. In other words, assign a_k to B_j

if
$$1-c(B_j) \geqslant a_k$$

and
$$1-c(B_i) < a_k \quad \text{for all } i<j .$$

Note that in the FF rule, we scan every nonempty bin from left to right and put a_k into the first bin it fits.

Another on-line rule is called the Best-Fit rule. In the BF rule, we scan every nonempty bin from left to right and put a_k into the bin so that the gap would be minimum. In other words, assign a_k to B_j

if
$$1-c(B_j) - a_k \leqslant 1-c(B_i) - a_k \quad \text{for all } i .$$

In case of tie, put a_k into the bin of lowest index.

If
$$1-c(B_i) < a_k \text{ for all nonempty bins,}$$

put a_k into an empty bin of lowest index.

Now we illustrate the packing of a list L by the FF rule where

$$L = (a_1,a_2,a_3,a_4,a_5,a_6,a_7,a_8,a_9) = (0.1,0.1,0.6,0.3,0.4,0.7,0.7,0.3,0.8)$$

The result is five bins as shown in Figure 6.3.

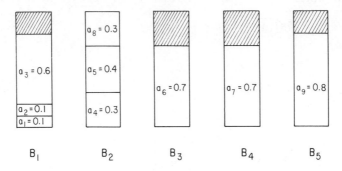

Figure 6.3

For this example, if we had used the BF rule, the result would have been the same.

Both the FF rule and the BF rule are on-line algorithms, and one can establish

$$\frac{17}{10}L^* - 2 \leqslant FF(L) \leqslant \frac{17}{10}L^* + 2 \tag{4}$$

$$\frac{17}{10}L^* - 2 \leqslant BF(L) \leqslant \frac{17}{10}L^* + 2 \;. \tag{5}$$

For the proof of (4) and (5), see Graham [2], Johnson et al. [8].

The 70% error is usually too high, although the performance would be better for most input lists L.

Now we turn to two off-line heuristic rules; one is called the First-Fit-Decreasing rule, the FFD rule. This rule first sorts all items on the list into decreasing sizes such that,

$$a_1 \geqslant a_2 \geqslant \cdots \geqslant a_n$$

and then applies the First-Fit rule.

Another heuristic rule is called the Best-Fit-Decreasing rule (abbreviated to the BFD rule); it first sorts the items into decreasing sizes and then applies the Best-Fit rule.

If we use the FFD rule or the BFD rule to the example in Figure 6.3, we have now a list

$$L = (a_1, a_2, ..., a_9) = (0.8, 0.7, 0.7, 0.6, 0.4, 0.3, 0.3, 0.1, 0.1)$$

and the result of the packing is shown in Figure 6.4.

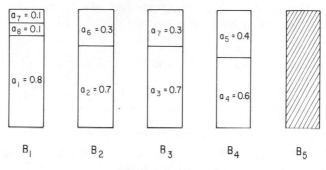

Figure 6.4

We can establish

$$\left\lfloor \frac{11}{9} \right\rfloor L^* \leqslant \text{FFD}(L) \leqslant \left\lfloor \frac{11}{9} \right\rfloor L^* + 4 \qquad (6)$$

$$\left\lfloor \frac{11}{9} \right\rfloor L^* \leqslant \text{BFD}(L) \leqslant \left\lfloor \frac{11}{9} \right\rfloor L^* + 4 \ . \qquad (7)$$

The interested reader is referred to Johnson [8].

Since (4), (5), (6) and (7) essentially describe the worst case behavior of these heuristic rules, any improvement must be made on more sophisticated heuristic rules. Now we shall describe a remarkable heuristic rule due to Yao [13] which is on-line and achieves the ratio $\frac{5}{3}$.

First, we shall classify items by their size. An item a_k is called an

$$\alpha \text{ item if } \frac{1}{2} < a_k \leqslant 1$$

$$\beta_1 \text{ item if } \frac{2}{5} < a_k \leqslant \frac{1}{2}$$

$$\beta_2 \text{ item if } \frac{1}{3} < a_k \leqslant \frac{2}{5}$$

$$\delta \text{ item if } 0 < a_k \leqslant \frac{1}{3} \ .$$

We also divide all the bins into four classes. All α items are packed into bins in class 1, all β_1 items are packed into bins in class 2. The majority of β_2 items (approximately 6/7 of the total) are packed into bins in class 3, while the remaining β_2 items are packed into bins in class 1. All δ items are packed into bins in class 4.

We first examine the size of a_k and then put it by first-fit into a bin in:

Class 1   If a_k is an α item

Class 2   if a_k is a β_1 item

Class 3   if a_k is a β_2 item (for every seventh β_2 item, we put it into class 1 instead. Thus, the 7th, 14th, ..., β_2 items are in class 1 while 6/7 or more of the total β_2 items are in class 3.)

Class 4   if a_k is a δ item.

The first-fit rule is modified when a β_2 item is packed into a class 1 bin, by disallowing a β_2 item in a bin already occupied by another β_2 item. Since $\frac{1}{2} < \alpha$, two α items cannot be put in a single bin, but we do not allow two β_2 items into a single bin even if they can fit. Thus, the resulting packing of a list has the structure as shown in Figure 6.5.

This rule is called the Refined-First-Fit rule by Yao [13], and we shall use RFF(L) to denote the amount of bins required under this rule.

Let Z_{11} denote the set of bins containing a single α item in class 1

Z_{12} denote the set of bins containing a single β_2 item in class 1

Z_{13} denote the set of bins containing both α and β_2 in class 1

Z_2 denote the set of nonempty bins in class 2

Z_3 denote the set of nonempty bins in class 3

Z_4 denote the set of nonempty bins in class 4

We shall let z_{11}, z_{12}, z_{13}, z_2, z_3, z_4 denote the number of bins of the above types, and a, b_1, b_2, d denote the total number of α, β_1, β_2, δ items, respectively.

We would like to establish a relation between RFF(L) and L*. From the RFF rule, we have

$$RFF(L) = z_{11} + z_{12} + z_{13} + z_2 + z_3 + z_4 \qquad (8)$$

where z_{11}, z_{12}, ..., z_4 are functions of a, b_1, b_2, d and the actual sizes of the items. It is easy to see that

$$z_{11} + z_{13} = a \qquad (9)$$

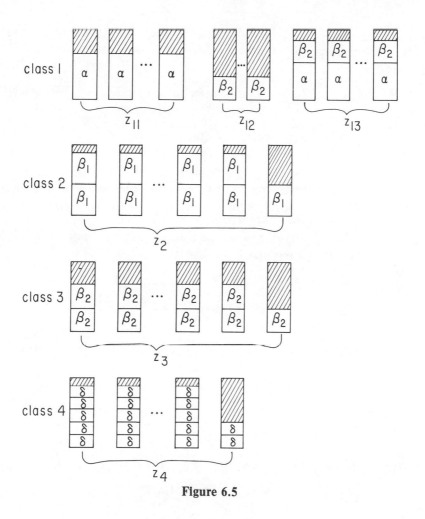

Figure 6.5

$$z_{12} + z_{13} = \left\lfloor b_2/7 \right\rfloor \tag{10}$$

$$z_2 = \left\lfloor b_1/2 \right\rfloor \tag{11}$$

$$z_3 = \left\lfloor \frac{1}{2}(b_2 - z_{12} - z_{13}) \right\rfloor \tag{12}$$

but it is hard to define z_4 in terms of d and δ. Thus we use the following approach.

If we know the sum of contents of bins in the first three classes, then the difference between L^* and the sum is an upper bound on the contents of Z_4. We shall prove that all bins in Z_4 have contents $\geqslant 3/4$. This fact and the upper bound on the contents of Z_4 give an expression of z_4 in terms of L^* and other quantities. Substituting this expression into (8), we have a relation between RFF(L) and L^*.

Lemma 1 All bins in Z_4, with the possible exception of two bins, have contents $\geqslant 3/4$, i.e.

$$c(B_j) \geqslant \frac{3}{4} \qquad (\text{for } j \neq i, m) \ .$$

Proof. Let B_i be the first bin in Z_4 that has contents $< 3/4$, then the δ-items in $B_{i+1}, B_{i+2}, \ldots$, must all have sizes $> 1/4$, otherwise the item would be fit into B_i according to first-fit rule. If all items in $B_{i+1}, B_{i+2}, \ldots$, have size greater than $1/4$ and less than or equal to $1/3$ (since $\delta \leqslant 1/3$), then every bin $B_{i+1}, \ldots$ has three items and has contents $> 3/4$ (except possibly the last bin). In other words, only B_i and the last bin may have contents $\leqslant 3/4$.

Theorem 3

$$\text{RFF(L)} \leqslant \frac{5}{3}L^* + 5$$

To get a relation between RFF(L) and L^*, we consider three cases:

(i) $z_{12} = 0$

(ii) $z_{11} \geqslant z_{12} > 0$

(iii) $z_{12} > z_{11} \geqslant 0$.

Case (i): $z_{12} = 0$.

In this case, the contents in the first three classes of bins is at least $\frac{1}{2}a + \frac{2}{5}b_1 + \frac{1}{3}b_2$, and the contents in Z_4 is at most

$$L^* - \frac{1}{2}a - \frac{2}{5}b_1 - \frac{1}{3}b_2 \ .$$

Using Lemma 1, we have

$$z_4 \leqslant 2 + \frac{4}{3}\left[L^* - \frac{1}{2}a - \frac{2}{5}b_1 - \frac{1}{3}b_2\right] \ . \tag{13}$$

Substituting (9) and (13) into (8), we have

$$\text{RFF(L)} \leqslant \frac{4}{3}L^* + \frac{1}{3}a + \left[z_2 - \frac{8}{15}b_1\right] + \left[z_3 - \frac{4}{9}b_2\right] + 2 \ . \tag{14}$$

Note that

$$z_2 - \frac{8}{15}b_1 = \left\lceil b_1/2 \right\rceil - \frac{8}{15}b_1$$

$$\leqslant 1 - \frac{1}{30}b_1$$

$$\leqslant 1 \tag{15}$$

$$z_3 - \frac{4}{9}b_2 = \left\lceil \frac{1}{2}\left(b_2 - \left\lceil b_2/7 \right\rceil\right) \right\rceil - \frac{4}{9}b_2$$

$$\leqslant \left\lceil \frac{1}{2}(b_2 - b_2/7) \right\rceil - \frac{4}{9}b_2 + 1$$

$$\leqslant \frac{1}{2}(b_2 - b_2/7) - \frac{4}{9}b_2 + 2$$

$$\leqslant 2 - \frac{1}{63}b_2$$

$$\leqslant 2 \ . \tag{16}$$

Substituting (15), (16) into (14) and using the fact that $a \leqslant L^*$, we have

$$RFF(L) \leqslant \frac{5}{3}L^* + 5 \ .$$

Case (ii): $z_{11} \geqslant z_{12} > 0$

The fact that z_{11} and z_{12} all have one item means

$$c(B_i) + c(B_j) > 1 \quad \text{for } B_i \in Z_{11}, B_j \in Z_{12} \ . \tag{17a}$$

In particular

$$\frac{3}{5} < c(B_i) \leqslant 1 \ \text{ and } \ \frac{1}{3} < c(B_j) \leqslant \frac{2}{5} \ \text{ for } B_i \in Z_{11}, B_j \in Z_{12} \ . \tag{17b}$$

Using (17a) and (17b), we see that the total contents of the first three classes of bins are at least

$$\frac{3}{5}z_{11} + \frac{2}{5}z_{12} + \left[\frac{1}{2} + \frac{1}{3}\right]z_{13} + \frac{2}{5}(2z_2 - 1) + \frac{1}{3}(2z_3 - 1)$$

$$> \frac{3}{5}a + \frac{2}{5}z_{12} + \frac{7}{30}z_{13} + \frac{4}{5}z_2 + \frac{2}{3}z_3 - 1 \tag{18}$$

(since $z_{11} + z_{13} = a$). The contents in Z_4 is at most $L^* - $ (18) or (by lemma 1)

$$z_4 \leqslant 2 + \frac{4}{3}\left[L^* - \frac{3}{5}a - \frac{2}{5}z_{12} - \frac{7}{30}z_{13} - \frac{4}{5}z_2 - \frac{2}{3}z_3 + 1\right] . \qquad (19)$$

Substituting (19) into (8), we have

$$\mathrm{RFF}(L) \leqslant \frac{4}{3}L^* + \frac{1}{5}a + \frac{7}{15}z_{12} - \frac{14}{45}z_{13} - \frac{1}{15}z_2 + \frac{1}{9}z_3 + 2\frac{4}{3}$$

$$= \frac{4}{3}L^* + \frac{1}{5}a + \frac{7}{15}z_{12} - \frac{14}{45}z_{13} - \frac{1}{15}z_2 + \frac{1}{9}\left[\frac{1}{2}(b_2 - z_{12} - z_{13})\right] + 2\frac{4}{3}$$

$$\leqslant \frac{4}{3}L^* + \frac{1}{5}a + \frac{37}{90}z_{12} + \frac{1}{18}b_2 + 4$$

$$\leqslant \frac{4}{3}L^* + \frac{1}{5}a + \left[\frac{37}{90} \cdot \frac{1}{7} + \frac{1}{18}\right]b_2 + 4 . \qquad (20)$$

Lemma 2

$$\frac{1}{5}a + \left[\frac{37}{90} \cdot \frac{1}{7} + \frac{1}{18}\right]b_2 \leqslant \frac{1}{3}L^* \qquad (21)$$

Proof. In an optimum packing, each bin can contain at most one α item and one β_2 item, or two β_2 items

$$\frac{1}{2}(a + b_2) \leqslant L^*$$

or $\qquad\qquad b_2 \leqslant 2L^* - a$. $\qquad\qquad\qquad\qquad\qquad (22)$

Substituting (22) into (21), we have

$$\frac{1}{5}a + \left[\frac{37}{90} \cdot \frac{1}{7} + \frac{1}{18}\right](2L^* - a)$$

$$= \left[\frac{37}{90} \cdot \frac{1}{7} + \frac{1}{18}\right]2L^* + \left[\frac{1}{5} - \frac{37}{90} \cdot \frac{1}{7} - \frac{1}{18}\right]a$$

$$\leqslant \frac{1}{3}L^* \qquad\qquad (\text{since } a \leqslant L^*) .$$

Substituting (21) into (20), we have the desired result

$$\mathrm{RFF}(L) \leqslant \frac{5}{3}L^* + 5 .$$

Case (iii): $z_{12} > z_{11} \geq 0$

In this case, (17a) and (17b) are still true. Thus the total contents of the first three classes is

$$\frac{2}{3}z_{11} + \frac{1}{3}z_{12} + \left[\frac{1}{2} + \frac{1}{3}\right]z_{13} + \frac{2}{5}(2z_2 - 1) + \frac{1}{3}(2z_3 - 1)$$

$$> \frac{2}{3}a + \frac{1}{3}z_{12} + \frac{1}{6}z_{13} + \frac{4}{5}z_2 + \frac{2}{3}z_3 - 1 \ .$$

The contents in Z_4 is at most

$$z_4 \leq 2 + \frac{4}{3}\left[L^* - \frac{2}{3}a - \frac{1}{3}z_{12} - \frac{1}{6}z_{13} - \frac{4}{5}z_2 - \frac{2}{3}z_3 + 1\right] \ . \tag{23}$$

Substituting (23) into (8), we have

$$RFF(L) \leq \frac{4}{3}L^* + \frac{1}{9}a + \frac{5}{9}z_{12} - \frac{2}{9}z_{13} - \frac{1}{15}z_2 + \frac{1}{9}z_3 + 4$$

$$\leq \frac{4}{3}L^* + \frac{1}{9}a + \frac{5}{9}z_{12} + \frac{1}{9}z_3 + 4$$

$$\leq \frac{4}{3}L^* + \frac{1}{9}a + \frac{5}{9}z_{12} + \frac{1}{9}\left[\left[\frac{1}{2}(b_2 - z_{12})\right]\right] + 4$$

$$\leq \frac{4}{3}L^* + \frac{1}{9}a + \frac{1}{18}b_2 + \frac{1}{2}z_{12} + 5$$

$$\leq \frac{4}{3}L^* + \frac{1}{9}a + \left[\frac{1}{18} + \frac{1}{2} \cdot \frac{1}{7}\right]b_2 + 5 \quad \left[\text{using } \frac{1}{2}(a+b_2) \leq L^*\right]$$

$$\leq \frac{5}{3}L^* + 5 \ .$$

Now we shall construct a list L such that the ratio 5/3 is actually achieved. The packing of β_1 and β_2 items in the RFF packing are actually quite efficient. The β_1 items are packed into Z_2 with 80% or better efficiency and β_2 items are packed into Z_3 with 66.67% or better efficiency. So we would like to construct a list consisting of δ-items followed by α-items of size $\frac{1}{2} + \epsilon$, for example, so that the combined efficiency is 60% for RFF(L).

In the list that we shall construct, there are basically two kinds of δ-items. Those slightly greater than 1/4 and those slightly less than 1/4.

$$\delta_j^+ = \frac{1}{4} + \epsilon_j \tag{24}$$

$$\delta_j^- = \frac{1}{4} - 2\epsilon_j \qquad (25)$$

where $\qquad \epsilon_j = 1/4^{(j+2)}$.

Also we have one kind of α item:

$$\alpha_j = \frac{1}{2} + \epsilon_j \ . \qquad (26)$$

Consider the list $L = L_1L_2$ where

$L_1 = (\delta_1^+, \delta_2^-, \delta_3^-, \delta_3^+, \delta_4^-, \delta_5^-, \ldots, \delta_{2j-1}^+, \delta_{2j}^-, \delta_{2j+1}^-, \ldots, \delta_{n-2}^+, \delta_{n-1}^-, \delta_n^-)$.

$L_2 = (\delta_2^+, \delta_4^+, \ldots, \delta_{n-1}^+, \alpha_1, \alpha_2, \ldots, \alpha_n, \delta_1^-, \delta_n^+)$.

Now, the total contents of the list is n and the optimum packing is shown in Figure 6.6(a), where the RFF will give the packing as shown in Figure 6.6(b).

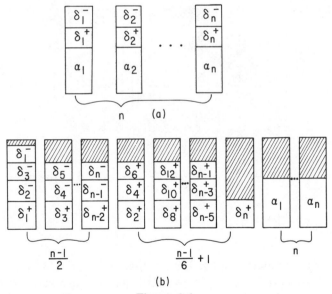

(b)

Figure 6.6

§6.3 JOB-SCHEDULING

In this section, we consider job-scheduling problems. A project consists of many jobs (tasks). These jobs have to be processed on machines or processors. The jobs are partially ordered due to technical restrictions, for example, the job of washing dishes must precede the job of drying the dishes. If we use nodes to represent jobs (tasks), and directed arcs to represent the order restrictions among jobs, then we can use an acyclic graph to represent the whole project.

In this class of problems, we have m identical machines (processors) $P_1, P_2, ..., P_m$; and we have n jobs $T_1, T_2, ..., T_n$ which are partially ordered. Each job T_j needs t_j units of time to execute. The problem is to assign the machines to the jobs in such a way so as to complete the entire project in the shortest time. We make the following assumptions about the scheduling:

i)   All m machines are identical, and any machine can work on any job.

ii)   Whenever a machine is idle and a job is available, then the machine must start working on the job.

iii)   Once a machine works on a job, the machine keeps working until that job is completed.

iv)   A priority list of jobs is arranged in the beginning which assigns the priorities among jobs. The priority list $L = (T_{i_1}, T_{i_2}, ..., T_{i_n})$ is a permutation of all the jobs. At any time, if a machine is idle, we shall assign the machine to the job that is highest on the priority list L if that job can be started. If the number of jobs available is more than the number of machines, then the machines are assigned to those available jobs with higher priority. Due to the partial ordering among jobs, a job with low priority may be processed before a job with higher priority. If there are more machines than jobs, then any machine can be assigned. (To make algorithms definite, we use the convention that the machine with smallest index will be assigned.)

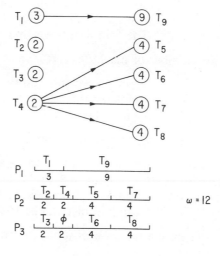

Figure 6.7

In Figure 6.7 we show a project with 9 jobs. The jobs are labeled $T_1, T_2, ..., T_9$. The time of completion of every job is written within the node, thus the job T_1 needs 3 units of time to complete, and the job T_9 needs 9 units of time to complete. None of the jobs T_5, T_6, T_7 and T_8 can be started until job T_4 is completed. On the other hand, T_1, T_2, T_3 and T_4 can be started at any time. We have three identical machines P_1, P_2, P_3. If we use the priority list $L = (T_1, T_2, ..., T_9)$ what would be the completion time?

Since there are three machines and four jobs available, the jobs with higher priority T_1, T_2, T_3 are processed first. We assign the machine with lowest index to the job with highest priority. When P_2 and P_3 have completed their jobs T_2 and T_3, there is only one job T_4 available, and T_4 is assigned to P_2. When P_1 completes T_1, there is only T_9 available, so P_1 is assigned to T_9. The whole assignment of machines to jobs are represented by three lines with total completion time $\omega = 12$ units. Note that P_3 is idle for two units because no job is available at that time.

Remember that we make the assumption that the execution of a job cannot be interrupted. Once a machine is assigned to a job, the machine must finish that job. This kind of non-interruptive scheduling is called non-preemptive scheduling. This is a realistic assumption. If a job of duration $(t_1 + t_2)$ can be interrupted after t_1 units of time, then the job can always be transformed into two jobs connected by a directed arc with the first job of duration t_1 and the second job of duration t_2. Thus, we lose no generality in assuming that all jobs cannot be interrupted. The assumption of no setup time, i.e., a machine finishing a job can immediately start on another, is not very realistic but we can combine the setup time with the execution time. We make the policy that no machine is allowed to be idle if a single job can be started. This "NO-IDLE POLICY" causes many strange phenomena to occur. The following are some of these phenomena:

i)   Increasing the number of machines can increase the completion time.

      In Figure 6.7, if we have increased the number of machines from three to four, everything else remains the same, then the completion time is *increased* from 12 to 15. (See Figure 6.8.)

ii)   Relaxing the partial order constraints can increase the completion time.

      If we remove the directed arcs from T_4 to T_5 and from T_4 to T_6, then the whole project is shown in Figure 6.9 while the dashed lines indicate constraints that have been removed from Figure 6.7. Under the priority list $L = (T_1, T_2, ..., T_9)$, the whole project takes 16 units instead of 12 units.

iii) Decreasing the execution time of jobs, can increase the completion time of the whole project.

In Figure 6.10 we show the same project as in Figure 6.7 except the execution time of every job has been decreased by 1. The reader can verify that the total completion time is $\omega = 13$.

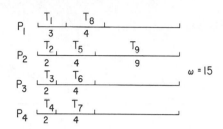

Figure 6.8

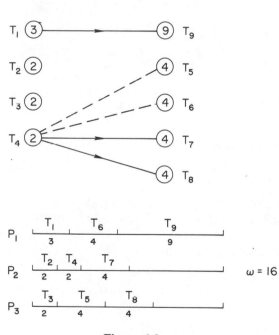

Figure 6.9

The reader may feel that the reason behind all these strange phenomena is due to the fact that we use a very stupid priority list L. In Figure 6.11, we show an example where the project takes 30 units to complete with two machines. If we use three machines, relax some constraints, decrease the execution time on every job, we need 31 units to complete the project *no matter what* priority list L we use!!!

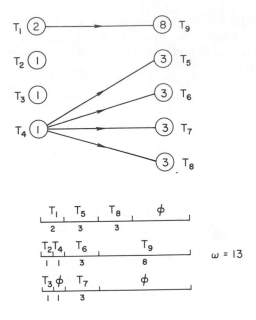

Figure 6.10

Even if all the jobs take one unit of time, increasing the number of machines can increase the completion time. This is shown in Figure 6.12 where the priority list L is $(T_1, T_2, ..., T_{12})$.

Despite these strange examples and phenomena, we can still get some general results. Let us assume that we have a project, a priority list L and the shortest completion time ω. If the priority list L is changed to L′ with resulting completion time ω' then ω' is bounded from above by

$$\omega' \leqslant \left\lceil \frac{2m-1}{m} \right\rceil \omega \qquad (1)$$

where m is the number of machines.

Proof. Before we give proof of (1), we want to show that (1) is a sharp upper bound. We shall show three examples in Figure 6.13 without ordering constraints and the reader can furnish the general case.

Consider an arbitrary example of three machines, although the argument applies to m machines.

We can make the following observations.

1. At most m-1 machines may be idle at a given time, at least one machine must be working during the whole period.

2. The end of each idle time ϕ coincides with completion of a job on another machine. (The reason that one machine P_i is no longer idle is due to the completion of a job T_k by another machine P_k which makes a job T_j available. The job T_k had a directed arc to T_j.) We use $T_i < T_j$ to denote that T_i must precede T_j.

3. If P_j has an idle time ϕ_j followed by a job T_j, then there exists a job T_i such that $T_i < T_j$; otherwise T_j could be started earlier. If T_i is longer that ϕ_j, T_i covers ϕ_j. If T_i is shorter than ϕ_j, then there exists a $T_q < T_i$; otherwise T_i could be started on P_j. Repeat this kind of reasoning, we have an ordered sequence of jobs whose duration covers the whole idle time.

    Using this observation, we see that

    $$T_6 < T_7 < T_2 < T_9 < T_{15} < T_{11} < T_{12} .$$

    We shall denote this set of constrained jobs by J*.

4. The execution time of J* must be less than or equal to the optimal execution time ω, of the full set of jobs J.

    $$\omega' = \frac{1}{m} \left[\sum_{j \in J} t(T_j) + \sum_i t(\phi_i) \right]$$

    $$\leqslant \frac{1}{m} \left[m\omega + (m-1) \sum_{i \in J*} t(T_i) \right]$$

    $$\leqslant \frac{1}{m} [m\omega + (m-1) \omega]$$

    $$= \left(\frac{2m-1}{m} \right) \omega .$$

Note

$$\frac{1}{m} \sum_{j \in J} t(T_j) \leqslant \omega \text{ since an optimal schedule may have some machine idle time}$$

and

$$\frac{\sum t(\phi_i)}{m-1} \leqslant \sum_{i \in J*} t(T_i) \leqslant \omega$$

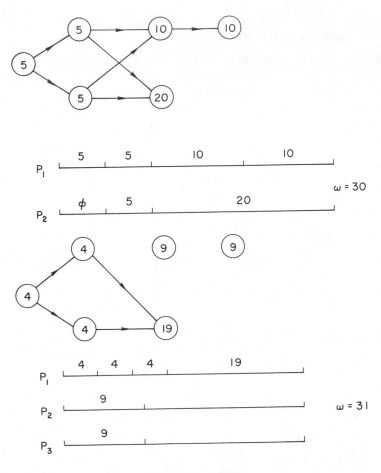

Figure 6.11

because at most $(m-1)$ machines could be idle and the observation that the total idle time for each machine must be less than ω.

§6.4 JOB-SCHEDULING (tree-constraints)

In the last section, we have seen many anomalies in job-scheduling. It is unlikely that an efficient optimum algorithm can be found for the general job-scheduling problem. Thus, we should try the following approaches:

a)   Heuristic algorithm: a heuristic algorithm may or may not obtain the optimum solution. We should characterize the cases where optimum solution is obtained and estimate the error bounds for other cases. This approach was used in § 6.1 for the greedy algorithm.

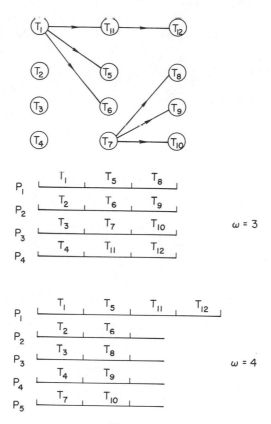

Figure 6.12

b)   Special cases: We have already seen a special case where there is no
ordering-constraint among the jobs (§ 6.2 Bin-Packing). There are many
other special cases, for example, the case of two processors was solved by
Coffman and Graham [4]. When the partial ordering forms a tree, the case
was solved by Hu [7].

In this section, we consider the special case where the partial ordering forms
a tree and all jobs need one-unit of time. Note that there is no priority among the
jobs except the ordering constraints. A typical partial ordering that forms a tree is
shown in Figure 6.15. Note that the root is at the bottom and at level one.

For the tree-constraint job-scheduling, we have an optimum algorithm for
m processors (m arbitrary) and a formula for calculating the minimum number of
processors needed to meet a given deadline.

Let us introduce some terminology using Figure 6.15. The node T_A is
called the root of the tree, and is considered to be at the lowest level, one. A

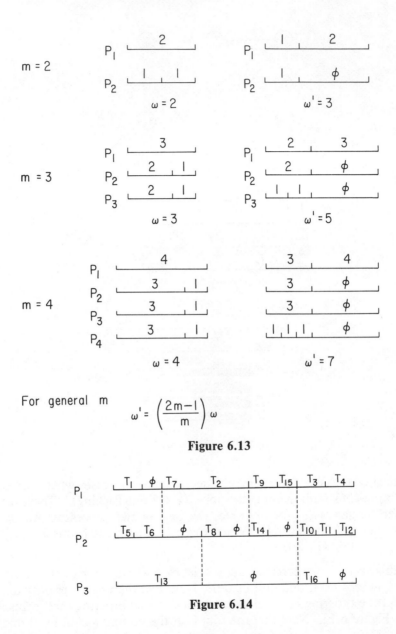

For general m

$$\omega' = \left(\frac{2m-1}{m}\right)\omega$$

Figure 6.13

Figure 6.14

node is at the level k if the unique path from the node to the root consists of k−1 arcs. Thus T_C is at level two and T_K is at level four. If there is a directed arc from T_i to T_j, then T_i is called the father of T_j. A node without a father is called a starting node. In Figure 6.15, T_I, T_J, T_K, T_L, T_G, T_H, and T_D are starting nodes. If a job is processed, then the node is considered to be removed from the graph. Thus if T_I, T_J, T_K are removed, then T_E becomes a starting node in the

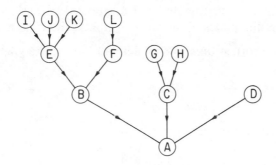

Figure 6.15

resulting graph. The graph is of *height* h if the maximum level is h.

Of course, the height of a graph changes as nodes are successively removed. When a definite algorithm is specified, we can define the height of the graph after t units of time, and also the total number of starting nodes as a function of time.

Let us introduce an algorithm that always removes the nodes of the maximum level and in the case of a tie, removes the leftmost ones. Thus, in Figure 6.15, for m = 3, T_I, T_J, T_k will be removed at the first step, T_L, T_E, T_G at the second step, T_F, T_H, T_D at the third step, etc.

It is obvious that a graph of height h cannot be completed in h−1 units of time no matter how many processors are available. So any path from a node of maximum level to the root is very critical, and the algorithm is called the critical-path algorithm. We shall prove that the critical-path algorithm is optimum for any tree-shaped graph.

Let us define $p(\alpha)$ to be the number of nodes at the level α, $s(\alpha)$ to be the number of starting nodes at the level α, $c(\alpha)$ is the number of covered nodes of level α (nodes with fathers are called covered nodes), thus

$$p(\alpha) = s(\alpha) + c(\alpha).$$

In Figure 6.15,

$$p(4) = p(3) = 4, \quad s(3) = c(3) = 2.$$

If the number of processors is fixed, and there is a definite algorithm of removing nodes in the graph, we shall use $p_t(\alpha)$, $s_t(\alpha)$ to denote $p(\alpha)$, $s(\alpha)$ of the remaining graph after t units of time. If the number of processors is 3 and we use the critical path algorithm, then $p_1(4) = 1$ after one unit of time where the subscript 1 indicates the time. Similarly, $s_2(3) = 2$ as (T_I, T_J, T_K), (T_L, T_E, T_G) are removed after two units of time. We define

$$S_t(\alpha) = \sum_{j \geqslant \alpha} s_t(j)$$

to be the total number of starting nodes at or above a certain level α. $S_t(1)$ is the total number of starting nodes in the entire graph at the time t.

Let ω_0 be the shortest time to complete all jobs in the graph. Then we have

$$\omega_0 \geqslant h \ . \tag{1}$$

This is called the *height constraint.*

Since the total number of nodes removed cannot exceed $\omega_0 m$, we have

$$\omega_0 \geqslant \left\lceil \sum_{j=1}^{h} p(j)/m \right\rceil , \tag{2}$$

which is called the *width constraint.*

Both (1) and (2) are special cases of the following bound

$$\omega_0 \geqslant \left\lceil \sum_{j=\gamma+1}^{h} p(j)/m \right\rceil + \gamma \quad (0 \leqslant \gamma \leqslant h) \ . \tag{3}$$

Note that (3) reduces to (1) when $\gamma=h$ and (3) reduces to (2) when $\gamma=0$. Roughly speaking, all the nodes above the level γ are removed "m" at a time and the remaining graph has the height γ, hence the lower bound (3). This is called the width-height constraint and it is the lower bound for all trees.

In Figure 6.15, with $m=3$, $\gamma=1$, and (3) gives $\lceil 11/3 \rceil + 1 = 5$, and the critical algorithm also uses 5 units of time. It is not obvious that there always exists a level $\gamma + 1$ in a tree, which makes the bound (3) satisfied. We have to prove that all nodes on or above the level $\gamma + 1$ are removed in groups of m nodes per step, except possibly in the last step in the level $\gamma + 1$. It is also not obvious how level $\gamma + 1$ is chosen.

To illustrate how the level $\gamma + 1$ is chosen, we apply the critical path algorithm to Figure 6.16 with $m = 3$.

The nodes removed at successive steps are

(A̲, B,C), (D̲, E̲, F̲), (G̲,I,J), (H̲,K,L), (M̲,N̲,O̲), (P̲,R,T) (Q̲), (S̲), (U̲)

where the underline indicates the nodes are the maximum level nodes in the current graph.

Note that certain levels have many nodes and cannot be removed in a single step when that level becomes the maximum level in the current graph. On the other hand, a level may have many nodes, most of which are starting nodes. These starting nodes are removed before the level becomes the maximum level. When the level becomes the maximum level, there are no more than m nodes in the level and hence all the nodes can be removed in one step.

Let us record whether a level is removed in a single step when the level

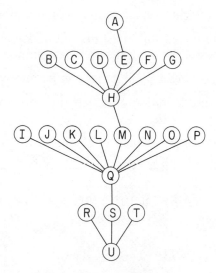

Figure 6.16

becomes the maximum level, then we have Table 6 where "Y" means Yes and "N" means Not in a single step. (See Figure 6.16.)

Table 6

Level	7	6	5	4	3	2	1
Removability	Y	N	Y	N	Y	Y	Y

We always set $\gamma+1$ equal to the lowest level with the "N". In this case,

$$\gamma + 1 = 4$$

so

$$\gamma = 3 \quad .$$

Using the lower bound (3), we have

$$\left\lceil \sum_{j=\gamma+1}^{h} p(j)/m \right\rceil + \gamma$$

$$= \lceil (1+6+1+8)/3 \rceil + 3$$

$$= 6 + 3 = 9 \quad .$$

To prove that the critical path algorithm is optimum we must prove

(i)   When nodes are removed "m" at a time, all nodes removed are at or above the level $\gamma + 1$ except for the last step which empties the $r+1$ level.

(ii)   When the graph has height γ, all nodes can be removed in γ steps.

(ii) follows from the definition of γ, we shall now prove (i) using the fact that the graph is a tree.

In a tree, no node has more than one son, so the total number of starting nodes above any level is monotonically decreasing as nodes are successively removed, i.e.

$$S_t(j) \geqslant S_{t+1}(j) \quad \text{for } t = 0,1,\dots \tag{4}$$

In particular

$$S_t(\gamma+1) \geqslant S_{t+1}(\gamma+1) \ . \tag{5}$$

If all levels are "N" then (i) is clearly satisfied. If a level "α" is "Y", i.e.

$$p_t(\alpha) = S_t(\alpha) \leqslant m \quad (\alpha > \gamma+1) \ ,$$

It is conceivable that some nodes below the level $\gamma+1$ are removed together with the nodes in the maximum level since the inequality may hold strictly, i.e., $p_t(\alpha) = S_t(\alpha) < m$. We shall show that it is impossible unless it is the last step.

By assumption, if level $\gamma+1$ becomes the maximum level at t',

$$p_t(\gamma+1) > m$$

or $$s_t(\gamma+1) > m$$

or $$S_t(\gamma+1) > m$$

which means

$$S_t(\gamma+1) > m \quad \text{as } t < t'.$$

This implies that there are m or more starting nodes available above the level γ at any time $t \leqslant t'$. Thus no nodes below level $\gamma + 1$ are removed before the time $t^* - 1$, where the tree has height γ first at t^*.

Thus, the lower bound (3) is always achieved. And if all levels are "Y" then we set $\gamma = h$ and (3) reduces to (1).

Having proved that the critical-path algorithm is optimum, we shall now consider the question: how many processors are needed if the project must be finished in h+c steps?

Let us define γ^* by the following equation

$$\max \frac{1}{h-\gamma+c} \sum_{j=\gamma+1}^{h} p(j) = \frac{1}{h-\gamma^*+c} \sum_{j=\gamma^*+1}^{h} p(j) \qquad (6)$$

and let m be the unique integer satisfying (7)

$$m - 1 < \frac{1}{h-\gamma^*+c} \sum_{j=\gamma^*+1}^{h} p(j) \leqslant m \qquad (7)$$

Lemma 3 If the ordering constraint forms a tree of height h, and γ^*, m, and c are defined by (6) and (7), then m is the minimum number of processors needed to complete the project in h+c units of time.

Proof. We shall first prove that (m−1) processors will not be sufficient. Note that the total number of nodes in the levels γ^*+1 to h exceeds $(m-1)(h-\gamma^*+c)$. If nodes are removed (m−1) at a step, then after $h-\gamma^*+c$ steps, there exists at least one node in the level γ^*+1. This means that we need at least γ^*+1 steps to finish the remaining graph, so we need at least

$$(h-\gamma^*+c) + (\gamma^*+1) = h+c+1 \text{ steps.}$$

This shows that m−1 processors will not be sufficient.

To show that m processors are sufficient, we argue as follows. If each level is removed in a single step, then the whole graph can be removed in h steps. If not all levels can be removed in single steps, then there must be a lowest level which cannot be removed in one step when it first becomes the maximum level. Let this be the level $\gamma + 1$.

Then according to the algorithm, all nodes are removed "m" at a time in levels h,h−1,...,$\gamma+1$. So the total time needed for removing nodes on and above the level $\gamma+1$ is

$$\left\lceil \frac{1}{m} \sum_{j=\gamma+1}^{h} p(j) \right\rceil \leqslant h - \gamma + c,$$

i.e., all the nodes on and above the level $\gamma+1$ are removed in $h-\gamma+c$ steps. The remaining graph has α levels for which each level can be removed in one step, and can all be removed in γ units of time. So the total time is

$$(h - \gamma + c) + \gamma = h + c \text{ units of time.}$$

EXERCISES

1. Assume that the weights of the coins are equal and their values are 1, 4, 7, 9. Does the greedy algorithm work? What happens if the values are 1, 5, 14, 18?

2. Construct a list of numbers such that the BF rule is better than the FF rule.

3. Draw the constraint graph among tasks shown in Figure 6.14.

4. In Yao's algorithm of bin-packing, we have to put m^{th} β_2 item in class 1 where m can assume the value 7, 8, or 9. What would be the worst ratio if there is no β_2 item? What would be the ratio if all β_2 items are put into class 3 bins.

5. Generalize the job-scheduling algorithm in § 6.4 to multiple trees, in-trees, and out-trees.

   (In an in-tree, every node has at most one son, whereas in an out-tree, every node has at most one father.)

6. Read the article by R. R. Muntz and E. G. Coffman in Journal of ACM, Vol. 17, No. 2, April 1970.

CHAPTER 6

BIBLIOGRAPHIC NOTES AND SUGGESTED READING

Theorem 1 is due to Magazine, Nemhauser and Trotter [10], the proof of the Theorem in section 6.1 is adopted from Hu and Lenard [6]. Error bounds on the heuristic algorithm are reported in [10] and [12]. If we consider the values of the coins as a sequence, then Theorem 1 gives the condition that a sequence would yield an optimum solution if its subsequence also yields an optimum solution. However, there are cases that a sequence will yield optimum solutions but its subsequence does not. This case is studied in Johnson and Kerninghan [9].

The first classical report on the bin-packing algorithm is the Ph.D. thesis of D. S. Johnson [8] where most of the bounds on NF, BF, FFD, etc., are obtained. For application of bin-packing to multiprocessing scheduling, see Coffman, Garey, and Johnson [3]. The Yao algorithm together with many other interesting results is in [13]. The bounds on heuristic scheduling can be improved if all tasks are approximately of the same length, see Achugbue and Chin [1].

The first paper on parallel sequencing (job-scheduling) is in Hu [7] and a very complete survey is reported in the book edited by Coffman [2]. A more recent survey is by Graham [5]. The two-processor problem for an arbitrary-constraint graph is solved in Coffman and Graham [4]. The proof of the critical-path scheduling in section 6.4 is new, a generalization of the critical-path scheduling is in Nett [11].

1.   J. O. Achugbue and F. Y. Chin, "Bounds on Schedules for Independent Tasks with Similar Execution Times", University of Alberta Tech. Report 79-2.

2.   E. G. Coffman, Jr. (ed.), "Computer and Job Shop Scheduling Theory", Wiley & Sons, 1976.

3.   E. G. Coffman, M. R. Garey, and D. S. Johnson, "An Application of Bin-Packing to Multi-Processing Scheduling", SIAM J. Computing 7(1) (1978), pp. 1-17.

4.   E. G. Coffman and R. L. Graham, "Optimal Scheduling for Two-Processor Systems", Acta Informatica 1 (1972), pp. 200-213.

5.   R. L. Graham, "The Combinatorial Mathematics of Scheduling", Scientific Amer. 238, No. 3 (1978), pp. 104-123.

6.   T. C. Hu and M. L. Lenard, "Optimality of a Heuristic Solution for a Class of Knapsack Problems", ORSA 24(1) (1976), pp. 193-196.

7.   T. C. Hu, "Parallel Sequencing and Assembly Line Problems", J. ORSA 9(6) (1961), pp. 841-848.

8.   D. S. Johnson, "Near-Optimal Bin-Packing Algorithms", MIT Report, MAC TR-109, June 1973.

9.   S. C. Johnson and B. W. Kernighan, "Making Change with a Minimum Number of Coins", Bell Telephone Report, Murray Hill, New Jersey.

10.   M. Magazine, G. L. Nemhauser, and L. E. Trotter, Jr., "When the Greedy Solution Solves a Class of Knapsack Problems", J. ORSA 23 (1975, pp. 207-217.

11.   E. Nett, "On Further Application of the Hu Algorithm to Scheduling Problems", Proceedings of 1976 International Conference on Parallel Processing, P. H. Enslow, Jr. (ed.).

12.   B. N. Tien and T. C. Hu, "Error Bounds and the Applicability of the Greedy Solution to the Coin-Changing Problem", J. ORSA 25(3) (1977), pp. 404-418.

13.   A. C. Yao, "New Algorithms in Bin-Packing", Stanford Univ. Report, STAN-CS-78-662.

CHAPTER 7. MATRIX MULTIPLICATION

Matrix computation is the arithmetic of higher mathematics.

§7.1 STRASSEN'S MATRIX MULTIPLICATION

Matrix computation is usually considered as a topic in linear algebra or numerical analysis. In this chapter, we give two results in the computation of matrices derived from combinatorial considerations. The first result, due to Strassen [15], deals with the multiplication of two square matrices. The second result, due to Hu and Shing [9] [10] [11], deals with the optimum order of multiplying a chain of matrices of different dimensions.

Consider the multiplication of two 2×2 matrices where

$$\begin{bmatrix} c_{11} & c_{12} \\ c_{21} & c_{22} \end{bmatrix} = \begin{bmatrix} a_{11} & a_{12} \\ a_{21} & a_{22} \end{bmatrix} \begin{bmatrix} b_{11} & b_{12} \\ b_{21} & b_{22} \end{bmatrix} \tag{1}$$

The elements c_{ij} are defined in the normal manner

$$c_{11} = a_{11}b_{11} + a_{12}b_{21} \tag{2}$$

$$c_{12} = a_{11}b_{12} + a_{12}b_{22}$$

$$c_{21} = a_{21}b_{11} + a_{22}b_{21}$$

$$c_{22} = a_{21}b_{12} + a_{22}b_{22}$$

Note that 8 multiplications and 4 additions are needed in (2). In general for two m×m matrices, we need m^3 multiplications and $m^2(m-1)$ additions.

The straightforward way of matrix multiplication has been accepted for many years. It is very surprising that a new way of multiplication was discovered by Strassen [15] in 1969. The new way of multiplying (1) requires 7 multiplications and 18 additions and subtractions. If we use this method recursively for two very large m×m matrices, we need $O(m^{\log_2 7})$ multiplications.

To introduce the new way of multiplication, we first define 7 products as follows.

$$d_1 = (a_{11} + a_{22})\ (b_{11} + b_{22})$$

$$d_2 = (a_{12} - a_{22})\ (b_{21} + b_{22})$$

$$d_3 = (a_{11} - a_{21})\ (b_{11} + b_{12})$$

$$d_4 = (a_{11} + a_{12})\ b_{22} \tag{3}$$

$$d_5 = (a_{21} + a_{22})\ b_{11}$$

$$d_6 = a_{11} \, (b_{12}-b_{22})$$

$$d_7 = a_{22} \, (-b_{11}+b_{21})$$

The elements c_{ij} can then be expressed in terms of d_k as follows

$$
\begin{array}{lllll}
c_{11} = d_1 + d_2 & & -d_4 & & +d_7 \\
c_{12} = & & d_4 & +d_6 & \\
c_{21} = & & & d_5 & +d_7 \\
c_{22} = d_1 & -d_3 & & -d_5 & +d_6
\end{array}
\qquad (4)
$$

It is easy to verify that (2) and (4) are the same and that there are 7 multiplications and 18 additions and subtractions in (3) and (4).

If we multiply two m×m matrices where m is a power of 2, then we can partition each matrix into four square matrices, namely

$$
\begin{bmatrix} C_{11} & C_{12} \\ C_{21} & C_{22} \end{bmatrix} = \begin{bmatrix} A_{11} & A_{12} \\ A_{21} & A_{22} \end{bmatrix} \begin{bmatrix} B_{11} & B_{12} \\ B_{21} & B_{22} \end{bmatrix}
\qquad (5)
$$

and process the submatrices recursively.

The submatrices C_{ij}, A_{ij} and B_{ij} are related in the same way as (2), (3) and (4).

Let $T(m)$ be the time required to multiply two m×m matrices. From (3) and (4), we have the following recurrence relation

$$T(m) = 7 \, T\left(\frac{m}{2}\right) + 18\left(\frac{m}{2}\right)^2 \text{ for } m \geqslant 2. \qquad (6)$$

Solving (6), we have

$$T(m) = O(m^{\log_2 7}) . \qquad (7)$$

The recent result of V. Ya. Pan [13] gives asymptotic improvement of Strassen's result. For other results in Arithmetic Complexity of Computation, see Winograd [16].

§7.2 OPTIMUM ORDER OF MULTIPLYING MATRICES

Consider the multiplication of four matrices

$$
\begin{array}{ccccccc}
M = & M_1 & \times & M_2 & \times & M_3 & \times & M_4 \\
& [10 \times 11] & & [11 \times 25] & & [25 \times 40] & & [40 \times 12]
\end{array}
\qquad (1)
$$

where the dimensions of M_i are written below each M_i in (1). Since matrix multiplication satisfies the associative law, the final result M is the same for all orders of processing (1). If we use the normal way to multiply a p×q matrix by a q×r matrix, we need p.q.r multiplications. Hence, if we multiply (1) as shown in (2)

$$M = (((M_1 \times M_2) \times M_3) \times M_4) \qquad (2)$$

we need

$$10 \times 11 \times 25 + 10 \times 25 \times 40 + 10 \times 40 \times 12 = 17550 \text{ multiplications}$$

However, if we multiply (1) as shown in (3)

$$M = (M_1 \times (M_2 \times (M_3 \times M_4))). \qquad (3)$$

we need

$$25 \times 40 \times 12 + 11 \times 25 \times 12 + 10 \times 11 \times 12 = 16620 \text{ multiplications.}$$

Examples can be constructed to show that a bad order of multiplication is very much worse than an optimum order of multiplication (see for example [1]).

So the general problem is to find an order of evaluating n−1 matrices

$$M = M_1 \times M_2 \times ... \times M_{n-1} \qquad (4)$$

where M_i is a $w_i \times w_{i+1}$ matrix such that the total number of multiplications is minimum. An order of multiplication corresponds to a way of putting brackets around n−1 symbols, and there are $\dfrac{[2(n-2)]!}{(n-2)! \, (n-1)!}$ ways to insert the n−2 pairs of brackets.

The dynamic programming approach can be used to find an optimum order (see Chapter 3, [1] [6] [8] [14]). This would require $O(n^3)$ time. An $O(n \log n)$ algorithm for finding an optimum order has been developed by Hu and Shing [11] but will not be described in this chapter. Here, we first transform the problem of matrix chain product problem into the problem of partitioning a convex polygon into non-intersecting triangles, then we state several theorems about the optimum partition problem. Based on these theorems, we develop an $O(n)$ heuristic algorithm [12] which has a 15% error in the worst case.

§7.3 PARTITIONING A CONVEX POLYGON

The problem of matrix chain product is to find an optimum order of multiplying n−1 matrices

$$M = M_1 \times M_2 \times ... \times M_{n-1} \qquad (1)$$

where M_i is a $w_i \times w_{i+1}$ matrix. For the moment, we shall devote attention to the seemingly unrelated problem of partitioning a convex polygon.

Given an n-sided convex polygon, such as the hexagon shown in Figure 7.1, the number of ways to partition the polygon into $(n-2)$ triangles by non-intersecting diagonals is the Catalan numbers (see for example, Gould [7]). Thus, there are two ways to partition a convex quadrilateral, five ways to partition a convex pentagon, and fourteen ways to partition a convex hexagon.

Let every vertex V_i of the convex polygon have a weight w_i. We can define the cost of a given partition as follows: The cost of a triangle is the product of the weights of the three vertices, and the cost of partitioning a polygon is the sum of the costs of all its triangles. For example, the cost of the partition of the hexagon in Figure 7.1 is

$$w_1w_2w_3 + w_1w_3w_6 + w_3w_4w_6 + w_4w_5w_6 \qquad (2)$$

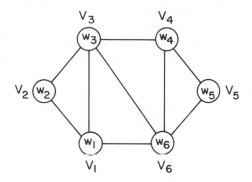

Figure 7.1. A partition of a hexagon.

If we erase the diagonal from V_3 to V_6 and replace it by the diagonal from V_1 to V_4, then the cost of the new partition will be

$$w_1w_2w_3 + w_1w_3w_4 + w_1w_4w_6 + w_4w_5w_6 \ . \qquad (3)$$

For brevity, we shall use w_i to denote the vertex V_i with the weight w_i, n-gon to mean a convex polygon with n sides, and the partition of n-gon to mean the partitioning of an n-gon into $(n-2)$ non-intersecting triangles.

The one-to-one correspondence between the orders of multiplying $(n-1)$ matrices and the partitions of a convex n-gon can be established as follows. For any n-gon, one side shall be drawn horizontally at the bottom, such as the side V_1-V_6 in Figure 7.1. This side is called the base. All other sides are considered in the clockwise direction. Thus, V_1-V_2 is the first side, V_2-V_3 the second side, ..., and V_5-V_6 the fifth side. The first side represents the first matrix in the matrix chain and the base represents the final result M in (1). The dimensions of a matrix are the two weights associated with the two end vertices of the side.

Since the adjacent matrices are compatible, the dimensions $w_1 \times w_2, w_2 \times w_3, ..., w_{n-1} \times w_n$ can be written inside the vertices of an n-gon as $w_1, w_2, ..., w_n$. The diagonals are the partial products. The cost of a partition equals the total number of operations needed to multiply the matrices in the corresponding order.

A partition of an n-gon corresponds to either an alphabetic tree of $n-1$ leaves or the parenthesis problem on $n-1$ symbols (see, for example, Gardner [5]). It is also easy to see the one-to-one correspondence between the multiplication of $n-1$ matrices to either the alphabetic binary tree or the parenthesis problem of $n-1$ symbols. However, the correspondence between the order of evaluating the matrix-chain product and the partition of a convex polygon is established directly here.

Theorem 1 Any order of multiplying $n-1$ matrices corresponds to a partition of an n-gon.

Proof. The proof is by induction on the number of matrices. For two matrices of dimensions $w_1 \times w_2$ and $w_2 \times w_3$, there is only one way of multiplication, this corresponds to a triangle where no further partition is required. The total number of operations in multiplication is $w_1 w_2 w_3$, the product of the three weights of the vertices. The resulting matrix has dimension $w_1 \times w_3$. For three matrices, the two orders of multiplication $(M_1 \times M_2) \times M_3$ and $M_1 \times (M_2 \times M_3)$ correspond to the two ways of partitioning a 4-gon. Assume that this lemma is true for k matrices where $k \leqslant n-2$, and we now consider $n-1$ matrices. The n-gon is shown in Figure 7.2.

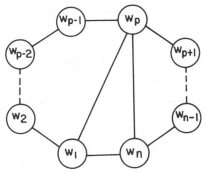

Figure 7.2.   Illustration for proof of Theorem 1.

Let the order of multiplication be represented by

$$M = (M_1 \times M_2 \times ... \times M_{p-1}) \times (M_p \times ... \times M_{n-1})$$

i.e., the final matrix is obtained by multiplying a matrix of dimension $(w_1 \times w_p)$ and a matrix of dimension $(w_p \times w_n)$. In the partition of the n-gon, let the triangle with vertices w_1 and w_n have the third vertex w_p. Then the polygon

$w_1-w_2-...-w_p$ is a convex polygon of p sides and its partition corresponds to an order of multiplying matrices $M_1,...,M_{p-1}$, giving a matrix of dimension $w_1 \times w_p$. Similarly, the partition of the polygon $w_p-w_{p+1}-...-w_n$ corresponds to an order of multiplying matrices $M_p,...,M_{n-1}$, giving a matrix of dimension $w_p \times w_n$. So the triangle $w_1 w_p w_n$ represents the multiplication of the two partial products, giving the final matrix of dimension $w_1 \times w_n$.

∎

The partitions corresponding to (2) and (3) of Section 2 are shown in Figure 7.5 on page 251.

Theorem 2 The minimum number of operations to evaluate the following matrix chain products are identical.

$$M_1 \times M_2 \times ... \times M_{n-2} \times M_{n-1}$$
$$M_n \times M_1 \times ... \times M_{n-3} \times M_{n-2}$$

$$\bullet$$
$$\bullet$$
$$\bullet$$

$$M_2 \times M_3 \times ... \times M_{n-1} \times M_n$$

where M_i has dimension $w_i \times w_{i+1}$ and $w_{n+1} \equiv w_1$. Note that in the first matrix chain, the resulting matrix is of dimension w_1 by w_n. In the last matrix chain, the resulting matrix is of dimension w_2 by w_1. But in all the cases, the total number of operations in the optimum order of multiplication is the same.

Proof. The cyclic permutations of the $n-1$ matrices all correspond to the same n-gon and thus have the same optimum partition.

∎

(This Theorem was obtained independently in [4] with a long proof.)

From now on, only the partitioning problem will be discussed.

The diagonals inside the polygon are called arcs. Thus, every partition consists of $n-2$ triangles formed by $n-3$ arcs and n sides.

In a partition of an n-gon, the degree of a vertex is the number of arcs incident to the vertex plus two (since there are two sides incident to every vertex).

Lemma 1 In any partition of an n-gon, at least two of the $n-2$ triangles are formed by two sides and one arc, i.e., these two triangles each has a vertex of degree two. (For example, in Figure 7.1, the triangle $V_1 V_2 V_3$ has vertex V_2 with degree 2 and the triangle $V_4V_5V_6$ has vertex V_5 with degree 2.)

Proof. In any partition of an n-gon, there are n−2 non-intersecting triangles formed by n−3 arcs and n sides. And for any $n \geqslant 4$, no triangle can be formed by 3 sides. Let x be the number of triangles with two sides and one arc, y be the number of triangles with one side and two arcs, and z be the number of triangles with three arcs. Since an arc is used in two triangles, we have

$$x + 2y + 3z = 2(n-3) \tag{4}$$

Since the polygon has n sides, we have

$$2x + y = n \ . \tag{5}$$

From (4) and (5), we get

$$3x = 3z + 6 \ .$$

Since $z \geqslant 0$, we have $x \geqslant 2$.   ∎

Lemma 2 Let P and P′ both be n-gons where the corresponding weights of the vertices satisfy $w_i \leqslant w_i'$ for $1 \leqslant i \leqslant n$, then the cost of the optimum partition of P is less than or equal to the cost of the optimum partition of P′.

Proof. Omitted.

    ∎

If we use $C(w_1,w_2,w_3...w_k)$ to mean the minimum cost of partitioning the k-gon with weights w_i, Lemma 2 can be stated as

$$C(w_1,w_2,...,w_k) \leqslant C(w_1',w_2',...,w_k') \text{ if } w_i \leqslant w_i' \ .$$

In the rest of this chapter, the following conventions will be adopted. The vertices denoted by $w_1,w_2,w_3,...$ are ordered according to their weights, i.e. $w_1 \leqslant w_2 \leqslant w_3 \leqslant ...$. The vertices denoted by $w_a,w_b,...$ are unordered. The product of any three vertices w_i, w_j and w_k is denoted by T_{ijk}.

To make the presentations and proofs easier to read, we can assume that all weights are distinct; in other words, we can perturbate the weights by ϵ to make all weights distinct. Even if all weights are distinct, an n-gon may still have more than one optimum partition in general. We shall use the following rule to deal with the non-uniqueness of optimum partitions.

After the vertices are labeled, we define an arc V_i-V_j to be <u>less than</u> another arc V_p-V_q

if $\min(i,j) < \min(p,q)$

or $\begin{cases} \min(i,j) = \min(p,q) \\ \max(i,j) < \max(p,q) \ . \end{cases}$

(For example, the arc V_3-V_9 is less than the arc V_4-V_5.) Every partition of an n-gon has $n-3$ arcs which can be sorted from the smallest to the largest into an ordered sequence of arcs, i.e., each partition is associated with a unique ordered sequence of arcs. We define a partition P to be lexicographically less than a partition Q if the ordered sequence of arcs associated with P is lexicographically less than that associated with Q.

When there are more than one optimum partition, we use the optimum partition to mean the lexicographically smallest optimum partition, and use an optimum partition to mean a partition of minimum cost.

We say that two vertices are connected in an optimum partition if two vertices are connected by an arc or if the two vertices are adjacent to the same side of the polygon.

Theorem 3 In every optimum partition of a polygon, the smallest vertex V_1 is always connected with the second smallest vertex V_2 and also with the third smallest vertex V_3 (i.e. both V_1-V_2 and V_1-V_3 exist in the optimum partition).

Proof. The proof is by induction. For the optimum partitions of any triangles and quadrilateral, the theorem is true. Assume that the theorem is true for all k-gons $(3 \leqslant k \leqslant n-1)$ and consider the optimum partitions of an n-gon.

From Lemma 1, there exists at least two vertices having degree two. Call these two vertices V_i and V_j. We have the following four cases.

(i)   One of the two vertices V_i (or V_j) is not V_1, V_2, or V_3. In this case, we can remove the vertex V_i with its two sides and obtain an $(n-1)$-gon. In this $(n-1)$-gon, V_1, V_2, and V_3 are the three vertices with smallest weights. By the induction assumption, both V_1-V_2 and V_1-V_3 exist in every optimum partition.

(ii) $V_i = V_2$ and $V_j = V_3$, i.e., both V_2 and V_3 have degree two. In this case, we can first remove V_2 with its two sides and show that V_1 and V_3 are connected. Then we can remove V_3 with its two sides and show that V_1 and V_2 are connected.

(iii) $V_i = V_1$ and $V_j = V_2$, i.e., both V_1 and V_2 have degree two. In this case, we can first remove V_1 and form an $(n-1)$-gon where V_2, V_3, and V_4 are the three vertices with smallest weights. By induction assumption, both V_2-V_3 and V_2-V_4 exist in the partition. Since V_2 has degree two, V_3 and V_4 must be connected to V_2 by sides in the n-gon. Similarly, we can remove V_2 and form a $(n-1)$-gon with V_1, V_3, and V_4 as the three vertices with smallest weights. Then V_1-V_3 and V_1-V_4 must also exist in the partition. Since V_1 is of degree two, the vertices V_3 and V_4 must also be connected to V_1 by sides. But for any n-gon $(n \geqslant 5)$, it is impossible to have V_3 and V_4 both adjacent to V_1 and V_2 at the same time.

(iv) $V_i = V_1, V_j = V_3$. By argument similar to (iii), we can show that V_2 must be adjacent to V_1 and V_3 in the n-gon. The situation is as shown in Figure 7.3a.

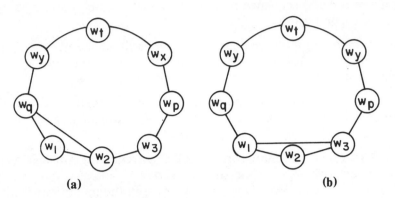

(a)   (b)

Figure 7.3. Illustration for proof of Theorem 3.

Then the partition in Figure 7.3b is cheaper because

$$T_{123} \leqslant T_{12q}$$

and

$$C(w_1, w_q, w_y, w_t, w_x, w_p, w_3) \leqslant C(w_2, w_q, w_y, w_t, w_x, w_p, w_3)$$

from Lemma 2.   ∎

Once we know that $V_1 - V_2$ and $V_1 - V_3$ always exist in every optimum partition, we can use this fact recursively. Hence, in finding the optimal partition of a given polygon, we can decompose it into subpolygons by joining the smallest vertex with the second smallest and third smallest vertices repeatedly, until each of these subpolygons has the property that its smallest vertex is adjacent to both its second smallest and third smallest vertices.

A polygon having V_1 adjacent to V_2 and V_3 by sides will be called a <u>basic polygon.</u>

Theorem 4 (i)   A necessary but not sufficient condition for $V_2 - V_3$ to exist in an optimum partition of a basic polygon is

$$\frac{1}{w_1} + \frac{1}{w_4} \leqslant \frac{1}{w_2} + \frac{1}{w_3} .$$

(ii) If V_2 and V_3 are not connected in an optimum partition, then V_1 and V_4 are always connected in that optimum partition.

Proof. If V_2 and V_3 are not connected in any basic polygon, the degree of V_1 is greater than or equal to 3. Let V_1-V_P be an arc of the partition, where V_4 is either in the subpolygon containing V_2 or in the subpolygon containing V_3. In either case, V_4 will be the third smallest vertex in the subpolygon. From Theorem 3, V_1 and V_4 are connected.

If V_2 and V_3 are connected, then we have an $(n-1)$-gon where V_2 is the smallest vertex and V_4 is the third smallest vertex. By Theorem 3, V_2 and V_4 are connected. Thus, we can assume that V_4 is adjacent to V_2 in the basic polygon as shown in Figure 7.4a.

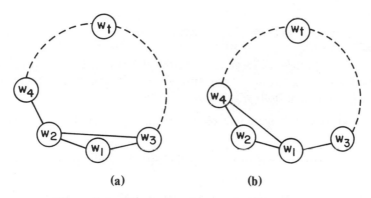

(a)   (b)

Figure 7.4. Illustration for proof of Theorem 4.

The cost of partitioning in Figure 7.4a is

$$T_{123} + C(w_2,w_4,...,w_t,...,w_3) \ . \tag{7}$$

And the cost of partitioning in Figure 7.4b is

$$T_{124} + C(w_1,w_4,...,w_t,...,w_3) \ . \tag{8}$$

According to Lemma 2,

$$C(w_1,w_4,...,w_t,...,w_3) \leqslant C(w_2,w_4,...,w_t,...,w_3) \ . \tag{9}$$

The difference between the LHS and RHS of (9) is at least

$$T_{234} - T_{134}$$

So the necessary condition for (7) to be less than or equal to (8) is

$$T_{123} + T_{234} \leqslant T_{124} + T_{134}$$

or

$$\frac{1}{w_1} + \frac{1}{w_4} \leqslant \frac{1}{w_2} + \frac{1}{w_3} \ . \qquad \blacksquare$$

Theorem 5 In an optimum partition of an n-gon, let V_x, V_y, V_z, and V_w be four vertices of an inscribed quadrilateral (where V_x and V_z are not adjacent in the inscribed quadrilateral). If there is an arc connecting V_x and V_z, then

$$\frac{1}{w_x} + \frac{1}{w_z} \geqslant \frac{1}{w_y} + \frac{1}{w_w} \tag{10}$$

Proof. The cost of partitioning the quadrilateral by the arc V_x-V_z is

$$T_{xyz} + T_{xz} \tag{11}$$

and the cost of partitioning the quadrilateral by the arc V_y-V_w is

$$T_{xyw} + T_{yzw} \tag{12}$$

For optimality, we have (11) $\leqslant$ (12) which is (10).   ∎

Note that this theorem is a generalization of Lemma 1 of Chin [3] where V_y is the vertex with the smallest weight and V_x, V_w, V_z are three consecutive vertices with w_w greater than both w_x and w_z.

A partition is called <u>stable</u> if every quadrilateral in the partition satisfies (10).

Corollary 1 An optimum partition is stable but a stable partition may not be optimum.

Proof. The fact that optimum partition has to be stable follows from Theorem 5. Figure 7.5 gives an example that a stable partition may not be optimum.   ∎

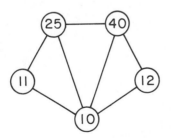   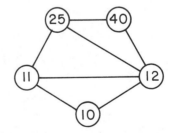

(a) A stable partition.   (b) An optimum partition.

Figure 7.5. An example showing that a stable partition may not be optimum.

In any partition of an n-gon, every arc dissects a unique quadrilateral. Let V_x, V_y, V_z, and V_w be the four vertices of an inscribed quadrilateral. Let V_x-V_z be the arc which dissects the quadrilateral. The arc V_x-V_z is said to be vertical if (13) or (14) is satisfied.

$$\min(w_x, w_z) < \min(w_y, w_w) \tag{13}$$

$$\left. \begin{array}{l} \min(w_x, w_z) = \min(w_y, w_w) \\[2em] \max(w_x, w_z) \leqslant \max(w_y, w_w) \end{array} \right\} \tag{14}$$

The arc $V_x - V_z$ is said to be horizontal if (15) is satisfied

$$\left. \begin{array}{l} \min(w_x, w_z) > \min(w_y, w_w) \\[2em] \max(w_x, w_z) < \max(w_y, w_w) \end{array} \right\} \tag{15}$$

For brevity, h-arcs and v-arcs are used to denote the horizontal arcs and vertical arcs from now on.

Corollary 2 All arcs in an optimum partition must be either vertical arcs or horizontal arcs.

Proof. Let $V_x - V_z$ be an arc which is neither vertical nor horizontal. There are two cases:

$$\text{Case 1.} \quad \begin{cases} \min(w_x, w_z) = \min(w_y, w_w) \\ \max(w_x, w_z) > \max(w_y, w_w) \end{cases}$$

$$\text{Case 2.} \quad \begin{cases} \min(w_x, w_z) > \min(w_y, w_w) \\ \max(w_x, w_z) \geqslant \max(w_y, w_w) \end{cases} .$$

In both cases, the inequality (10) in Theorem 5 cannot be satisfied. This implies that the partition is not stable and hence cannot be optimum. ■

Theorem 6 Let V_x and V_z be two arbitrary vertices in a polygon and V_w be the smallest vertex from V_x to V_z in the clockwise manner ($V_w \neq V_x$, $V_w \neq V_z$), and V_y be the smallest vertex from V_z to V_x in the clockwise manner ($V_y \neq V_x$, $V_y \neq V_z$). This is shown in Figure 7.6. Without loss of generality, we can assume that $w_x < w_z$ and $w_y < w_w$. The necessary condition for $V_x - V_z$ to exist as an h-arc in an optimum partition is

$$w_y < w_x \leqslant w_z < w_w .$$

Proof. The proof is by contradiction. If $w_x \leqslant w_y$, the vertex w_x must be equal to the smallest weight w_1 and $V_x - V_z$ can never satisfy (15). Hence, in order that $V_x - V_z$ exists as an h-arc in the optimum partition, we must have $w_y < w_x \leqslant w_z$. Since V_y is the smallest vertex from V_z to V_x in the clockwise manner and $w_x < w_w$, we must have $V_y = V_1$.

Figure 7.6. Illustration for Theorem 6.

Assume for the moment that $w_3 < w_x < w_z$. From Theoem 3, both V_1-V_2 and V_1-V_3 exist in every optimum partition, and the two arcs would divide the polygon into subpolygons. If V_x and V_z are in different subpolygons, then they cannot be connected in any optimum partition. Without loss of generality, we can assume that the polygon is a basic polygon. In this basic polygon, either V_2-V_3 or V_1-V_4 exists in an optimum partition (Theorem 4).

If V_2, V_3 are connected, then V_x and V_z are both in a $(n-1)$-gon and we can treat V_2 as the smallest vertex and repeat the argument. If V_1, V_4 are connected, the basic polygon is again divided into two subpolygons and V_x and V_z both have to be in one of the subpolygons and the subpolygon has at most $n-1$ sides. (Otherwise V_x-V_z can never exist in an optimum partition.) The successive reduction in the size of the polygon will either make the connection V_x-V_z impossible, or force V_x and V_z to become the second smallest and the third smallest vertices in a basic subpolygon. Let V_m be the smallest vertex in this basic subpolygon. In order that V_x-V_z appear as an h-arc, we must have $w_x > w_m$. From Theorem 4, the necessary condition for V_x-V_z (i.e. V_2-V_3) to exist in an optimum partition of the subpolygon is

$$\frac{1}{w_x} + \frac{1}{w_z} \geqslant \frac{1}{w_m} + \frac{1}{w_w} .$$

Since $w_x > w_m$, the inequality holds true only if $w_z < w_w$.   ∎

We define an arc V_x-V_z as defined in Theorem 7 to be a <u>potential</u> h-arc if its weights satisfy the following condition

$$w_x \leqslant w_z < w_w .$$

Note that this condition is a weaker condition than the necessary condition stated in Theorem 6. We call this a potential h-arc because it could exist as an h-arc in an optimum partition.

Corollary 3 Let V_w be the maximum vertex in the polygon and V_x and V_z be its two neighbors and $\max(w_x, w_z) < w_w$, then the arc V_x-V_z is a potential h-arc.

Proof. Omitted.
∎

Corollary 4 Let $V_x - V_z$ dissect the polygon into two subpolygons. The arc $V_x - V_z$ is a potential h-arc if all vertices in one of the subpolygons are greater than $\max(V_x, V_z)$.

Proof. It follows from the definition of potential h-arcs.
∎

We shall call the subpolygon with vertices of weights greater than $\max(w_x, w_z)$ the <u>upper</u> subpolygon of $V_x - V_z$.

Two arcs are called compatible if both can exists simultaneously in a partition. Two arcs are said to cross each other if both cannot exist simultaneously in a partition.

Assume that all weights of vertices are distinct, then there are $(n-1)!$ distinct permutations of the weights around an n-gon. For example, the weights in Figure 7.5(b) 10, 11, 25, 40, 12 correspond to the permutation w_1, w_2, w_4, w_5, w_3 (where $w_1 < w_2 < w_3 < w_4 < w_5$). There are infinitely many values of the weights which correspond to the same permutation. For example, 1, 16, 34, 77, 29 also correspond to w_1, w_2, w_4, w_5, w_3 but its optimum partitions are different from that of 10, 11, 25, 40, 12. However, all the potential h-arcs in all optimum partitions corresponding to the same permutation of weights are compatible. We state this remarkable fact as Theorem 7.

Theorem 7 All potential h-arcs in all optimum partitions of an n-gon with the same permutation of weights (same relative ordering of weights) are compatible.

Proof. Assume that $x_1 - z_1$ is a potential h-arc in one optimum partition and $x_2 - z_2$ is a potential h-arc in another optimum partition and the two arcs cross each other. Without loss of generality, we shall assume that

$$x_1 < z_1 \text{ and } x_2 < z_2 \quad \text{(note that } x_1 \text{ denotes the vertex as well as its weight.)}$$

Since $x_1 - z_1$ and $x_2 - z_2$ cross each other, the vertex x_2 must be in one of the two subpolygons dissected by $x_1 - z_1$ and z_2 must be in the other subpolygon.

It follows from Corollary 4, all the vertices in one of the subpolygons must all be larger than $\max(x_1, z_1)$ if $x_1 - z_1$ is a potential h-arc in some optimum partition. Thus

$$z_2 > \max(x_1, z_1) = z_1$$

Similarly, in order for $x_2 - z_2$ to be a potential h-arc in some optimum partition, we must have

$$z_1 > \max(x_2, z_2) = z_2$$

This contradicts $z_2 > z_1$.
∎

Using Corollary 3 and Theorem 7, we can generate all the potential h-arcs of a polygon.

Let $V_x - V_z$ be the arc defined in Corollary 3. The arc $V_x - V_z$ is a potential h-arc compatible to all other h-arcs in all optimum partitions. Furthermore, there is no other potential h-arcs in its upper subpolygon. Now consider the $(n-1)$-gon obtained by cutting out V_w. In this $(n-1)$-gon, let $V_{w'}$ be the largest vertex and $V_{x'}$ and $V_{z'}$ be the two neighbors of $V_{w'}$. The $V_{x'} - V_{z'}$ is again a potential h-arc compatible to all other h-arcs in other optimum partitions and there is no other h-arc in its upper subpolygon which has not been generated. This is true even if V_w is in the upper subpolygon of $V_{x'} - V_{z'}$. If we repeat the process of cutting out the largest vertex, we get $n-3$ arcs, all arcs satisfy the definition of potential h-arcs.

The h-arcs of any optimum partition must be a subset of the $n-3$ arcs.

The process of cutting out the largest vertex can be made into an algorithm which is $O(n)$. This algorithm is called the one-sweep algorithm.

The algorithm starts from the smallest vertex V_1 and checks the weights of vertices of the polygon in a clockwise manner. The weights of the vertices are pushed into a stack in the following way.

(i)   Let V_t be the top element on the stack, V_{t-1} be the element immediately below V_t, and V_c be the element to be pushed onto the stack. If there are two or more vertices on the stack and $w_t > w_c$, record $V_{t-1} - V_c$ as a potential h-arc, pop V_t off the stack; if there is only one vertex on the stack or $w_t \leqslant w_c$, push w_c onto the stack. Repeat this step until the nth vertex has been pushed onto the stack.

(ii)   If there are more than three vertices on the stack, record $V_1 - V_{t-1}$ as a potential h-arc. Pop V_t off the stack and repeat this step, else stop.

§7.4 THE HEURISTIC ALGORITHM

A partition which is made up entirely of v-arcs joining the smallest vertex to all other vertices is called a fan. A fan in the polygon $w_1 - w_b - w_c - w_d - ... - w_m - w_n$ is denoted by

$$\text{Fan}(w_1 \mid w_b, w_c, w_d, ..., w_m, w_n)$$

and the smallest vertex w_1 is called the center of the fan. The cost of the fan equals

$$w_1 \bullet (w_b w_c + w_c w_d + ... + w_m w_n) = w_1 \bullet (w_b : w_n)$$

where $w_b : w_n$ is a shorthand notation indicating the sum of the products going from w_b to w_n in a clockwise manner.

The algorithm to find a near-optimum partition of a convex polygon is based on two intuitions:

(i)   if a vertex has a very large weight, it should be cut out in the optimum partition, i.e. its degree should be equal to two;

(ii) if none of the vertices has a very large weight, the fan with the smallest vertex w_1 as its center should be near-optimum.

In [3], Chin gave a sufficient condition to determine whether two matrices are associated in the optimum order. Based on his idea, a similar sufficient condition for connecting two vertices in the optimum partition of a polygon is stated in Theorem 8.

If there are two or more vertices with weights equal to the smallest weight w_1, we can arbitrarily choose one to be the vertex V_1. Once the vertex V_1 is chosen, further ties in equal weights are resolved by regarding the vertex which is closer to V_1 in the clockwise direction to be of less weight. A vertex is called a local maximum vertex if its weight is larger than its two neighbors. A vertex is called a local minimum vertex if its weight is smaller than its two neighbors.

Theorem 8 [3] Let w_1 be the minimum vertex of a general convex polygon, and w_m be a local maximum vertex, with w_p and w_q as its two neighbors, i.e., $w_m > w_p$ and $w_m > w_q$. If

$$\frac{1}{w_p} + \frac{1}{w_q} > \frac{1}{w_1} + \frac{1}{w_m} , \tag{16}$$

then $w_p - w_q$ will exist in the optimum partition of the polygon.

Proof. The proof is by contradiction. Suppose there exists a local maximum vertex w_m such that (16) is satisfied and $w_p - w_q$ is not present in any optimum partition of the polygon. There will exist at least two triangles. each has w_m as one of its vertices, as shown in Figure 7.7a. (If w_p and w_q are connected to the same vertices, stability cannot be achieved.)

Let the triangle with w_p and w_m as two of its vertices have w_i as its third vertex, and the triangle with w_m and w_q as two of its vertices have w_j as its third vertex. Hence we can divide the polygon into five subpolygons and the optimum partition of the polygon can be obtained by combining the optimum partitions of these subpolygons together. Let us denote the cost of the optimum partition of the subpolygon P_i by C_i. Hence, the cost of the optimum partition of the polygon is

$$C_1 + C_2 + C_3 + C_4 + C_5 \tag{17}$$

where

$$C_1 = C(w_i,...,w_p),$$

$$C_2 = C(w_q,...,w_j),$$

$$C_3 = C(w_j,...,w_i,w_m),$$

$$C_4 = T_{ipm}, \quad \text{and}$$

$$C_5 = T_{jqm}.$$

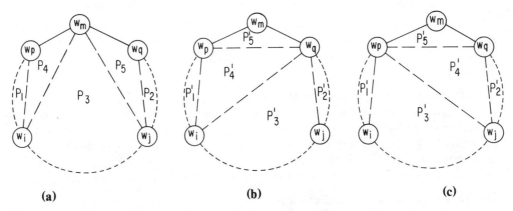

(a)   (b)   (c)

Figure 7.7.   Illustration for proof of Theorem 8.

Case 1 $w_i \leqslant w_j$

Consider the partition shown in Figure 7.7b. The cost of the partition is

$$C_1' + C_2' + C_3' + C_4' + C_5' \tag{18}$$

where

$$C_1' = C(w_i,...,w_p) = C_1,$$

$$C_2' = C(w_q,...,w_j) = C_2,$$

$$C_3' = C(w_j,...,w_i,w_q),$$

$$C_4' = T_{ipq}, \quad \text{and}$$

$$C_5' = T_{pmq} \ .$$

Since w_m is a local maximum vertex, we have $w_m > w_q$ and by Lemma 2,

$$C(w_j,...,w_i,w_m) > C(w_j,...,w_i,w_q) \leftrightarrow C_3 > C_3'. \tag{19}$$

From (16),

$$\frac{1}{w_p} + \frac{1}{w_q} > \frac{1}{w_1} + \frac{1}{w_m}$$

$$\rightarrow \quad \frac{1}{w_p} + \frac{1}{w_q} > \frac{1}{w_i} + \frac{1}{w_m} \qquad (\because w_i \geqslant w_1)$$

$$\rightarrow \quad T_{ipm} + T_{iqm} > T_{ipq} + T_{pqm}$$

$$\rightarrow \quad T_{ipm} + T_{jqm} > T_{ipq} + T_{pqm} \qquad (\because w_i \leqslant w_j)$$

$$\rightarrow \quad C_4 + C_5 > C_4' + C_5' \tag{20}$$

From (19) and (20), we have (18) < (17) which is a contradiction.

Case 2 $w_i > w_j$

Consider the partition shown in Figure 7.7c. The cost of the partition is

$$C_1' + C_2' + C_3' + C_4' + C_5' \tag{21}$$

where

$$C_1' = C(w_i, ..., w_p) = C_1,$$

$$C_2' = C(w_q, ..., w_j) = C_2,$$

$$C_3' = C(w_j, ..., w_i, w_p),$$

$$C_4' = T_{jpq}, \quad \text{and}$$

$$C_5' = T_{pqm}.$$

Since w_m is a local maximum vertex, we have $w_m > w_p$ and by Lemma 2,

$$C(w_j, ..., w_i, w_m) > C(w_j, ..., w_i, w_p) \leftrightarrow C_3 > C_3'. \tag{22}$$

From (16),

$$\frac{1}{w_p} + \frac{1}{w_q} > \frac{1}{w_1} + \frac{1}{w_m}$$

$$\rightarrow \quad \frac{1}{w_p} + \frac{1}{w_q} > \frac{1}{w_j} + \frac{1}{w_m} \qquad (\because w_j \geqslant w_1)$$

$$\rightarrow \quad T_{jpm} + T_{jmq} > T_{jpq} + T_{pqm}$$

$$\rightarrow \quad T_{ipm} + T_{jmq} > T_{jpq} + T_{pqm} \qquad (\because w_i > w_j) \tag{23}$$

$$\rightarrow \quad C_4 + C_5 > C_4' + C_5'$$

From (22) and (23), we have (21) < (17) which is a contradiction. ∎

Now we give the details of the heuristic algorithm to find a near optimum partition of an n-sided convex polygon.

We start from the smallest vertex w_1, travel in the clockwise direction around the polygon, and push the weights of the vertices successively onto the stack. (w_1 will be at the bottom of the stack.)

1. Let w_t be the top element on the stack, w_{t-1} be the element immediately below w_t, and w_c be the element to be pushed onto the stack. If there are two or more vertices on the stack and $\dfrac{1}{w_{t-1}} + \dfrac{1}{w_c} > \dfrac{1}{w_1} + \dfrac{1}{w_t}$, then join $w_{t-1}-w_c$ and pop w_t off the stack, else push w_c onto the stack. (Note that the inequality implies $w_t \geqslant w_{t-1}$ and $w_t > w_c$.) Repeat this step until the nth vertex has been pushed onto the stack.

2. If there are more than 3 vertices on the stack, join w_1-w_{t-1}, pop w_t off the stack and repeat this step, else Stop.

Note that step 1 cuts out a vertex if its weight is sufficiently large and step 2 joins w_1 to all vertices which have not been cut off.

In order to derive the upper bound for the error ratio, we shall first prove that, for any n-gon, we can find a monotone polygon of n-sides with an error ratio no less than the given n-gon. Then we shall prove that the maximum error ratio is achieved in a strictly monotone pentagon.

A <u>monotone</u> polygon is a convex polygon with only one local minimum vertex and one local maximum vertex. Let w_1 be the smallest vertex in a monotone n-gon, w_i be the ith vertex from w_1 in the clockwise direction, and w_i' be the ith vertex from w_1 in the counterclockwise direction. Then a monotone n-gon is said to be <u>strictly</u> <u>monotone</u> if for all i, $1 \leqslant i \leqslant \left\lfloor \dfrac{n}{2} \right\rfloor$, either $w_{i+1} \geqslant w_i' \geqslant w_i$ or $w_{i-1} \leqslant w_i' \leqslant w_i$. A typical strictly monotone basic polygon with ten vertices would be one with w_1, w_2, w_4, w_6, w_8, w_{10}, w_9, w_7, w_5 and w_3 in a clockwise manner.

Let P be the smallest convex polygon which gives the worst error ratio in the heuristic algorithm. P must consist of five vertices or more, because we always obtain the optimum partition of a quadrilateral by the heuristic algorithm.

Lemma 3 None of the local maximum vertices of P satisfies (16).

Proof. The proof is by contradiction. Suppose there exists a local maximum vertex w_m in P and it satisfies (16), as shown in Figure 7.8. Since the arc w_p-w_q is present in both the optimum partition and the partition produced by the heuristic algorithm, we can decompose P into two subpolygons P_1 and P_2. Let C_1 be the cost of partitioning P_1 optimally and F_1 be the cost of partitioning P_1 according to the heuristic algorithm.

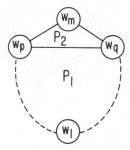

Figure 7.8

The error ratio of P

$$= \frac{F_1 - C_1}{(T_{pmq} + C_1)}$$

$$< \frac{F_1 - C_1}{C_1}$$

= the error ratio of P_1.

Hence, P_1 is a smaller polygon which gives a larger error ratio. This contradicts the assumption that P is the smallest polygon which gives the maximum error ratio.

Lemma 4 None of the arcs which appear in the optimum partition of P can be present in the fan produced by the heuristic algorithm.

Proof. The proof is by contradiction. Assume $w_1 - w_j$ is an arc present in both the optimum partition and the fan of P, as shown symbolically in Figure 7.9.

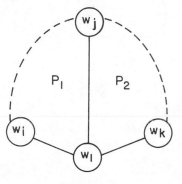

Figure 7.9

We can decompose P into two subpolygons P_1 and P_2. Let the cost of the optimum partition of P_i be C_i and the cost of a fan in P_i be F_i.

The error ratio of $P_1 = \dfrac{F_1-C_1}{C_1} = R_1$,

The error ratio of $P_2 = \dfrac{F_2-C_2}{C_2} = R_2$, and

The error ratio of the whole polygon

$$= \frac{(F_1-C_1) + (F_2-C_2)}{C_1+C_2} = R .$$

Let $R_1 = \max\{R_1,R_2\}$ and hence $R \leqslant R_1$. For maximum R, $R = R_1 = R_2$ and R_1 is a smaller basic polygon which produces the same error ratio. Hence, we have a contradiction.

∎

Lemma 5 Let V_x-V_y be an h-arc in the optimum partition of P. Then none of the v-arcs which appear in the fan of the upper subpolygon of V_x-V_y can be present in the optimum partition of P.

Proof. The proof is by contradiction. Let V_x-V_y be an h-arc in the optimum partition of P. Without loss of generality, we can assume $w_x \leqslant w_y$. Let V_x-V_j be the v-arc which is common to both the optimum partition of P and the fan in the upper subpolygon of V_x-V_y. Hence, P can be divided into 3 subpolygons as shown in Figure 7.10a. In Figure 7.10b P can also be divided into 3 subpolygons by the v-arcs in the fan produced by the heuristic algorithm. Let the optimum cost of partitioning P_i be C_i, and the cost of the fan in P_i' be F_i'.

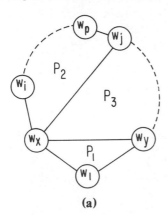

(a)

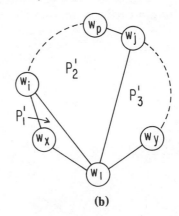

(b)

Figure 7.10.

The error ratio of P

$$= \frac{(F_1' + F_2' + F_3') - (C_1 + C_2 + C_3)}{C_1 + C_2 + C_3}$$

$$= \frac{[(F_1' + F_2') - (C_1 + C_2)] + (F_3' - C_3)}{(C_1 + C_2) + C_3}$$

$$= R \ .$$

Let $\dfrac{(F_1' + F_2') - (C_1 + C_2)}{C_1 + C_2}$ be R_1 and $\dfrac{F_3' - C_3}{C_3}$ be R_3. We have $R \leqslant \max\{R_1, R_3\}$.

Case 1 $R_1 \leqslant R_3$

Consider the subpolygon P_3' in Figure 7.11b.

The error ratio of P_3'

$$= \frac{w_1 \bullet (w_j : w_y) - C(w_1, w_j, \ldots, w_y)}{C(w_1, w_j, \ldots, w_y)}$$

$$\geqslant \frac{w_1 \bullet (w_j : w_y) - C(w_x, w_j, \ldots, w_y)}{C(w_x, w_j, \ldots, w_y)} \qquad (\because w_x \geqslant w_1)$$

$$= \frac{F_3' - C_3}{C_3}$$

$$= R_3$$

$$\geqslant R \ .$$

This contradicts the assumption that P is the smallest polygon which gives the worst error ratio.

Case 2 $R_1 > R_3$

Consider the polygon which is made up of $w_1 - w_x - w_i - \ldots - w_p - w_y$, i.e., the polygon obtained by deleting all vertices between w_p and w_y exclusively. By Corollary 4, we have $w_x \leqslant w_y \leqslant$ (all other vertices in the polygon). The error ratio of this polygon is

$$\frac{[w_1 \bullet (w_x : w_p) + T_{1pu}] - C(w_1, w_x, w_i, \ldots, w_p, w_y)}{C(w_1, w_x, w_i, \ldots, w_p, w_y)}$$

$$\geqslant \frac{[w_1 \bullet (w_x : w_p) + T_{1pu}] - [T_{1xy} + C(w_x, w_i, ..., w_p, w_y)]}{T_{1xy} + C(w_x, w_i, ..., w_p, w_y)}$$

Since $C(w_x, w_i, ..., w_p, w_j) - C(w_x, w_i, ..., w_p, w_y)$

$$\geqslant w_x \bullet w_p \bullet (w_j - w_y)$$

$$\geqslant w_1 \bullet w_p \bullet (w_j - w_y) \ ,$$

i.e. $T_{1pu} - C(w_x, ..., w_p, w_y) \geqslant T_{1pj} - C(w_x, ..., w_p, w_j)$. Hence, the error ratio is greater than or equal to

$$\frac{[w_1 \bullet (w_x : w_p) + T_{1pj}] - [T_{1xy} + C(w_x, w_i, ..., w_p, w_j)]}{T_{1xy} + C(w_x, w_i, ..., w_p, w_j)}$$

$$= \frac{[T_{1xi} + w_1 \bullet (w_i : w_j)] - [T_{1xy} + C(w_x, w_i, ..., w_p, w_j)]}{T_{1xy} + C(w_x, w_i, ..., w_p, w_j)}$$

$$= \frac{(F_1' + F_2') - (C_1 + C_2)}{C_1 + C_2}$$

$$= R_1$$

$$\geqslant R \ .$$

This again contradicts the assumption that P is the smallest polygon which gives the largest error ratio. ∎

Lemma 6 P is a strictly monotone n-gon and for all i. $1 \leqslant i \leqslant \left\lfloor \frac{n}{2} \right\rfloor$, either $w_i - w_i'$ and $w_{i-1} - w_i'$ or $w_i - w_i'$ and $w_{i+1} - w_i'$ will exist in the optimum partition of P, where $w_i (w_i')$ is the ith vertex from w_1 in the clockwise (counterclockwise) direction.

Proof. The proof is by induction. From Theorem 3 and Lemma 4 we can prove that w_1 is adjacent to both w_2 and w_3 and $w_2 - w_3$ is present in the optimum partition of P. From Theorem 3 and Lemma 5, we can prove that w_4 is adjacent to w_2 and $w_4 - w_3$ exists in the optimum partition of P. Using the same argument, we can show that w_5 is adjacent to w_3 with w_4 and w_5 connected, w_6 is adjacent to w_4 with w_6 and w_5 connected, and so on. Since n is finite, we can show in finite number of steps that for $1 \leqslant i \leqslant \left\lfloor \frac{n}{2} \right\rfloor$,

(i) $w_i \leqslant w_i' \leqslant w_{i+1}$, and

(ii) w_i and w_{i+1} are connected to w_i'. ∎

Theorem 9 P must be a strictly monotone 5-gon.

Proof. From Lemma 6, P must be a strictly monotone n-gon where $n \geqslant 5$.

Let the n vertices of P be $w_1, w_2, \ldots, w_n$ such that $w_1 \leqslant w_2 \leqslant w_3 \leqslant \ldots \leqslant w_{i-1} \leqslant w_i \leqslant w_{i+1} \leqslant \ldots \leqslant w_n$. P must have one of the following forms:

(i) $w_1 - w_2 - w_4 - \ldots - w_{n-2} - w_n - w_{n-1} - \ldots - w_5 - w_3$ if n is even,

or

(ii) $w_i - w_2 - w_4 - \ldots - w_{n-1} - w_n - w_{n-2} - \ldots - w_5 - w_3$ if n is odd.

Without loss of generality, let us assume n to be even. By Lemma 9, the optimum partition of P consists of the arcs $w_{i-1} - w_i$ and $w_{i+1} - w_i$, for all i which is odd and $3 \leqslant i \leqslant n-2$. This is shown symbolically in Figure 7.11a. In Figure 7.11b, a fan which is produced by the heuristic algorithm is shown.

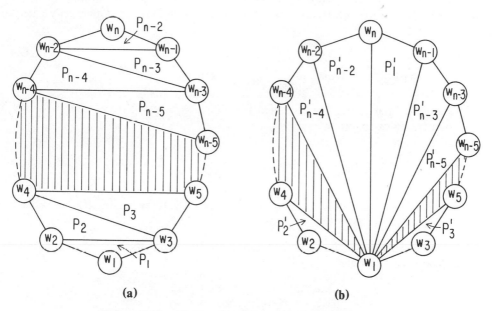

(a)   (b)

Figure 7.11. Illustration for proof of Theorem 9.

Let us denote the n−2 triangles in Figure 7.11a by $P_1,P_2,...,P_{n-2}$. Except P_1 and P_{n-2}, all the other n−4 triangles are made up of one side and two diagonals each. Hence, for each of these n−4 triangles, we can find a unique triangle in Figure 7.11b such that they both consist of the same side. P_i' is used to denote the image of P_i in Figure 11b. The only two triangles left unmatched in Figure 7.11b is $w_1w_{n-2}w_n$ and $w_1w_nw_{n-1}$ and they can be denoted as P_{n-2}' and P_1'. Let the cost of P_i be C_i and the cost of P_i' be F_i'. The error ratio is given by

$$\frac{\left(\sum_{i=1}^{n-2} F_i'\right) - \left(\sum_{i=1}^{n-2} C_i\right)}{\sum_{i=1}^{n-2} C_i} = R \ .$$

In the optimum partition, w_2 is involved in two triangles, namely $w_1w_2w_3$ and $w_2w_3w_4$, whereas in the heuristic partition, w_2 is involved in the triangle $w_1w_2w_4$ only. Reducing the weight w_2 would certainly increase the error ratio R. So we may assume that $w_2 \cong w_1$.

For the vertices w_3, w_4, ..., w_{n-2}, each of these vertices is involved in three triangles in the optimum partition and is involved in two triangles in the heuristic partition. Consider the vertex w_i, $3 \leqslant i \leqslant n-2$, the triangles involving w_i in the optimum partition are $w_{i-2}w_{i-1}w_i$, $w_{i-1}w_iw_{i+1}$ and $w_iw_{i+1}w_{i+2}$. These three triangles together cost

$$T_{(i-2)(i-1)(i)} + T_{(i-1)(i)(i+1)} + T_{(i)(i+1)(i+2)} \tag{24}$$
$$= w_i \bullet (w_{i-2} w_{i-1} + w_{i-1} w_{i+1} + w_{i+1} w_{i+2}) \ .$$

In the heuristic partition, the triangles involving w_i are $w_{i-2}w_iw_1$ and $w_iw_{i+2}w_1$. These two triangles together cost

$$T_{(i-2)(i)(1)} + T_{(i)(i+2)(1)} \tag{25}$$
$$= w_i \bullet (w_{i-2}w_1 + w_{i+2}w_1) \ .$$

Since (24) > (25), we can increase R by successively reducing the weights of $w_3,w_4,...,w_{n-2}$ and we have $w_2 \cong w_4 \cong ... \cong w_{n-2} \cong w_1$.

From Theorem 5, the necessary condition for w_{n-2}, w_{n-1} to be connected in the optimum partition is

$$\frac{1}{w_{n-2}} + \frac{1}{w_{n-1}} \geqslant \frac{1}{w_{n-3}} + \frac{1}{w_n} \ .$$

Since $w_{n-2} \cong w_{n-3} \cong w_1$, we have

$$\frac{1}{w_1} + \frac{1}{w_{n-1}} \geqslant \frac{1}{w_1} + \frac{1}{w_n} \ . \tag{26}$$

From Lemma 1, the local maximum vertex does not satisfy the sufficient condition of Theorem 4, we have

$$\frac{1}{w_1} + \frac{1}{w_n} > \frac{1}{w_{n-2}} + \frac{1}{w_{n-1}} \tag{27}$$

From (26) and (27), we have

$$w_{n-1} \cong w_n \quad .$$

For any n-gon, the maximum error ratio is achieved where all the vertices have two kinds of weights

$$w_{n-2} \cong w_{n-1} \cong \ldots \cong w_2 \cong w_1 = x \geqslant 1$$

and $\quad w_{n-1} \cong w_n = tx \quad$ where $t \geqslant 1$

So the cost of the optimum partition is

$$t^2 x^3 + t x^3 + (n-4) x^3$$

while the cost of the heuristic partition is

$$t^2 x^3 + 2t x^3 + (n-5) x^3$$

So the error ratio is given by

$$\frac{t x^3 - x^3}{t^2 x^3 + t x^3 + (n-4) x^3} = \frac{t-1}{t^2 + t + (n-4)} = R \tag{28}$$

Hence, the error ratio is inversely proportional "to" n and R is maximum when n = 5.

■

Now, it has been proved that P is a strictly monotone pentagon with the optimum partition as shown in Figure 7.12.

To find maximum R, we equate $\dfrac{\partial R}{\partial t} = 0$ and solve for t. For a given n, the worst error ratio is given by

$$t^2 - 2t - (n-3) = 0$$

or $\quad t = 1 + \sqrt{n-2}$

The maximum ratio occurs when n = 5 and t = $1 + \sqrt{3}$, which gives $\cong 0.1547$, as conjectured by Chin [3]. In Figure 7.13, a pentagon which achieves this maximum error ratio is shown. Hence, the upper bound is tight.

As n approaches ∞, $t \cong \sqrt{n}$ and $R = \dfrac{1}{2\sqrt{n}}$. In general, if t is given, i.e. $\dfrac{w_n}{w_1}$ is bounded, then we can calculate the maximum error ratio for any given n directly. For example, if $t = 2$, $R = \dfrac{1}{n+2}$.

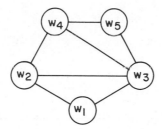

Figure 7.12. The partition of a pentagon which gives the maximum error ratio.

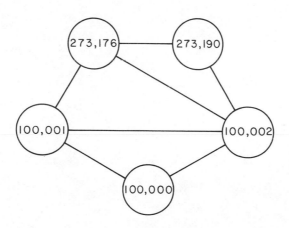

Figure 7.13. An example for maximum error ratio.

EXERCISES

1.   Prove the following theorem:

If the weights of vertices satisfy the following condition

$$w_1 = w_2 < w_3 \leqslant w_4 \leqslant \dots w_n$$

then every optimum partition of the n-gon must contain a triangle $V_1 V_2 V_p$ for some vertex V_p with weight equal to w_3.

2.   Prove the following theorem:

If the weights of vertices satisfy

$$w_1 = w_2 = \dots = w_k < w_{k+1} \leqslant w_{k+2} \leqslant \dots \leqslant w_n$$

$(3 \leqslant k \leqslant n)$, then every optimum partition of the n-gon contains the k-gon $Vs_1 - V_2 - \dots - V_k$.

3.   Formulate the optimum partition problem as a linear programming problem where each column corresponds to a triangle and each row corresponds to an arc.

CHAPTER 7

BIBLIOGRAPHIC NOTES AND SUGGESTED READING

Since matrix theory has been an important subject in all branches of mathematics, numerous papers and books have been written on the subject. The paper by Strassen [15] is considered to contain very important and surprising results. The algorithm of Pan [13] is an asymptotic improvement of Strassen's famous algorithms.

The matrix chain product problem must have existed for a long time. The dynamic programming approach has been used in finding the optimum order (see [1] [6] [8] [14]).

A heuristic algorithm was suggested in [2] and a further improvement was made by Chin [3]. The $O(n)$ heuristic algorithm is based on the paper by Hu and Shing [12]. For the $O(n\log n)$ optimum algorithm see [10] [11].

1.   A. V. Aho, J. E. Hopcroft and J. D. Ullman, "The Design and Analysis of Computer Algorithms", Addison-Wesley, 1974, p. 67.

2.   A. K. Chandra, "Computing Matrix Chaing Product in Near Optimum Time", IBM Res. Report RC5626 (#24393), IBM Thomas J. Watson Research Center, Yorktown Heights, NY, 1975.

3.   F. Y. Chin, "An O(n) Algorithm for Determining a Near Optimal Computation order of Matrix Chain Product", Communication of ACM, Vol. 21, No. 7, July 1978, pp. 544-549.

4.   L. E. Deimel, Jr. and T. A. Lampe, "An Invariance Theorem Concerning Optimal Computation of Matrix Chain Products", North Carolina State Univ. Report TR79-14.

5.   M. Gardner, "Catalan numbers", Scientific American, June 1976, pp. 120-124.

6.   S. S. Godbole, "An Efficient Computation of Matrix Chain Products", IEEE Trans. Computers C-22, 9 Sept. 1973, pp. 864-866.

7.   H. W. Gould, "Bell and Catalan Numbers", Combinatorial Research Institute, Morgantown, W. Va., June 1977.

8.   E. Horowitz and S. Sahni, "Fundamentals of Computer Algorithms", Computer Science Press, 1978, pp. 242-243.

9.   T. C. Hu and M. T. Shing, "Computation of Matrix Chain Product", Abstracts of AMS, Vol 1, No. 3., April 1980, Issue 3, 80T-A72, pp. 336.

10. T. C. Hu and M. T. Shing, "Some Theorems about Matrix Multiplications", 21st Symposium on Foundations of Computer Science, Oct. 1980, pp. 28-35.

11. T. C. Hu and M. T. Shing, "Computation of Matrix Chain Products, Part I and Part II", to appear in J. of SIAM on Computing, 1981.

12. T. C. Hu and M. T. Shing, "An O(n) algorithm to Find a Near-optimum Partition of a convex polygon", J. of Algorithms, Vol. 2, No. 2, June 1981, pp. 122-138.

13. V. Y. Pan, "New Fast Algorithms for Matrix Operations", SIAM J. on Computing, Vol. 9, No. 2, May 1980, pp. 321-342.

14. E.M. Reingold, J. Nievergelt, and N. Deo, "Combinatorial Algorithms: Theory and Practice", Prentice Hall, 1977, p. 156.

15. V. Strassen, "Gaussian Elimination is not optimal", Numer. Math. 13, (1969), pp. 354-356.

16. S. Winograd, "Arithmetic Complexity of Computations", CBMS--NSF regional conference in Applied Math, No. 33., SIAM publisher, 1980.

ANSWERS TO EXERCISES - CHAPTER 7

1.&2.   See later part of Hu and Shing [11].

3.   See the forthcoming paper by Dantzig, Hoffman and Hu.

CHAPTER 8. NP-COMPLETE PROBLEMS

God Grant me the serenity
To accept the problems that I cannot solve
The persistence to solve the problems that I can
And the wisdom to know the difference.

§8.1 INTRODUCTION

In the previous chapters, we have described many algorithms for solving various problems. Some algorithms are very efficient, others, quite tedious. A natural question is why do some problems seem to have no efficient algorithms. Are some problems intrinsically more difficult than others, or is it that efficient algorithms for these problems have not yet been found? If different problems have different degrees of difficulty, can problems be classified according to their degree of difficulty? The purpose of this chapter is to expand upon the concept "degree of difficulty of problems*. There are at least two reasons for classification of problems. First, if we know that a problem belongs to a very difficult class, we should not concentrate on getting optimum solutions. We may try to get approximate solutions, upper and lower bounds, heuristic approaches, etc. Second, when two problems belong to one class, the technique of solving one problem sometimes can be transformed to the other problem. It is not easy to identify which problem belongs to what class. Two problems may appear very similar and yet one can be much more difficult than the other.

Let us consider two problems for example.

Given a set of n distinct positive integers $x_1, x_2, ..., x_n$ (n even).

(i)   Partition the set into two subsets each of cardinality n/2 such that the difference between the sums of the two subsets is maximized.

(ii)   Partition the set into two subsets such that the difference between the sums of the two subsets is minimized.

Problem (i) can be solved by sorting all the integers $x_1, x_2, ..., x_n$ and putting the n/2 smaller integers into a subset and the n/2 larger integers into another set. This would take $O(n \log n)$ time. A better way is to find the median and use that integer to partition the two subsets. The algorithm of finding the kth largest integer among n integers is $O(n)$, so the algorithm takes $O(n)$ time. Since any algorithm presumably has to check each integer, $O(n)$ is a lower bound. In fact,

---

* For a complete treatment of the theory of NP-complete problems, see the book by Garey and Johnson [4]. The purpose of this chapter is to introduce some of the concepts on a more intuitive level.

we can solve this problem for two subsets of arbitrary sizes by finding the kth largest integer and then partitioning the set into two subsets of size k and n-k.

We can solve problem (ii) by partitioning the set into size k and n-k and recording their sums. If we try all possible combinations of k, then we can certainly find the minimum difference. This algorithm needs

$$\sum_{k=1}^{n/2} \binom{n}{k} \text{ time or } O(2^n) \ .$$

Of course, there are better algorithms than we have just described, but none has yet found a polynomial algorithm, or a bound where n does not appear in the exponential.

We have just skipped over several points worthy of consideration. First, when we say a problem of partitioning integers $x_1, x_2, \ldots, x_n$, we mean all possible values of integers. If $x_1, x_2, \ldots, x_n$ are specified, then it is an instance of the problem. To solve a problem means to solve all possible instances of the problem.

For a given instance, we may have a very efficient algorithm, but we are interested in how an algorithm behaves under the worst possible input data. If no confusion should arise, we shall use the word problem instead of "all possible instances of a problem."

Second, we are interested in large problems. To describe a problem, we need to encode the input data into a string of binary digits for example. And we will assume that the string is of length n. Then the amount of time needed by an algorithm is a function of n, $f(n)$. We are interested in the asymptotic behavior of $f(n)$.

In reality, we do not actually encode the input data and then measure the length of the encoded string. In theory, we should encode the input data and then measure the length of the encoded string. For many problems in graph theory, we can use the number of nodes or the number of arcs as the measure of the size of the problem, since they are polynomially equivalent. The choice of a parameter to represent the size of a problem is commonly accepted, and will not alter the classification of a problem.

Third, there are various ways of encoding data to describe the same problem. For example, a graph could be described by a node-arc incidence matrix, or a list of all the nodes and their adjacent neighboring nodes. Let the input data be encoded and have length n, and the algorithm need $f(n)$ time. We would like to know if $f(n)$ is a polynomial function, or an exponential function. [A function is considered an exponential function if n appears in the exponent, thus $n^{\log n}$ is considered an exponential function.] This classification of $f(n)$ into polynomial and exponential functions does not depend on encodings; i.e., the function $f(n)$ will never be a polynomial function for one reasonable encoding and an exponential function for another reasonable encoding. In this sense, all reasonable encodings will give the same result.

Fourth, what computer is needed to execute the algorithm so that $f(n)$ units of time is needed? The most primitive computer is called a Turing Machine. It is an artificial computer, an abstract machine model that can read symbols from a tape, erase a symbol, and halt. We also have many realistic random-access-machine models which are like the very high speed computers on the market. It turns out that if an algorithm needs exponential time on a Turing Machine, then the algorithm also needs exponential time on any real computer, and vice versa. In other words, the polynomial time or exponential time is independent of the computer selected. Thus, we can assume that we have a computer with a single central processing unit and unlimited memory space.

We shall classify problems into four classes according to their degrees of difficulty.

1. Undecidable problems (unsolvable problems): These are the problems for which no algorithm can be written. For example, it was proved that the problem of deciding whether a program will halt on a Turing Machine belongs to this class. We shall not discuss this class of problems in this book.

2. Intractable problems (provably difficult problems): These are the problems which no polynomial algorithm can possibly be developed to solve them. In other words, only exponential algorithms can be expected to solve them.

3. NP problems: (Here NP stands for nondeterministic polynomial.) This class includes problems that can be solved in polynomial time if we can *guess* correctly what computational path that we should follow. The concept of *guessing* is strange since all computer programs are deterministic. Roughly speaking, this class includes all problems that have exponential algorithms but we have not proved that they cannot have polynomial-time algorithms. This will be discussed fully in the next section.

4. P-problems: (Here P stands for polynomial). This class includes all problems that have polynomial-time algorithms. Most people consider this class as a proper subclass of class 3. The relationships between NP-problems and P-problems are the main topics of the next section.

§8.2 POLYNOMIAL ALGORITHMS

In this section, we shall discuss problems that have polynomial algorithms.

As we have mentioned in 8.1 all problems having polynomial algorithms belong to the class P. Thus a problem requiring $n \log n$ units of time belongs to the class P, as does the problem requiring $(n^{116} + 3n^4 + 7739)$ units of time. The unit of time is not specified. The unit could be a microsecond or an hour. In either case, only a constant multiple of 3,600,000,000 is involved. There are three reasons for concentrating on the class P. First, the addition or the multiplication of two polynomials yields a polynomial, thus polynomials are invariant under substitution. It is easy to count the number of steps in an algorithm to see if a polynomial amount of time is needed. Second, the polynomial function is insensitive to detailed implementation. An implementation by a different data structure may lower the degree of a polynomial but we have not yet found an example in which two implementations of the same algorithm result in one polynomial function and one exponential function. In this sense, the property of having polynomial time becomes an intrinsic property of an algorithm. The third reason for concentrating on polynomial algorithms is that polynomial algorithms are better than exponential algorithms when the problem is large. Consider the algorithms A and B. The algorithm A needs n^5 operations and the algorithm B needs 2^n operations. If each operation takes a microsecond, then the algorithm A needs 0.1 second for n = 10 and 13 minutes for n = 60. On the other hand, the algorithm B needs 0.001 second for n=10 and 366 centuries for n=60. For this reason, Edmonds called polynomial algorithms good algorithms. Even if a polynomial algorithm is worse than an exponential algorithm for certain n, the polynomial algorithm always catches up in speed for large n. Note that the comparison is for the worse case only, there are exponential algorithms that are faster than polynomial algorithms in average cases.

We do not partition the class P into subclasses, such as n, n log n, n^3, etc., just as we use the big O-notation without worrying about the coefficients of n. The reader should be aware of the beauty of the theory as well as its shortcomings.

Let us consider the problem of deciding if a graph has a Euler circuit. A graph has a Euler circuit if and only if

(i)   the graph is connected,

(ii)   the degree of every node is even.

We shall not prove that the two conditions are necessary and sufficient, but shall only estimate the amount of work involved in checking these two conditions.

Assume that the graph is given as an n×n matrix where the entry in the ith row and jth column is 1 if the ith vertex is adjacent to the jth vertex, and the entry is 0 if otherwise. (For our purpose, we define all entries in the diagonals to be zero.) To check if all nodes have even degrees, we add all 1's in each row to see if the sum is even. Since there are n rows, there are n operations. If we consider looking at each entry as one operation, then we need n^2 operations. In any case, a polynomial time is needed. To check if the graph is connected, we shall assume that the graph is given in adjacent-list form, i.e. a list of nodes together with all the neighboring nodes of each node. We can first construct an adjacency list from the matrix in $O(n^2)$ time, and then we can use depth-first-search to see if the graph is connected. Since every arc of the graph is traversed at most twice (twice if the arc is in the tree, once if it is not), the algorithm needs an additional $O(m+n)$ time, where m is the number of arcs. Since $m = O(n^2)$, we again have a polynomial time algorithm in terms of n, the number of nodes in the graph. One thing should be emphasized here, the algorithm can give the answer "yes" - the graph has a Euler circuit or the answer "no" - the graph does not have a Euler circuit both in polynomial time.

It is customary to formulate a problem in such a way that the answer is either yes or no. For the travelling salesman's problem of finding the shortest circuit in a graph, we recast the question as follows.

Does the graph have a tour of total distance less than B? If we can always decide this question in polynomial time, then we can also answer the travelling salesman's problem in polynomial time by asking a set of different B's. (It is easy to establish the upper and lower bounds of the shortest distance, and we can then use binary search to try different values of B.)

From now on, we shall assume all problems have the answer "yes" or "no". All these problems are called decision problems while the problems of maximizing or minimizing a function are called optimization problems.

Let us consider an algorithm as a computer program. For a given input data, the computer program will do various computations. Depending on the intermediate results of the computations, the computer program will execute various successive computations until the final answer is obtained. For decision problems, the answer is either "yes" or "no".

We can imagine the whole computation process as a rooted tree*. where each node represents some computation, and the leaves are labeled with "yes" or "no".

For an algorithm to have a polynomial time, the height of this rooted tree for any parameter n must be a polynomial of n; furthermore, the amount of time needed by each node must also be a polynomial.

When the input data is given, the computer program will do some computation, the result of this computation then decides which computational path to follow next. A polynomial algorithm has the property that all its computational paths are bounded by polynomial time.

The requirement that all computational paths be bounded by polynomials is

---

* Other books use trees to represent nondeterministic computations. This use of trees is different and should not be confused with such trees of nondeterministic computation.

very stringent. For a graph problem, an algorithm may need polynomial time if the graph is planar, but will need exponential time if the graph is not planar. It is of great importance to select a special class and solve it with an efficient algorithm where the general class has only exponential algorithms. Within the class P, new efficient algorithms or better implementation of existing algorithms can change the time from n^3 to n^2, n^2 to $n\log n$. These are very important areas of research but are not our main concern in this chapter.

§8.3 NONDETERMINISTIC ALGORITHMS

In this section, we discuss problems that belong to the class NP.

Here NP stands for nondeterministic polynomial. Let us discuss the concept of nondeterministic algorithms. Take the travelling salesman's problem, for example, a deterministic algorithm like backtracking will specify which arc to travel from a given node. For the question, does there exist a tour with total distance less than B, the backtrack algorithm implicitly tries all possible tours and gives the answer yes if indeed such a tour exists, and no otherwise.

Since the tours are tried one by one, and the last one may be the tour with the desired property, the backtrack algorithm for solving the travelling salesman's problem is considered to be $O(c^n)$.

For a nondeterministic algorithm, the algorithm can *correctly guess* which arc should be travelled next. So if there exists a tour with total distance less than B, the nondeterministic algorithm takes $O(n)$ to compute the total distance of the tour and verify that such a tour exists. And we can consider the travelling salesman's problem can be solved by a nondeterministic algorithm in polynomial time if the answer is "yes".

Roughly speaking, if the "yes" answer can be verified in polynomial time, then we consider the problem can be solved by a nondeterministic algorithm in polynomial time or the problem belongs to the class NP.

On the other hand, if there does not exist a tour with total distance less than B, to be able to answer "no" seems to require more than the ability to guess correctly. Thus the problem of answering "no" probably does not belong to NP.

When a problem belongs to P, its complement also belongs to P. It is believed that this is not true for problems in NP (although the question is technically still open).

By definition if a problem belongs to the class P, then it also belongs to the class NP. So the class P is a subclass of NP. A leading question in theoretical computer science today is

$$P = NP?$$

In other words, is the inclusion relationship a proper one?

To prove that $P = NP$, we must prove all problems in NP can be solved in polynomial time by deterministic algorithms. And no one has done this. To prove that $P \neq NP$, we must show a problem in NP which cannot be solved deterministically in polynomial time. No one has done this either.

Most people believe that $P \neq NP$, and that we need new mathematical techniques to settle this question.

§8.4 NP-COMPLETE PROBLEMS

The Hamiltonian circuit problem asks if there is a tour which visits every vertex exactly once. The traveling salesman problem asks if there is a tour of sufficiently short distance which visits every vertex of the graph. An algorithm for the traveling salesman problem can be used for solving the Hamiltonian circuit problem, since we can *transform* the Hamiltonian circuit problem to the traveling salesman problem as follows.

Let each arc of the graph have distance "one", and the distance between two vertices be ∞ if there is no direct arc connecting the vertices. Since there are n vertices in the graph, the existence of a tour of distance n means the existence of a Hamiltonian circuit.

Note that this transformation takes polynomial amount of time; i.e., specifying the distances for the $n(n-1)/2$ pairs. If we should discover a polynomial algorithm for the traveling salesman problem, we have effectively discovered a polynomial algorithm for the Hamiltonian circuit problem also.

We shall say problem L_1 transforms to L_2 (or L_1 reduces to L_2), written

$$L_1 \propto L_2$$

if any algorithm for L_2 can be used for L_1. It is understood that this transformation takes polynomial time. If L_2 can also be transformed into L_1, then we say the problems L_1 and L_2 are polynomially equivalent; i.e., $L_1 \equiv L_2$.

The relationships $\propto$ and $\equiv$ are both transitive. For example, $L_1 \propto L_2$, $L_2 \propto L_3$, then $L_1 \propto L_3$. If $L_1 \propto L_2$, then the problem L_2 is at least as hard as L_1.

It turns out that there is a subset of problems in NP which are the hardest problems in the following sense (the problems in the subset are polynomially equivalent):

Any problem in NP can be reduced to any problem in the subset. So if we have a polynomial algorithm for a problem in the subset, we can solve all the problems in NP in polynomial time.

The problems in this subset are called *NP-complete problems*. So within the class NP, there are two subsets of problems, the subset P which can be solved in polynomial time in a deterministic manner, and the subset NP-complete problems which are the hardest problems within NP. We draw this symbolically as in Figure 8.1.

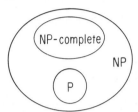

Figure 8.1

The first NP-complete problem was discovered in the remarkable paper by Cook [1], and then Karp [8] showed there are many other problems which are also NP-complete.

To prove that P = NP, we can prove that a NP-complete problem can be solved in polynomial time in a deterministic manner.

To prove that P ≠ NP, we can show a problem in NP which is not in P. In fact, it follows from a paper by Ladner [15], if P ≠ NP, there must exist a problem which is neither P nor NP-complete.

There were two problems which were prime candidates for problems in NP but not NP-complete. One was the linear programming problem which has been proved to be actually in P. (See [1] [11]) The other problem is the prime number problem [17] which is conjectured to be in the class P also.

If we find a new problem L to be NP-complete, then we have little chance to invent a new polynomial algorithm. To prove that our new problem L is NP-complete, we should prove:

(i)   The problem L belongs to NP.

(ii)   A known NP-complete problem reduces to L.

Following are three standard NP-complete problems and their variations.

1. Partition Problem: Given numbers $x_1, x_2, ..., x_n$, can a subset of size k exist such that the total sum of numbers in this subset is exactly B? A more general version of this problem is the knapsack problem discussed in previous chapters.

2. Hamiltonian Circuit: A more general version is the traveling salesman problem.

3a. Vertex Cover Problem: Given a graph $G = (V, E)$, find a subset $V' \subseteq V$ of minimum cardinality such that every edge is adjacent to at least one vertex in V'.

There is one version of Problem 3 which is essentially equivalent.

3b. Maximum Independent Set Problem: Find a subset $V'' \subseteq V$ of maximum cardinality such that no edge is adjacent to two vertices in V''. It can be verified that $V'' = V - V'$. For example, the subset of vertices labeled α in Figure 8.2 form a vertex cover, and the subset of vertices labeled β form a maximum independent set.

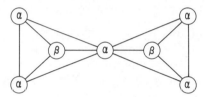

Figure 8.2

To show the importance of encoding of input data, let us consider the decision version for the knapsack problem for given w_i, does there exist x_i such that

$$\sum_{i=1}^{n} w_i x_i = b$$

$$x_i = 0, 1 \ .$$

We can construct an $n \times b$ table and solve the problem by dynamic programming as shown in Chapter 3. If we use n, b as a measure of the size of the problem, then we have a polynomial algorithm for the knapsack problem. Unfortunately, under the assumption of reasonable encoding of the input data, the number b does not need b digits to represent it, but $O(\log_2 b)$ digits to represent it. Now we have no algorithm which is a polynomial function of n, $\log_2 b$. On the other hand, if we restrict the maximum magnitude of b, then $\log_2 b$ is bounded by a constant, and we have a polynomial algorithm in terms of n. For this reason, we call the dynamic programming approach to a knapsack problem, a pseudo-polynomial algorithm. Many NP-complete problems involving numbers do have pseudo-polynomial algorithms, and are solved quite efficiently in practice.

For vertex cover problems, there is no natural bound on any number, and the number of vertices n is a good measure of the problem. So there is no pseudo-polynomial algorithm.

§8.5 FACING A NEW PROBLEM

When we face a new problem we certainly would like to invent a new efficient algorithm that always obtains an optimum solution. The book (Garey and Johnson [4]) has a list of current NP-complete problems and we may find out that the new problem is NP-complete. What should we do then? Or the new problem is not in the list, but we suspect that it may be. Proving that our problem is NP-complete does not solve our problem. From a practical point of view, we have to invent a new algorithm or use existing algorithms even if the problem is NP-complete. If the algorithm is polynomial but has power higher than n^3, then it is probably not efficient enough. The following are some suggestions.

1.   Ignore whatever is known and invent your own algorithm:

The best example of this is the Simplex Method (Dantzig [3]). Although the simplex method is not a polynomial algorithm in the worst case, *a simple fact is that the simplex method works.* One of the outstanding problems in operations research and applied mathematics today is, "Why does the simplex method work so well". When we specify a linear program, we allow all possible values for the entries in the matrix A, the vectors b and c. There are probably conditions on the entries of A, b, c, which make the simplex method so efficient.

2.   Special cases of the problem:

We have shown many cases of this approach. In the scheduling problems of m processors and n unit-time jobs partially ordered, the problem is NP-complete. But if we restrict to the special case that the constraint is a "tree" then the problem can be solved in linear time in Chapter 6. Another special case is m=2, see Coffman and Graham [4] in Chapter 6. For any unsolved problem it is better to consider special cases or extreme cases first, and then gradually generalize the results. It is customary to reduce our new problem to a known problem, but we might lose some special structure during the process. A great many combinatorial problems can be reduced to integer programs (i.e., linear programs with the additional constraint that variables be integers). But many of these problems should not be solved by a general integer programming algorithm.

A knapsack problem is a special integer program and can be solved by a tailor-made algorithm. The optimum alphabetic tree (Chapter 5) can be solved by dynamic programming but the Hu-Tucker algorithm is much more efficient and reveals the special structure of the problem. A general algorithm is like a size 48 cloth, it can cover everybody but it does not fit very well.

3.   Heuristic approach:

The partition problem is a special case of bin-packing which is again an NP-complete problem. Here we use a heuristic algorithm such as First-Fit and establish a performance bound. These approaches are described in Chapter 6. Normally, we try a few small numerical examples and build up our intuition. Then if the heuristic algorithm succeeds in some cases and fails in other cases, we should characterize the input data which guarantees that the heuristic algorithm works.

In Figure 8.3 we draw symbolically a large circle to represent the general input data, and a smaller circle to represent the subset of data which guarantees that the heuristic algorithm works.

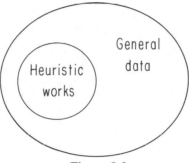

Figure 8.3

An example of this approach is the greedy algorithm for the coin-changing problem in Chapter 6. When the input data does not belong to the smaller circle, we should establish the maximum error bound.

4.   Decomposition approach:

When a problem is large and complicated, we may decompose the problem into several small problems and solve the small problems individually. Later, after these small problems are solved, we somehow piece them together to get the optimum solution for the original problem. The best example is the decomposition approach to linear programming by Dantzig and Wolfe [3]. In fact, most large linear programming problems are solved by column or row generating techniques (for a survey of this approach, see Gomory [5], Hu [7]). In Chapter 2, we have shown one such approach in getting the shortest paths between all pairs of nodes in a large network. Dynamic programming uses this approach, so is Divide-and-Conquer.

5.   Use general methods:

When we are pressed for time, and do not feel like doing much research, we can use general methods for solving combinatorial problems. Some are:

(i)   Backtrack   (Chapter 4)

(ii)   Dynamic programming   (Chapter 3)

(iii)   Cutting plane method of Gomory.   (see Hu [7], Johnson [8]).

Even for the backtrack method, special modifications such as in the case of game-tree, can greatly increase the efficiency of the method. The cutting plane method (due to Gomory) is a method of solving integer programs. This method has been very successful in some cases and behaves poorly in others.

In general, there is no systematic method for discovering new combinatorial algorithms. Hopefully, this book will arouse interest in combinatorial algorithms.

CHAPTER 8

BIBLIOGRAPHIC NOTES AND SUGGESTED READING

In this chapter, we have given a very brief overview of NP-complete problems. The reader is strongly urged to read the book by Garey and Johnson which deals exclusively with NP-complete problems. This book also includes an appendix listing of currently known NP-complete problems and related references. The expository paper by Lewis and Papadimitriou [16] is also highly recommended.

For general survey and review papers, see Klee [12], Knuth [13], Tarjan [18], and Weide [19].

Many combinatorial problems can be formulated as linear or integer programs, see for example [3], [7], and [8].

1.   B. Aspvall and R. E. Stone "Khachiyan's Linear Programming Algorithm", Computer Science Report CS-79-776, Nov. 1979, Stanford University.

2.   S. A. Cook, "The Complexity of Theorem-proving Procedures", Proceedings of 3rd Annual ACM Symposium on Theory o Computing (1971), pp. 151-158.

3.   G. B. Dantzig, "Linear Programming and Extensions", Princeton University Press, 1963.

4.   M. R. Garey and D. S. Johnson, "Computers and Intractability", Freeman Co., 1979.

5.   R. E. Gomory, "Large and Non-Convex Problems in Linear Programming", Proceedings of Symposium in Applied Math. Vol. XV, AMS, 1963.

6.   R. L. Graham, "The Combinatorial Mathematics of Scheduling", Scientific American, 238, no. 3 (1978), pp. 124-132.

7.   T. C. Hu, "Integer Programming and Network Flows", Addison-Wesley, 1969.

8.   E. L. Johnson, "Integer Programming", IBM Research Report, RC7450, Dec. 26, 1978.

9.   R. M. Karp, "Reducibility Among Combinatorial Problems", in R. E. Miller and J. W. Thatcher (eds.), Complexity of Computer Computations, Plenum Press, New York, 1972, pp.

10.   R. M. Karp, "On the Complexity of Combinatorial Problems", Networks, 5 (1975), pp. 45-68.

11.   L. G. Khachiyan, "A Polynomial Algorithm in Linear Programming", Doklady Academiia Nauk SSSR Novaia Seriia 244:5 (1979), pp. 1093-1096 (English Translation in Soviet Mathematics Doklady 20:1 (1979) pp. 191-194).

12.   V. Klee, "Combinatorial Optimization: What is the State of the Art?", Math. of O.R., Vol. 5, no. 1, (Feb. 1980), pp. 1-26.

13.   D. E. Knuth, "Combinatorial Algorithms", Vol. 4, Addison-Wesley, 19 .

14. D. E. Knuth, "Mathematics and Computer Science: Coping with Finiteness", Stanford University Report, CS-76-541 (1976).

15. R. E. Ladner, "The Computational Complexity of Provability in Systems of Modal Propositional Logic", SIAM J. Computing, Vol. 6, (1977), pp. 467-480.

16. H. R. Lewis and C. H. Papadimitriou, "The Efficiency of Algorithms", Scientific American, 238, no. 1 (1978), pp. 96-109.

17. V. Pratt, "Every Prime Has a Succinct Certificate", SIAM J. Computing, Vol. 4 (1975), pp. 214-220.

18. R. E. Tarjan, "Complexity of Combinatorial Algorithms", SIAM Review 20(3) (1978), pp. 457-491.

19. B. Weide, "A Survey of Analysis Techniques for Discrete Algorithms", Computing Survey, 9(4) (1977), pp. 291-313.

INDEX